Foundations of AOP for J2EE Development

■ ■ ■

Renaud Pawlak, Lionel Seinturier, and
Jean-Philippe Retaillé

Foundations of AOP for J2EE Development

Copyright © 2005 by Renaud Pawlak, Lionel Seinturier, and Jean-Philippe Retaillé

ISBN: 1-59059-507-6

Printed and bound in the United States of America 9 8 7 6 5 4 3 2 1

Lead Editor: Steve Anglin
Technical Reviewer: Houman Younessi
Editorial Board: Steve Anglin, Dan Appleman, Ewan Buckingham, Gary Cornell, Tony Davis, Jason Gilmore, Jonathan Hassell, Chris Mills, Dominic Shakeshaft, Jim Sumser
Associate Publisher: Grace Wong
Translator: Chelsea Creekmore
Project Manager: Sofia Marchant
Copy Edit Manager: Nicole LeClerc
Copy Editors: Linda Harmony, Ami Knox, Nicole LeClerc
Assistant Production Director: Kari Brooks-Copony
Production Editor: Katie Stence
Compositor and Artist: Wordstop Technologies Pvt. Ltd., Chennai
Proofreader: Elizabeth Berry
Indexer: John Collin
Interior Designer: Van Winkle Design Group
Cover Designer: Kurt Krames
Manufacturing Director: Tom Debolski

Distributed to the book trade worldwide by Springer-Verlag New York, Inc., 233 Spring Street, 6th Floor, New York, NY 10013. Phone 1-800-SPRINGER, fax 201-348-4505, e-mail orders-ny@springer-sbm.com, or visit http://www.springeronline.com.

For information on translations, please contact Apress directly at 2560 Ninth Street, Suite 219, Berkeley, CA 94710. Phone 510-549-5930, fax 510-549-5939, e-mail info@apress.com, or visit http://www.apress.com.

The source code for this book is available to readers at http://www.apress.com in the Source Code section.

To our families and friends

Contents at a Glance

Contents

Foreword

Aspect orientation as a concept and aspect-oriented programming (AOP) as a technology have emerged as an attempt to provide further separation of concerns in the way we compose software. Aspects modularize concerns that otherwise would pervade and crosscut many areas of a program or application. As such, they can be thought of as a second-dimension modularization of operational nature, where the structural idea of a component would be the first.

Although the ideas, concepts, and approaches (e.g., reflection) behind AOP are not new, the approach as it stands is novel in applying these ideas to form the aforementioned second dimension of modularization. AOP therefore is an important development in modern software engineering.

The book in your hands, *Foundations of AOP for J2EE Development*, provides an excellent overview of this technology, its features, and its limitations. Dr. Pawlak, Mr. Retaillé, and Dr. Seinturier have provided detailed discussion of aspect orientation as an approach, AOP as a technology, and various implementations of AOP and how they might be used.

It would be mere speculation to attempt to predict the future of AOP, or indeed its impact on software engineering or its longevity. What we can say about it with certainty, however, is that all students, investigators, and serious practitioners of software engineering should become familiar with this technology and assess its potential in their own work. *Foundations of AOP for J2EE Development* is an excellent resource to begin to do so.

—Houman Younessi
Professor of Computer Science and Chairman of the Department of Engineering and
Science Rensselaer Polytechnic Institute, Hartford Graduate Campus
Hartford, Connecticut

About the Authors

RENAUD PAWLAK holds a PhD in computer science and is currently a computer science researcher at INRIA, a public research institute in France. In 2003–2004, he was a postdoctorate fellow at Rensselaer Polytechnic Institute (RPI), Hartford Graduated Campus, where he taught software engineering and AOP to graduate students. His research focuses on the separation of concerns (SoC) in software engineering, reflection, distributed middleware, and AOP. He developed an original programming model that is directly applicable to distributed environments (the Aspect Component Model). In January 2000, he cofounded the company AOPSYS, with the primary goal of supporting the use of AOP and SoC-related techniques in industry. He is the founder and main programmer of the JAC framework, which is currently being used by AOPSYS to develop projects for a variety of customers. He is the author of more than 20 publications, including international research papers, popular science articles, and tutorials for JAC and AOP.

JEAN-PHILIPPE RETAILLÉ holds qualifications in several areas of computer science and business, including a degree in computer science engineering (MEng) and an MBA from the Sorbonne (France). He currently works as an IT architect for a large European insurance company. His main focus is on thin client architectures using J2EE as a means to improve developer productivity during software development. He is involved in several projects using J2EE in the French banking and insurance sectors. Jean-Philippe is particularly interested in all technologies that improve software quality, including AOP.

LIONEL SEINTURIER received his PhD degree in computer science from the CNAM, Paris (France), in December 1997 and currently holds a research position in computer science at LIFL, a computer science research laboratory that is jointly owned by the University of Lille (France) and INRIA (the French research agency for computer science). He is also an assistant professor in computer science at the University of Paris 6. Before joining academia, Seinturier worked as a research engineer for France Telecom's R&D department on the integration of ATM network technology and CORBA middleware. Seinturier's research interests include AOP and systems, middleware, and distributed algorithms. He is one of the programmers of the JAC AOP framework and the author of more than 25 international publications, including articles and tutorials on AOP.

About the Technical Reviewer

 **HOUMAN YOUNESSI** is an internationally renowned educator, practitioner, consultant, and investigator. Officially recognized by his peers as one of the world's top authorities in object-oriented software engineering (a field in excess of 100,000), he is probably best known for being one of the three main inventors of the OPEN methodology. Dr. Younessi combines world-class research-based knowledge with recognized industry experience to bring forth innovations in research as well as in the classroom and to industry, where his consultation is regularly sought by many leading organizations. A multidisciplinarian, he has expertise and publications in many fields, including electrical engineering, software engineering, information systems, business process, and business process re-engineering (for which he has written the CRC handbook encyclopedic entries), as well as molecular biology, bioinformatics, and biochemistry. Recently, he co-invented (with one of his postdoctoral students) the new paradigm of recombinant programming, which is likely to have a profound effect on how large-scale software systems are designed in the future.

Dr. Younessi is currently Professor of Computer Science and Chairman of the Department of Engineering and Science at Rensselaer Polytechnic Institute (RPI), Hartford Graduate Campus. Prior to joining academia, Dr. Younessi held a number of positions of responsibility and leadership in industry. He has led both technical and marketing efforts, and has been responsible for projects, budgets, staff, and revenue. In his last role in industry, he founded, staffed, and grew (in less than five years) an IT consulting firm from an initial size of two (himself and an employee) to a sizeable organization of 16 consulting staff and a revenue of several million dollars. He has also provided consulting services to some of the largest companies and government organizations around the world (the state governments of New York and Michigan, BHP, Royal Dutch Shell Oil Corp., Maersk, and Hitachi, to name a few).

Dr. Younessi is frequently asked to many prestigious venues and to participate in national and international committees and boards. He was the U.S. head of delegation to the ISO SC7 meeting in Malaga, Spain, and a member of the Australian Research Council (the Australian equivalent of the NSF) IT grant-proposal review board. He has also been part of the Australian team to promulgate and validate the ISO 15504 standard. Dr. Younessi is also the category editor for the ACM Computing Reviews and serves on the editorial or review board of several international journals.

Introduction

*A*spect-oriented programming (*AOP*) is a programming paradigm that was defined at the Xerox Palo Alto Research Center (PARC) in the mid-1990s. The roots of this paradigm can be traced back to several works designed to improve code modularity and facilitate reuse and maintenance.

The benefits of AOP for modularizing code have drawn attention from many application developers, especially those in the domain of web applications. Indeed, AOP is an excellent complement to Internet-oriented application servers such as Sun Microsystems's J2EE or Microsoft's .NET. With AOP, developers can facilitate the development and boost the productivity of these types of applications. However, AOP is not limited to the domain of web-centric applications. Similar to other programming paradigms (such as objects), AOP is a general technique that can be applied to any kind of application.

This book defines and explains the concepts of AOP. The implementation of these concepts is illustrated by a presentation of four major existing AOP products (AspectJ, JAC, JBoss AOP, and Spring AOP). In addition, this book shows how you can use AOP for programming J2EE applications.

Target Audience

This book aims to present the concepts of AOP in a clear and pedagogical way. No prior knowledge of the domain is needed. Instead of focusing on the advanced programming concepts of a particular AOP language, this book provides a broad overview of the existing products available for programming with aspects.

Many readers, including the following, will be interested in this book:

- Programmers curious about gaining insight into a new domain of computer science

- IT project managers wishing to learn what the expected benefits of AOP are

- Application developers seeking accurate information about AOP products

- PhD and MSc students needing an introduction to AOP and a state-of-the-art comparison of existing implementations

How to Read This Book

The chapters of this book were written to be as independent as possible; therefore, it is not necessary to read the chapters sequentially from the first to the last to gain valuable information about AOP. Each reader can choose his or her own reading plan.

That said, we will outline some recommended reading for each target audience listed in the previous section:

- *Programmers*: Chapters 1 and 2 are recommended for gaining an overview of what AOP is and for learning its basic concepts. Reading Chapter 3 on AspectJ is also recommended, since this chapter shows how the concepts of Chapter 2 are implemented in the leading tool of the domain. The three last chapters (10, 11, and 12) illustrate the use of AspectJ for developing J2EE applications.

- *IT project managers*: Chapter 1 is recommended for obtaining a quick overview of AOP. The first pages of Chapter 2 are also useful to learn the main motivations for the introduction of this new programming paradigm. We also recommend reading Chapter 9 to understand how AOP can help to improve Quality of Service, which has a direct impact on an application's use. Chapter 10 gives a typical example of a J2EE application that can benefit from being developed with aspects.

- *Application developers*: Chapter 2, which covers the concepts of AOP, is recommended. Chapters 3 through 6 are recommended, as they provide an overview of how the concepts of AOP are implemented in existing tools. Chapters 8 and 9 show how AOP can be used for programming design patterns, contracts, and application managements. Finally, Chapters 11 and 12 present a case study of programming a J2EE application with AOP.

- *PhD and MSc students*: Chapters 1 and 2 are recommended for gaining an overview of AOP and for learning its basic concepts. Chapters 3 through 6 are recommended, as they provide an overview of how the concepts of AOP are implemented in existing tools. We recommend reading the comparison in Chapter 7, which explores the differences and similarities between these tools. Finally, Chapter 8 illustrates the power of AOP for implementing crosscutting structures, such as the well-known design patterns of software engineering.

Book Road Map

The first two chapters introduce AOP and present the main new concepts of this paradigm. The three major notions of AOP—aspects, pointcuts, and joinpoints—are defined. These chapters are recommended for readers without any prior knowledge of AOP.

The major existing products of AOP are presented in Chapters 3 through 7. Each chapter in this section is dedicated to a particular product: AspectJ (the leading language of the domain), JAC, JBoss AOP, and Spring AOP. These chapters can be read independently. Each chapter assumes only that you are familiar with the concepts presented in the first part. Chapter 7 compares the features of the four presented products.

Chapters 8 and 9 present the uses of AOP for programming design patterns, for improving software quality and for supervising and administering applications. These chapters are independent and can be read separately. AspectJ is the language chosen to illustrate the concepts introduced in these chapters. Reading Chapter 3 on AspectJ beforehand may help you understand the examples presented.

A case study of an aspect-oriented J2EE application is presented in Chapters 10 to 12. Chapter 10 is a general presentation of the application, independent of a solution (AOP or not) for implementing it. The next two chapters show how AOP can improve the implementation of the business tier of the application, and then the presentation tier. Chapters 11 and 12 are stand-alone and can be read separately.

About the Code Examples

The code examples provided in this book assume some basic knowledge of the Java programming language. The case study presented in Chapters 10 through 12 assumes knowledge of the principles of programming applications with J2EE.

All code examples from this book can be downloaded from Source Code area of the Apress web site (http://www.apress.com). In some cases (especially the J2EE case study), the programs presented in the text are truncated and only selected relevant excerpts are presented. The downloadable source code for this book contains the full version of all programs.

Frequently Asked Questions

The following series of questions and answers will help you gain a first insight into AOP, and understand its impacts on other programming paradigms and its role on enterprise application developments.

What Is AOP?

Several kinds of concerns need to be addressed when developing applications. These concerns can be classified in two categories: functional concerns, which deal with the business logic of the application, and technical concerns, which are related to the executing environment (operating system, network, etc.).

The principle known as the *separation of concerns* aims to decouple and separate each concern as much as possible to foster modularity. Object-oriented programming (OOP) has provided a good solution for separating many business concerns, and as a result applications are more reusable since the separated concerns can be easily reused in several different applications. However, technical or functional concerns that are said to be crosscutting are not easily dealt with using OOP.

AOP is a paradigm for separating concerns and for modularizing crosscutting concerns in well-identified software entities called *aspects*.

Does AOP Replace OOP?

AOP does not replace OOP. AOP complements OOP by modularizing crosscutting concerns. Therefore, programming an AOP application is still a matter of writing classes with fields and methods. AOP adds a new dimension of modularity in the sense that these classes are complemented with aspects, which implement concerns not efficiently modularized with classes.

Is AOP Used in Enterprise Applications?

AOP is a relatively new technique that appeared in the mid-1990s. As far as we know, no major software editor sells applications that were developed with AOP. However, many vendors, such as IBM, are investigating the use of AOP to improve the efficiency of developing J2SE and J2EE applications.

Compared to OOP, the adoption of AOP appears to be faster. Indeed, even though the first versions of object-oriented languages appeared in 1967 with Simula 67, it was not until the mid-1980s that objects were used for developing enterprise applications with C++. The cost of adopting AOP is less than the cost of adopting OOP because AOP languages complement existing OOP languages. Aspects can then be smoothly integrated in existing applications without the need for any major redevelopment of the existing code.

CHAPTER 1

■■■

Introducing AOP

This book presents *aspect-oriented programming (AOP)*, which defines a new programming paradigm. By the word *paradigm*, we mean a set of principles that structure the modeling of programs and, as a consequence, the development of programs.

As its name suggests, aspect-oriented programming introduces a new concept—that of the *aspect*. Some years ago, object-oriented programming (OOP) introduced the concept of the object, which initiated a new way to structure applications and write programs. The same idea applies to the concept of the aspect.

In 1996, Gregor Kiczales and his team at the Palo Alto Research Center (PARC), a subsidiary of Xerox Corporation that is located in California, originally defined the concept of the aspect. Although this definition made 1996 the official birthday of AOP, many of AOP's underlying ideas preceded this date. Some of OOP's limitations motivated the introduction of the aspect, which also originated in research domains, such as those of reflection and the meta-object protocol.

After the concept of the aspect was defined, an aspect-oriented language, named AspectJ, was soon implemented, with the first versions made available in 1998. AspectJ, which remains the most popular AOP language, extends the Java language with new keywords that make it possible to program aspects.

Above and beyond AspectJ, AOP itself has remained a subject of great interest since 1998 within the research community. As a result, many other languages and tools, the majority of which are constructed around Java, have been developed. These include Java Aspect Components (JAC), JBoss AOP, and AspectWerkz.

Despite the focus on Java, it's important to keep in mind that nothing about AOP is specific to OOP in general or Java in particular. The notion of the aspect is an abstract concept that, like the notion of the object, can be applied to different languages. Tools of varying completeness exist to support AOP in C, C++, C#, and Smalltalk. Furthermore, any existing language could be extended to support the concepts of AOP.

Because the concept of the aspect is relatively new, encouraging a large community of developers to adopt AOP is an important task.

Looking at Programming Paradigms

Viewed as a programming paradigm, you can see AOP as OOP's successor. However, the aim of AOP is not to replace OOP, but to complement it, allowing you to create clearer and better-structured programs.

Since the introduction of assembly language, a family of programming paradigms has been developed that allows programmers to create software of increasing complexity. The concepts of the procedure and the object have, each in their own ways, contributed to better code structuring and greater manageability of large programs. Think of AOP, which aims to continue this tradition, as the latest addition to this family of paradigms.

For example, the concept of the procedure, which languages such as Pascal embody, allows you to partition a program into entities called procedures. As you know, each procedure is simpler to write and understand than the program as a whole is. You therefore build a program as a set of procedures that call one another. The use of procedures aids the development of large applications because individuals on a team can independently develop procedures. Individuals can also test procedures independently, allowing programming errors to be more easily located.

Although the transition was not instantaneous, procedural programming contributed to the disappearance of the goto instruction. This instruction, which transferred execution to a specific line of the program, tended to cause "spaghetti code." In other words, the program would quickly become tangled—preventing the ability to reuse some parts of the program independently of others.

Procedural programming, on the other hand, allows you to code elementary tasks that each contain clearly identified beginning and end points. This type of programming makes it possible to create libraries of procedures that can be reused by many different programs.

Procedural programming simplifies the coding process. It allows programmers to develop modular—hence more understandable—programs by giving a clearer structure to the code. However, procedural programming does not provide a secure structure for any of the data. Indeed, one of the great weaknesses of this paradigm is that global variables can be accessed from anywhere in the program—and doing so improperly can lead to unexpected side effects.

The Origins of AOP

Like all programming paradigms, AOP is based on pre-existing concepts that had already been exploited in the past—but in limited, specific situations. While recognizing the importance of the work of Gregor Kiczales, who integrated the ideas that underpin AOP, the programming community must not forget that many other projects served as foundations for this work.

AOP uses ideas from various domains of information technology—specifically, those of meta programming, reflection, and meta-object protocols. These domains were developed by Mehmet Aksit, Jean-Pierre Briot, Shigeru Chiba, Pierre Cointe, Jacques Ferber, Patricia Maes, Brian Smith, and many others. Additionally, some of AOP's key mechanisms relate to features of object-oriented languages that never became popular, such as the before and after instructions of CommonLoops and Flavors. Also apparent are the similarities between AOP and certain recent techniques that generative programming and model-driven architectures (MDA) use.

However, the AOP approach as a whole remains original. Therefore, AOP must not be seen as competing with the techniques that it was developed from, but as presenting a logical and coherent structure that integrates these techniques for solving real-world problems.

OOP: A Promising Paradigm

The aim behind the development of OOP was to organize the data of an application and its associated processing into coherent entities. Doing so was achieved by having objects that encapsulate data along with the methods that manipulate the data and carry out the processing.

From a conceptual point of view, an application is broken down according to the real-world objects that it models. In a stock-management application, for example, you might find supplier, article, customer, and other types of objects.

By grouping together all the objects that possess the same characteristics, the concept of a class complements the concept of the object. In the stock-management application, all the supplier objects belong to the same class, which is named supplier.

When designing a solution to a concrete problem, deciding how to split up the program into classes and, therefore, objects is far from simple. Many variations are possible, so different developers may come up with very different solutions. Approaches such as that of the Rational Unified Process (RUP) platform aim to rationalize the conceptual choices you need to make.

Regardless of the design process, the way you divide an application into classes and objects must be guided, above all, by the real-world data that the application models. The most important factor that influences how you choose the classes is the way you want to organize—in other words, group together—the business data of the application. Classes first and foremost provide a grouping mechanism for the data, with the associated processing included as the methods.

The OOP concepts of the class and the object allow you to write programs that feature more of the following than programs that use the procedural paradigm:

Modularity: Because the processing that concerns an item or set of data is grouped together with the data in the same software entity (the class), a certain degree of modularity is achieved.

Reusability: As a result of modularity, only the extent to which a class is well designed, self-sufficient, and targeted at a precise goal determines its likelihood of being reusable in different software contexts.

Reliability: Because the data is encapsulated within objects, it can be manipulated only through the methods that define the object's interface. (Directly manipulating the data is not possible.) The valid ways to access the objects are therefore clearly identified, and programmers can safely use any of them.

Extendability: The concept of inheritance allows you to create new classes from those that already exist. A new class can extend an existing class by adding data or processing, or it can specialize the existing elements. For example, you could extend a class that manages data lists so that it manages only stacks. (A stack is a list that requires specific rules for adding and removing elements).

Because of these advantages, OOP has undeniably improved software engineering. Developers have built more-complex programs in a simpler fashion than would have been possible through procedural programming. Furthermore, developers have written large applications in object-oriented languages. For example, the Java 2 Platform, Enterprise Edition (J2EE) application servers were programmed in the Java language. Similarly, developers have implemented complex class hierarchies to construct graphical user interfaces. The Swing API, included in Java 2 Platform, Standard Edition (J2SE), falls into this category.

However, the transition from procedural programming to OOP occurred with considerable effort, with developer training representing a significant cost. Now that OOP is just starting to be widely understood, it is legitimate to ask whether introducing a new paradigm such as AOP is desirable.

To answer that question, we can begin by affirming that AOP does not call into question what has been achieved through OOP. Applications that are programmed according to AOP remain organized into classes and objects. AOP simply adds new concepts that allow you to improve object-oriented applications by making them more modular. In addition, AOP streamlines the development process by allowing the separation of development tasks. For example, highly technical functionalities, such as security, can be developed by specialized experts, and aspects allow you to more easily integrate these functionalities into the rest of the application.

No doubt the adoption of AOP will take a long time and require effort, but it can be done gradually when the need is clearly identified.

The Limitations of OOP

The importance of OOP for developing complex programs is undeniable. However, we will show that writing clear and elegant programs using only OOP is impossible in at least two cases: when the application contains *crosscutting functionalities*, and when the application includes *code scattering*.

The Case of Crosscutting Functionalities

Previously, we mentioned that when you analyze how to organize an application into classes, the analysis must be driven by the need for separating and encapsulating the data and its associated processing into coherent entities.

Although the classes are programmed independently of one another, they are sometimes behaviorally interdependent. Typically, this is the case when you implement rules of referential integrity. For example, a customer object must not be deleted while an outstanding order remains unpaid; otherwise, the program risks losing the contact details for that customer. To enforce this rule, you could modify the customer-deletion method so that it initially determines whether all the orders have been paid. However, this solution is deficient for several reasons:

- Determining whether an order has been paid does not belong to customer management but to order management. Therefore, the customer class should not have to manage this functionality.

- The customer class should not need to be aware of all the data-integrity rules that other classes in the application impose.

- Modifying the customer class to take these data-integrity rules into account restricts the possibilities of reusing the class in other situations. In other words, once the customer class implements any functionality that is linked to a different class, customer is no longer independently reusable, in many cases.

Despite the fact that the customer class is not the ideal place to implement this referential-integrity rule, many object-oriented programs work this way for lack of a better solution. You might be thinking about integrating this functionality into an order class instead, but this solution is no better. No reason exists for the order class to allow the deletion of a customer. Strictly speaking, this rule is linked to neither the customers nor the orders but cuts across these two types of entities.

One of the aims of dividing the data into classes is making the classes independent from one another. However, crosscutting functionalities, such as the rules of referential integrity, appear superimposed on the division—violating the independence of the classes. In other words, OOP does not allow you to neatly implement crosscutting functionalities. As a compromise, you can resign yourself to implementing them in individual classes, but remain conscious that this solution is not ideal.

The Case of Code Scattering

In OOP, the principal way that objects interact is by invoking methods. In other words, an object that needs to carry out an action invokes a method that belongs to another object. (An object can also invoke one of its own methods.) OOP always entail two roles: that of the invoker and that of the invoked.

When you write the code to call a method, you do not need to worry about *how* the service is implemented because the call interacts only with the interface of the invoked object. You need only ensure that the parameters in the call correspond to those of the method's signature.

Because methods are implemented within classes, you write each method as a block of code that is clearly delimited. To change a method, you obviously modify the file that contains the class where the method is defined. If you alter just the body of the method, the modification is transparent because the method will still be called in exactly the same way.

However, if you change the method's signature (for example, by adding a parameter), further implications arise. You must then modify all the calls to the method, hence you must modify any classes that invoke the method. If these calls exist in several places in the program, making the changes can be extremely time-consuming.

The main point is this: Even though the implementation of a method is located in a single class, the calls to that method can be scattered throughout the application. This phenomenon of code scattering slows down maintenance tasks and makes it difficult for object-oriented applications to adapt and evolve. Any change in the way that a service is used requires many other changes—a costly process that can also introduce errors.

The Benefits of AOP

AOP complements OOP by offering solutions to the two challenges just explained—solutions that implement crosscutting functionalities and eliminate code scattering. Chapter 2 will show that the concept of an aspect allows you to integrate crosscutting functionalities and code scattering into an object-oriented application by using the new concepts of the pointcut, the joinpoint, and the advice.

In procedural programming, you divide the application according to the functionalities that you need to implement. OOP goes one step further by obliging you to group related data items and their associated processing tasks into coherent entities. AOP then establishes a certain balance by allowing you to superimpose a new layer onto the data-driven composition of OOP. This layer corresponds to the crosscutting functionalities that are difficult to integrate directly through the OOP paradigm.

An aspect-oriented application consists of the following two parts:

- *Classes*: These constitute the base of the application and implement the business logic. In other words, the classes implement those parts of the application that deal directly with the real-world problem to be modeled.

- *Aspects*: These integrate the supplementary elements (classes, methods, and data) that correspond to crosscutting functionalities and code scattering.

Designing an aspect-oriented application thus begins by breaking down the problem to define the classes and the aspects. No universal rule exists for deciding whether a functionality should be implemented in a class or in an aspect. Furthermore, you can implement the same functionality in either one or the other, depending on the context. For example, you might implement the constraints of real-time execution as aspects in a management application but as classes in an application that supervises industrial processes.

The second design stage consists of putting the classes and the aspects together to obtain an operational application. You carry out this process by using the AOP concepts of the crosscut and the joinpoint. These concepts allow you to decide where in the program to insert the aspects and, therefore, which functionalities these aspects will implement.

On another note, remember that when OOP was introduced, the object-oriented languages were either extensions of existing languages (C++ is an extension of C) or completely new languages (such as Smalltalk and Java). In both cases, new compilers had to be developed.

AOP presents a slightly different situation because the tools exist either as frameworks or as extensions to existing languages. An example of the latter is the AspectJ language, which Chapter 3 presents in detail. AspectJ adds new keywords to the Java language that allow the use of AOP concepts, such as the aspect, the crosscut, and the joinpoint.

Examples of AOP frameworks are JAC, JBoss AOP, and AspectWerkz, all of which Chapters 4, 5, and 6 present. These frameworks use the syntax of an existing programming language, which in these cases is Java. You use the AOP concepts by means of the classes and methods in the framework. For example, defining an aspect through JAC comes down to extending a class that the framework contains.

Since the introduction of AOP, a hot debate has raged between those in favor of language extensions and those in favor of frameworks. In one case, you need to learn a language's new keywords; in the other case, you need to learn a new framework's API. Regardless, both cases require a learning phase.

Summary

This chapter introduced the concept of the aspect which, as its name suggests, serves as the main contribution to the AOP paradigm. Gregor Kiczales and his team at the Palo Alto Research Center (PARC) defined the concept of the aspect in 1996. Several existing ideas led to the emergence of AOP, and research domains such as those of reflection and the meta-object protocol actively contributed.

Although the concept of the aspect is a general programming concept that could be applied to any programming paradigm (functional, procedural, or object-oriented), the history of AOP is tightly linked to that of the OOP paradigm. Most of the existing AOP languages are extensions of OOP ones, such as Java and C#. Furthermore, the motivation for defining the concept of the aspect originated from the limitations of OOP.

This chapter described the two main OOP limitations: crosscutting functionalities and code scattering. The former refers to the fact that you cannot keep certain functionalities clearly modular when you implement them in classes. The latter refers to the fact that you can use classes to keep the implementation—but not the use—of functionalities modular. Because AOP provides a solution to these limitations, AOP complements rather than replaces OOP as a programming paradigm.

By analyzing why these limitations occur, this chapter introduced the benefits that you can expect from the AOP paradigm—benefits that stem from the clear and modular implementation of crosscutting functionalities and code scattering.

CHAPTER 2

■■■

The Concepts of AOP

This chapter introduces the basic concepts of AOP. Although AOP is relatively new, many of the basic concepts are already well established. This chapter gives a general introduction to the concepts of AOP, and the rest of the chapters demonstrate the use of these concepts with the four most advanced tools that are currently available: AspectJ/AspectWerkz, JAC, JBoss AOP, and Spring.

Every new programming paradigm brings with it a set of concepts and definitions. This was the case for the procedural approach, with the notions of the module and the procedure, and for the object-oriented approach, with the concepts of encapsulation, inheritance, and polymorphism. Important changes accompanied each of these new paradigms. From a technical point of view, the structure of the programs changed radically, so those involved in software development were required to learn new techniques. As with the previous paradigms, AOP brings a set of new concepts to the table. However, improvements in the quality of applications and the increased modularity that AOP allows counterbalance the costs of learning the new concepts.

Since the majority of AOP environments (including AspectJ/AspectWerkz, JAC, JBoss AOP, and Spring) are built on Java, this book uses the terminology and the concepts of Java; however, none of the concepts of AOP are specific to this language. In the same way that the concept of the object can be applied with success to various languages, the concept of the aspect can be implemented with C++ (AspectC++), C# (AspectC#), Smalltalk (Apostle), and even procedural languages such as C (AspectC). Furthermore, the concepts of AOP are important not only during the coding phase but earlier in the software development—during the conceptual program-design phase. Tools such as Theme/UML and JAC UML Aspectual Factory (UMLAF) propose Unified Modeling Language (UML) notations to model AOP concepts.

The Concept of an Aspect

To understand and manage a complex program, you generally divide it into smaller subprograms. Optimal partitioning criteria have been the subject of numerous studies—the aim of these studies being to help developers with the design, development, maintenance, and evolution of software.

When a program is written with the procedural approach, the application is modularized according to the actions or procedures to be carried out. With the object-oriented approach, on the other hand, the modularization is based on the data to be encapsulated in the classes.

With both paradigms, certain functions are more difficult to modularize than others. We say that the code related to such a function is scattered.

Code Scattering

The issue of code scattering is not linked to a particular language and has been shown to be a problem in numerous applications, whether OOP or another paradigm has been used. In fact, code scattering can appear in any environment—from Java with J2SE or J2EE, to C# with .NET, to additional languages. However, the most extensive study of this phenomenon has been carried out using Java.

For example, the AspectJ team analyzed the Tomcat servlet container. They realized that if some functionalities, such as URL pattern matching and XML parsing, were cleanly modularized in one or two classes each, others, such as the logging functionality and the management of user sessions, were highly scattered throughout the application.

Analysis of Code Scattering

Having established that code scattering occurs, it is normal to ask whether you could eliminate the problem by composing the class structure differently or designing the application in another way.

The main reason that code scattering occurs has to do with the differences in the way that a service is made available and the way that it is used. A class gives access to one or more services through its methods. It is relatively easy to group the available services together in the same place—in other words, in the same class. However, once these services have been used from several classes, it is difficult to re-engineer the application to group the calls to those methods together. It is therefore not surprising that a fundamental and well-known service is called from all over the application.

Code scattering is an effect that manifests itself in any complex program. However, the exact way it manifests itself depends on the application, the modeled concerns, the used libraries, and the frameworks. Because it heavily depends on a concrete problem, code scattering is difficult to remove.

Code scattering in an application slows down the development, maintenance, and evolution of the program. When several functionalities are scattered, the situation worsens because the code starts to contain many calls to multiple concerns that are a priori loosely coupled but that need to be integrated together. This phenomenon is apparent in many applications.

A New Dimension in Modularity

The main contribution of AOP is to provide a way of bringing together—in an aspect—code that would otherwise have been scattered throughout the application.

■**Definition** Aspect—A programming unit designed to capture a functionality that crosscuts an application.

An aspect is often described as being a *crosscutting structure*. In fact, Gregor Kiczales, the inventor of the concept of the aspect, stated that, "AOP is about capturing a crosscutting structure."

The definition of an aspect is almost as general as that of a class. When you model a problem, you use classes to represent the types of objects (customers, orders, suppliers, and so on), and each object contains the appropriate data (attributes) and processes (methods). In the same way, aspects are used to implement functionalities (security, persistence, logging, and so on) within an application, and these functionalities similarly require data and processing.

With AOP, an application consists of classes and aspects. An aspect differs from a class in that it implements a crosscutting functionality. As you saw earlier, a crosscutting functionality within the procedural or object-oriented paradigm is one that is called throughout the code of the application. Including classes and aspects in the same application means that modularity can occur in two dimensions: the base functionalities that are implemented by classes (this dimension could be called structural), and the crosscutting functionalities that are implemented by aspects (this dimension could be called operational).

Figure 2-1 illustrates the effect of an aspect on the code of an application. The left side of the figure represents an application consisting of three classes. The horizontal lines show the lines of code that correspond to a crosscutting functionality, such as logging. This functionality crosscuts the application because it affects all the classes. The right side of the figure shows the same application using an aspect to manage the logging functionality (the shaded rectangle). The code of this functionality is now entirely contained within the aspect, and the classes are now separate from the code. An application designed in this way is simpler to write, maintain, and adapt than one without aspects.

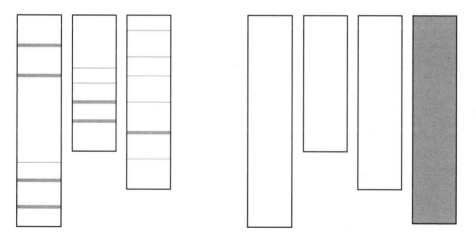

Without an Aspect   With an Aspect

Figure 2-1. *The impact of an aspect on the location of a crosscutting functionality*

The rest of this section presents some of the characteristics of aspects. We then introduce the concept of aspect weaving.

The Integration of Crosscutting Functionalities

You will see later in this chapter that an aspect itself is composed of two parts: the pointcut and the advice code. The *advice code* contains the code to be executed, whereas the *pointcut* defines the points in the program where this code should be implemented.

Clearly, the code of an aspect—or, more precisely, the advice code—depends on the operation you want to implement. For example, if you want to ensure data persistence, you need to write code that saves the data in a database. Although you could code this functionality from first principles directly within the aspect, you would rarely choose to do this. It is considered good practice to use a dedicated API, such as Hibernate. With this type of framework, the code of the aspect simply makes calls to the API. This way of working means that the aspect does not need to know how the services are implemented, and the aspect is therefore kept independent from a particular implementation.

Following this best practice, an aspect simply allows you to integrate a crosscutting functionality that is implemented using a dedicated API into an application. In Figure 2-2, the PersistenceAspect aspect uses Hibernate to integrate the data-persistence functionality into Class1 and Class3.

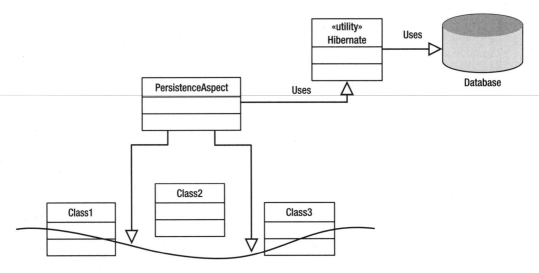

Figure 2-2. *Integration of a crosscutting data-persistence functionality using an aspect*

Strictly speaking, an aspect does not directly implement a crosscutting function but uses a dedicated API to achieve this. However, for ease of readability in this book, we shall just say that an aspect implements a crosscutting functionality.

Nonfunctional Services and Aspects

Most applications are comprised of two types of concerns: business and nonfunctional. *Business concerns*, also called *functional requirements*, correspond to the real-world behavior that you want to model. *Nonfunctional concerns*, or *nonfunctional requirements*, are additional services that the application must implement—essentially, technical or system-level concerns. For example, in an application that manages human resources, the functionalities for adding and deleting an employee are business concerns, whereas application security and privileges are nonfunctional concerns.

However, you need to be careful when using this distinction because a service can be nonfunctional in one application but functional in another.

In most cases, the nonfunctional services are called throughout the code of the business layer. Nonfunctional services are therefore fundamentally crosscutting. Consequently, nonfunctional services are implemented as aspects in AOP, whereas business concerns are implemented as classes. In some cases, however, the business concerns are crosscutting—making it appropriate to implement them as aspects.

Dependency Inversion

With object-oriented or procedural programming, as soon as an application uses a technical service from an API, a dependency is created between the application and the service. A link is generated for every explicit call the application makes to the API. When the API changes or its semantics evolve, calls to its services must be changed throughout the application. Such modifications are potentially costly—especially when the API is used in many different locations in the application.

In addition, you must understand the main principles of the API to be able to use it. You must know which methods to call, the order to call them in, and the parameters to pass to them. The nonfunctional service has to be integrated into every new application that is developed. So, even though the API is developed only once, it may be integrated into many different applications.

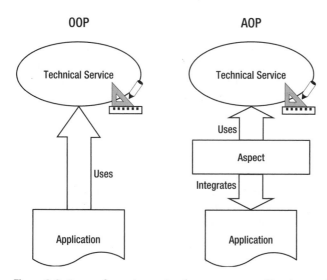

Figure 2-3. *Dependency inversion between an application and a nonfunctional API*

Figure 2-3 illustrates the direction of dependency in OOP and how this changes in AOP. The left side shows that, in OOP, the application uses and thus depends on the nonfunctional service. The situation is the same with procedural programming.

The right side shows the situation in AOP. An aspect uses the nonfunctional service and integrates it into an application. Contrary to OOP, the application no longer depends on the service—it is the aspect that depends on the application. This change in the direction of the links between the service and the application is not specific to AOP; it is sometimes the case for frameworks, as well. The principal advantage of this inversion is that it makes the work of the application developer easier.

With AOP, the application developer does not need to worry about the nonfunctional services. It is the aspect developer who, in addition to writing the code of the service itself, manages the integration of that service into the application. The advantage is that the specialized aspect developer has a better understanding of the service than the application developer, who is only a user of this API. This lowers the risk of a service being used incorrectly. In particular, the aspect developer can make sure that the service integration is correct by implementing some constraints on the way the service can be used.

Aspects and Frameworks

Like AOP, frameworks show dependency inversion, as previously described, whereby the code of the application does not depend on the library.

A framework[1] is a set of classes that offers a reusable structure for writing applications. Frameworks are used in numerous areas of application development, especially user interfaces. A J2EE application server can be considered a framework that manages the execution of applications based on web or Enterprise JavaBeans (EJB) components.

Developing an application with a framework consists of writing code that is handled by the framework. This code is not run directly—instead, the framework invokes it according to the context. In other words, the framework forms a set of services that extends the code that you write.

The situation is similar with AOP. Services are provided by aspects that extend the business layer of the application. The difference is that frameworks provide a set of fixed services, whereas those provided by AOP are entirely programmable within the aspects. AOP therefore offers a much more general mechanism for dependency inversion than frameworks, which are limited to the application domain that they were initially conceived for.

Aspect Weaving

An aspect-oriented application contains classes and one or several aspects. The operation that takes these classes and aspects as input and produces an application that integrates the functionalities of the classes and the aspects is known as *aspect weaving*. The program that performs this operation is called an *aspect weaver* or just a *weaver*. The resulting application is said to be *woven*.

■**Definition** Aspect weaver—A program that integrates classes and aspects. The weaving can be performed at either compile time or run time.

---

1. Ralph Johnson, "Framework = (compopnents + patterns)," *Communications of the ACM*, 40(10), (1997) 39–42.

Compile-Time Weaving

With compile-time weaving, the weaver is a program that, prior to any execution, produces an application code in which the classes are extended by the aspects. AspectJ, which is presented in detail in Chapter 3, is the most well-known compile-time aspect weaver.

A compile-time weaver is very similar to a compiler and is often referred to as an *aspect compiler* or even as a compiler.

With modern object-oriented languages, such as Java and C#, applications are compiled into intermediate bytecode. When weaving aspects with these applications, two solutions can be envisioned: weaving the aspects with the source code, or weaving them with the bytecode.

Bytecode weaving is more common than source-code weaving. A bytecode weaver can weave commercial and third-party applications that do not make their source code available. Furthermore, a bytecode weaver is generally simpler to program. The structure and the grammar of a source language such as Java are much more complex than that of the associated bytecode. The bytecode is therefore simpler to parse and analyze. A direct consequence of this increased simplicity is that the performance of a bytecode weaver is often superior to that of a source-code weaver.

The output of a compile-time weaver can be either source code or bytecode. However, in the case of bytecode weaving, the output is always bytecode. The advantage of generating source code is that it can be easily read by a programmer, who can then study the weaving process and understand what the weaver has done. The disadvantage of generating source code is that this code must then be compiled into bytecode, which slows down the code-production chain. In many cases, fast weaving strategies are preferred. That is why early versions of AspectJ generated source code, but versions 1.1 and later generate bytecode.

With compile-time weaving, aspects are added to the application code. When executed, this new code does not make any distinction between the original code and the code that comes from the aspects. This weaving is thus said to be static. To remove or add an aspect, a total reweaving of the application is needed.

Run-Time Weaving

With run-time weaving, the distinction between application objects and aspects is clearly established during the execution. A run-time weaver is a program that is able to orchestrate the execution of these two types of entities. In other words, the weaver executes either the application code or the aspect code, depending on the defined weaving directives.

The process of weaving aspects at run time can be compared to maintaining a relationship between a set of application objects and a set of aspect instances. An application object that is bound to an aspect instance is *aspectized* by this aspect. An aspect instance can be bound to several application objects (the aspect crosscuts several locations of the application) and, conversely, an application object can be bound to several aspect instances (more than one aspect applies to the same location).

The advantage of run-time weaving is that the relationships between objects and aspects can be dynamically managed. By adding or removing a binding, you can weave or unweave a concern while the application is running. This dynamic quality is particularly useful for applications, such as web servers, that must be highly available and that cannot be stopped for long time frames.

In most cases, run-time weavers transform the application's code or its bytecode before running it. The purpose of this adaptation is to make the classes ready for run-time weaving. All the code elements that can be adapted at run time are modified to introduce hooks. A *hook* is a piece of code that redirects the execution flow of the application toward an aspect. Hooks are introduced at the beginnings of methods, for example, or just before method calls. The types of locations where hooks can be introduced depend on the weaver. Note that hooks are not necessarily locations where aspects apply but locations where aspects *potentially* apply. Among all the hooks introduced by a run-time weaver, only a selected subset will redirect the execution flow toward an aspect. The aspect programmer decides which hooks effectively perform this redirection.

Instead of using a weaver to transform the application code, you can take advantage of an alternative solution that consists of running the application in a supervisory mode. This technique is similar to running the application in a debugger in that whenever the execution reaches a location where an aspect applies, the supervisor interrupts the normal execution flow and runs the aspect. The advantage of this technique is that it leaves the application free from any transformation. The disadvantage is that the supervisory mode introduces a cost that slows down the execution of the application.

In several implementations, the insertion of hooks is performed just before the execution—while the application is being loaded into the virtual machine. With the Java language, the class-loading mechanism can be customized and associated to a bytecode-engineering library, such as the Byte Code Engineering Library (BCEL) (see `http://jakarta.apache.org/bcel`), ASM (see `http://asm.objectweb.org`), or the Java Programming Assistant (Javassist) (see `http://www.csg.is.titech.ac.jp/~chiba/javassist/index.html`). For example, the run-time weaver of JAC uses BCEL, whereas that of JBoss AOP uses Javassist.

The notion of hooks that are inserted by a run-time weaver is closely related to the notion of the joinpoint, which is presented in the next section.

Joinpoints

In the previous section, you learned that an aspect is a software entity that implements a crosscutting functionality. The definition of an aspect, or crosscutting structure, relies on the notion of a *joinpoint*.

■**Definition** Joinpoint—A point in the control flow of a program where one or several aspects apply.

Although the notion of a joinpoint is general (potentially, each instruction of a program can be a joinpoint), all the points in the control flow are not considered useful for AOP. Joinpoints are grouped according to their types, and only a subset of all possible joinpoint types are supported by aspect-oriented languages.

Furthermore, the notion of the joinpoint is tightly related to a particular execution of a program (the control flow). Two different executions of the same program may give different sets of joinpoints.

Different Types of Joinpoints

Although the definition of a joinpoint occurs at run time, that definition is based on the structure of a program (its classes, methods, fields, and so on). The following chapters present in detail the various joinpoint types that are supported by existing aspect-oriented languages. The following categories describe the commonly encountered types that are independent of any implementation.

Methods: With object-oriented languages, the execution of a program can be seen as a sequence of method calls and method executions. The various execution scenarios of an application can be expressed in terms of sequences of messages that trigger method executions. Method calls and method executions are thus two commonly used joinpoint types. Note that method executions are considered joinpoints even if they are not, strictly speaking, "points." A method starts, continues, and ends—its execution spans a time period. Instead of considering the beginning and end as two separate points, the execution as a whole is a type of joinpoint.

Constructors: Constructors are the main entities used to create the objects of an application. As with methods, the calls and executions of a constructor correspond to joinpoint types.

Exceptions: An exception is thrown to signal an abnormal run-time situation, and it is caught to execute a particular treatment. These two events are major points in the execution of an application. They can be both considered joinpoint types.

Fields: Many aspects, such as the persistence aspect, need to deal with the application's data. Fields are the main code elements that implement this data. Hence, aspect-oriented languages consider read and write operations on fields as joinpoint types.

Method calls and executions are clearly the most widely used joinpoint types in AOP. Other code elements, such as code blocks like for loops and if statements, define the structure of a program. With the exception of static code blocks in AspectJ, these elements are considered too fine grained to be used when defining aspects. Even though these elements define useful treatments for method bodies, it is assumed that the crosscutting nature of a functionality can be captured with higher-level elements, such as the ones mentioned in the previous list.

Aspect-oriented-compiler designers often use the term *joinpoint shadow*. Like a hook for run-time weavers, a joinpoint shadow is a place in the program where an aspect can potentially apply. Hence, the joinpoints—as the points where the aspects *actually* apply—are a subset of the set of joinpoint shadows. Depending on the information needed by the aspects, several pieces of data can be constructed during run time when a joinpoint is reached. A joinpoint object can even be provided by the language.

Finally, all programs, even the simplest ones, contain many different joinpoints. The task of the aspect programmer is to select the joinpoints that are useful for implementing a given aspect. This selection is performed with the notion of a pointcut, which is presented in the next section.

Pointcuts

In the previous section, you learned that joinpoints are the points in the control flow of a program where one or several aspects apply. Yet, the notion of a joinpoint is not sufficient by itself to define which joinpoints are pertinent for a given aspect. An entity is needed for describing joinpoints. This entity is defined by the notion of a *pointcut*.

Definition Pointcut—A set of joinpoints where an aspect applies.

Above all, the crosscutting nature of an aspect is expressed with a pointcut because a pointcut groups joinpoints that are located in different source files. Of course, these joinpoints are not chosen randomly. They share the "common secret" in that they are located in the parts of the program where a given aspect applies. Pointcuts are thus a way of "talking about" the application. It is often said that a pointcut defines the "where" of an aspect. On the other hand, the "what" of an aspect is defined by the advice code, as we will explain in the next section.

It is important to note that most pointcuts are application dependent. When an aspect needs to be reused for a different application, it is likely that the definition of the pointcuts will need to be adapted to the locations in the new application.

As illustrated by the previous definition, the notions of the pointcut and the joinpoint are linked. A pointcut is defined by a set of joinpoints and, conversely, a set of joinpoints define a specific pointcut. However, note that the natures of these two notions are somewhat different. Joinpoints are well-defined run-time entities (they occur in the control flow of a program), whereas pointcuts cannot be attached to a particular structure or time slot of the running program. Instead, pointcuts are to be seen as structural code elements that participate in the definition of an aspect.

As illustrated in the following chapters, a language for defining pointcuts is included in every existing aspect-oriented tool. Although each tool defines its own syntax, the principles remain the same. The ultimate goal of a pointcut language is to provide a simple and flexible way to query the joinpoints about a given program's structure—so an aspect can be applied to the joinpoints. Typically, the language is a kind of pattern language with quantification operators, wildcard symbols (such as *), and Boolean operators. Keywords are also included for designating joinpoint types.

EXAMPLES OF POINTCUTS

To familiarize you with AOP syntax, the following examples of widely used pointcut types show implementations in AOP pseudocode (with a syntax that is similar to that of AspectJ):

- *Data-modification pointcut*: This type of pointcut designates all the write operations on a set of fields. When data that is represented as a set of fields needs to be saved in a database, such a pointcut can be used for persistence aspects, for example. This type of pointcut can also be used in GUIs to update views that are associated with data. Here is an example of a data-modification pointcut:

```
// all the field set operations on all the fields (*) of class C
pointcut dataModification(): set(C.*)
```

- *Method-calls pointcut:* This type of pointcut designates all the calls to a set of methods. Such a pointcut can be used to compute a message-sequence chart, for example. Here is an example of a method-calls pointcut:

```
// all the calls to the methods of C returning void
// and taking any parameters (..)
pointcut calls(): call(void C.*(..))
```

- *Method-executions pointcut:* This type of pointcut designates all the executions of a set of methods. Such a pointcut can be used to compute method-execution times, for example. Here is an example of a method-executions pointcut:

```
// all the executions of the methods of C returning any type (*)
// and taking any parameters (..)
pointcut executions(): execution(void A.*(..))
```

Advice Code

In the previous section, you learned that a pointcut defines *where* an aspect applies. The advice code defines *what* the instructions of an aspect are.

■**Definition** **Advice code**—The definition of the behavior of an aspect.

Advice code is associated with a pointcut to implement a crosscutting functionality. The treatments that are defined in the advice code are performed for all the joinpoints that are included in the associated pointcut.

Much like a method, the advice code owns a body that contains instructions. However, unlike a method, the advice code is never called directly but is woven into the joinpoints that are specified in the associated pointcut.

Different Types of Advice Code

Three main types of advice code exist:

- *before*: The advice code is executed before the joinpoints.

- *after*: The advice code is executed after the joinpoints.

- *around*: The advice code is executed before and after the joinpoints.

For "around" advice code, you need to separate the instructions that must be executed before the joinpoints from the ones that must be executed after. This is done with a special instruction, which in most cases is named proceed. The proceed instruction provides a way of resuming the normal execution of the program and executing the code that is contained in the joinpoint. To intuitively understand "around" advice code, think of a decorator design pattern in which a decorating method is the "around" advice code, and proceed is the call to the next decorator or decorator object.

The execution of a program with "around" advice code can be summed up as follows:

1. The program executes normally.

2. Just before a joinpoint that is included in a pointcut, the "before" part defined in the "around" advice code is executed.

3. A call to proceed is made.

4. The piece of code that is defined in the joinpoint is executed.

5. The "after" part defined in the "around" advice code is executed.

6. The program execution is resumed just after the joinpoint.

The call to proceed is optional. If proceed is not called, the code of the joinpoint is not executed, and the program execution resumes just after the joinpoint.

Advice code blocks can be classified according to whether they always call proceed, never call it, or call it under certain conditions. For example, a trace aspect always calls proceed because its purpose is to keep track of the application's execution—not to modify its normal execution. A security aspect calls proceed when access is granted to the user; it doesn't call proceed when access is denied. An optimization aspect never calls proceed if it replaces the original implementation of a functionality with an optimized version.

In addition to the three previously listed advice-code types, some languages (including AspectJ) define two other types: "after returning" and "after throwing." The idea is that a method can either return normally or throw an exception. The first case corresponds to the execution of the "after returning" advice code, whereas the second one leads to the execution of the "after throwing" advice code.

Here is a simple example (still using pseudocode) of "around" advice code, which prints some tracing messages before and after the execution of the joinpoint:

```
around void a() {
    System.out.println("before joinpoint");
    proceed();
    System.out.println("after joinpoint");
}
```

Then, in an aspect, this advice code can be linked to pointcuts. For example, the following aspect links the previous advice code to the pointcuts that were defined in the previous section:

```
aspect MyAspect {
    a() : dataModification();
    a() : calls();
    a() : executions();
}
```

This aspect prints the specified messages around the executions of all the joinpoints that are denoted by the `dataModification`, `calls`, and `executions` pointcuts.

The Introduction Mechanism

The notions of the pointcut and the advice code allow you to reason about the structure of an application and to implement crosscutting functionalities through *behavioral* modifications. The control flow of the program deviates to the advice code, which adds, removes, or modifies behavior. The *introduction* mechanism is complementary and allows you to extend the static structure of a program.

■**Definition** Introduction—An extension mechanism for bringing new structural code elements into an application.

The two most common code elements that are *introduced* by aspects are fields and methods. In relation to methods, interfaces can also be introduced—the idea is to let a target class implement a new interface. In some aspect-oriented frameworks, such as JAC (see Chapter 4), exception handlers can also be introduced. The idea is to define handlers for exceptions that are not caught by the application.

Like the inheritance relationship of OOP, the introduction mechanism allows for the extension of existing classes. However, contrary to inheritance, the introduction mechanism does not allow for the redefinition of existing elements—it can only add new ones. This limitation is due to the goal of conserving the program's integrity, especially when several aspects are composed together. Next, we elaborate on the well-known problem of aspect composition.

Aspect Composition

The concepts that have been defined so far deal with the definition of aspects and their integration with applications. This section raises the issue of aspect interactions—for example, how distinct aspects that are woven into the same application interact. This issue is known as *aspect composition*.

The study of aspect composition can be carried out from two complementary points of view: that of design time (when choosing the aspects for an application), and that of weave time (when applying several aspects to the same joinpoints).

Design

Like classes, aspects can be independently programmed and then reused and integrated into an application. The aspect programmer must therefore verify that aspects do not conflict nor introduce inconsistencies in the execution of the application.

Several kinds of conflicts can arise:

Incompatibility: Two aspects can introduce incompatible functionalities. For example, a transaction aspect and a persistence aspect can conflict. Indeed, when programmed with persistence frameworks, such as Hibernate, a persistence aspect uses a database to store data that is modified during a so-called *persistent session*. Most of the time, transactions involve data that is also stored in databases. Hence, the database is a resource that is shared by the two aspects. When developed separately, the aspects might not be aware of the operations performed on the database by one another.

Dependence: Two aspects can be linked. In this case, if one aspect is used, the other must also be used.

Redundancy: Two aspects might implement the same functionality differently. For example, several data-compression algorithms can be implemented. The joint utilization of two data-compression aspects might be useless and should be avoided.

These kinds of conflicts occur at the semantic level and cannot be simply addressed at the programming level with the existing aspect-oriented tools. For example, existing aspect weavers cannot automatically detect that two aspects implement data-compression algorithms. The weavers reason about the instructions that must be appended to the joinpoints, but they usually cannot reason about the semantics of these instructions. (However, some research prototypes are currently being developed.) Therefore, the job of detecting whether two aspects are incompatible, dependant, or redundant is entirely the responsibility of the aspect programmer.

Weaving

In addition to posing potential semantic conflicts, the composition of several aspects might require the execution of the distinct aspects that must be woven into an application.

For example, a security aspect and a trace aspect might define pointcuts that include the same set of joinpoints. In this case, the execution order of the two aspects should be defined. There is no automatic solution to this problem. For example, you might want to trace all requests—even those that will be rejected because the user is not authorized. (In this case, the trace aspect must be applied first). Or, you might want to trace only the requests from authorized users. (In this case, the security aspect must be applied first.) Hence, given two aspects, you must decide on and define the correct execution order.

Summary

This chapter introduced the basic concepts of AOP. The concepts that were presented are independent of any implementation by a specific language or framework. This chapter provided a reference for the following chapters in this book, where the concepts will be illustrated specifically with AspectJ, JAC, JBoss AOP, and Spring.

The concept of an aspect aims to modularize a crosscutting functionality. A functionality is said to be crosscutting when its implementation is not cleanly located in one file but is scattered throughout many different files of an application. By locating these scattered elements in one place, the concept of an aspect improves modularity and leads to applications that are easier to understand, debug, and maintain.

AOP is a technique that complements OOP. The purpose of AOP is not to replace classes and objects. Hence, an aspect-oriented application is still organized around a set of classes. Aspects enhance these classes by implementing crosscutting functionalities.

Implementing an aspect consists of defining advice code and pointcuts. The advice code defines *what* the behavior of the aspect is, and pointcuts define *where* this behavior is to be applied in the application. The point in the program execution where an aspect applies is called a joinpoint. AOP provides the additional notion of introduction, which is the mechanism for extending an application.

CHAPTER 3

■ ■ ■

AspectJ

In the previous chapter, we presented the basic concepts of AOP with the notions of the aspect, the pointcut, the joinpoint, and the advice code.

In this chapter, we will illustrate the way that these concepts are implemented in AspectJ. The syntax and concepts presented here correspond to version 1.2.1 of the language.

Gregor Kiczales and his team, who are credited with the creation of AOP at the Palo Alto Research Center (PARC), are responsible for the invention and development of AspectJ— which is now the leading tool for AOP. The first versions of AspectJ were released in 1998 and, as of December 2002, the AspectJ project has left PARC and joined the open-source Eclipse community. Today, AspectJ is the most widely used aspect-oriented language.

THE HISTORY OF ASPECTJ

The histories of AspectJ and AOP are closely related. AspectJ has always been considered by Gregor Kiczales as the project that would illustrate the concepts of AOP. Although the notion of the aspect dates back to 1996, and the first versions of AspectJ were released in 1998, the ideas and research that culminated in AOP date back to before this time. Research in reflection in the 1980s and work on open implementations in the 1990s served as background for the development of AOP.

Invented in 1984 by Brian Smith, and studied and popularized by Patricia Maes in 1997, reflection is a programming technique that introduces a two-level architecture. The first level, called the *base level*, consists of the application. The second level, called the *meta level*, controls and supervises the base level. Although the notions of the aspect and the meta level differ, they share a common goal: to separate business functionalities from technical concerns. This separation aims to result in better modularization of programs. Prior to inventing the concept of the aspect, Kiczales spent time conducting research in the domain of reflection. In 1991, he was coauthor of *The Art of the Metaobject Protocol* (MIT Press, 1991).

The founding document of AOP was published and presented in 1997 by Kiczales during the European Conference on Object-Oriented Programming (ECOOP). Presentations had been held previously, in 1996, but the 1997 article is considered seminal. Simultaneously, the first prototypes of AOP languages appeared in 1996–97.

Christina Lopez, a member of Kiczales's team at the time and an important contributor, developed the D language and its implementation, DJava. The D language contained two types of aspects: distribution and concurrency-management. Soon after, Lopez and Kiczales realized that this new approach could be generalized and applied to other aspects. A general-purpose language that could implement any kind of aspect was needed.

In 1998, Kiczales and his team made the decision to switch from D to AspectJ. Soon after, the first implementations of AspectJ were released. At almost the same time, Aspect-Oriented Tcl Object System (A-TOS),

23

which was the first prototype of Java Aspect Components (JAC), was implemented. Since then, several versions of AspectJ have been released, and each one has included new features and/or bug fixes. The first major version of AspectJ, designated version 1.0, was released in November 2001. This was also the year during which AOP was fully recognized by the international computer-science community. A special edition of the leading journal, *Communications of the ACM*, was devoted to AOP.

In December 2002, the AspectJ project left PARC and joined the open-source Eclipse community. Since then, the AspectJ Development Tools (AJDT) plug-in has been developed. It enables you to write, compile, and run an aspect-oriented program within the IBM Eclipse IDE.

A First Application with AspectJ

This section presents a simple example of an aspect-oriented application with AspectJ. This example introduces the syntax for writing aspects, pointcuts, and advice code.

The example is an order-management application that manages client orders. The application implements a trace aspect, which traces the execution of the application and determines which methods are called and the order that they are called in.

The Order-Management Application

The order-management application enables a client to add items to an order and to compute the amount of that order. References to the items and their prices are stored in a catalog.

This application defines three classes: Customer, Order, and Catalog. The Customer class, which is shown in Listing 3-1, is the main entry point of the application.

Listing 3-1. *The Customer Class for the Order-Management Application*

```
package aop.aspectj;
public class Customer {

  public void run() {
    Order myOrder = new Order();
    myOrder.addItem("CD",2);
    myOrder.addItem("DVD",1);
    double amount = myOrder.computeAmount();
    System.out.println("Order amount: US$"+amount);
  }

  public static void main(String[] args) {
    new Customer().run();
  }
}
```

The main method creates an object from the Customer class and calls the run method. The latter method creates an order (a myOrder object), calls the addItem method two times with a reference and a quantity, computes the amount of the order, and displays the amount.

The orders are managed by the Order class, which is shown in Listing 3-2.

Listing 3-2. *The Order Class for the Order-Management Application*

```
package aop.aspectj;

import java.util.*;

public class Order {

  private Map items = new HashMap();

  public void addItem(String reference,int quantity) {
    items.put(reference,new Integer(quantity));
    System.out.println(
      quantity+" item(s) "+reference+ " added to the order" );
  }

  public double computeAmount() {
    double amount = 0.0;
    Iterator iter = items.entrySet().iterator()
    while ( iter.hasNext() ) {
      Map.Entry entry = (Map.Entry) iter.next();
      String item = (String) entry.getKey();
      Integer quantity = (Integer) entry.getValue();
      double price = Catalog.getPrice(item);
      amount += price*quantity.intValue();
    }
    return amount;
  }
}
```

The Order class records the items and the ordered quantities in a hash map (in the items field). This map is indexed with the item references. The associated map values are the quantities of the ordered items. The addItem method adds an item to the order and displays a message that reports on the operation. The computeAmount method iterates over the ordered items, determines each price, and returns the total amount of the order.

The price of each item is determined by the Catalog.getPrice method, which is shown in Listing 3-3.

Listing 3-3. *The Catalog Class for the Order-Management Application*

```
package aop.aspectj;

import java.util.*;

public class Catalog {

    private static Map priceList = new HashMap();
```

```
    static {
      priceList.put( "CD", new Double(15.0) );
      priceList.put( "DVD", new Double(20.0) );
    }

    public static double getPrice( String reference ) {
      Double price = (Double) priceList.get(reference);
      return price.doubleValue();
    }
}
```

The Catalog class records the price of each item in the priceList hash map. This table is indexed by the item references. The associated values are the item prices. The static code block initializes the priceList map with two items: a CD that costs US$15 and a DVD that costs US$20. The getPrice method returns the price of the item that was given as a parameter.

Execution

The order-management application has so far been written purely in Java. The principle of AOP is to leave applications unpolluted by code that is not related to the main functionality. As a result, AOP allows you to focus on the core business, which in this case is the management of orders.

The nonfunctional concerns, such as security, tracing, and the management of transactions, can be independently added through aspects. The output of the order-management application is shown in Listing 3-4.

Listing 3-4. *The Output of the Order-Management Application*

```
2 item(s) CD added to the order
1 item(s) DVD added to the order
Order amount: US$50.0
```

A First Trace Aspect

The business core of the application has now been developed. We will now proceed with the development of a first aspect. This aspect, developed separately from the classes, monitors each ordered item by displaying messages before and after the addItem method, which is defined in the Order class.

The AspectJ code for this aspect is shown in Listing 3-5.

Listing 3-5. *A First Trace Aspect for the Order-Management Application*

```
1 package aop.aspectj;
2
3 public aspect TraceAspect {
4
5   pointcut toBeTraced():
```

```
 6    call( public void Order.addItem(String,int) );
 7
 8  void around(): toBeTraced() {
 9    System.out.println("-> Before calling addItem");
10    proceed();
11    System.out.println("<- After calling addItem");
12  }
13 }
```

The AspectJ language extends the Java syntax with new keywords. In Listing 3-5, the first new keyword you encounter is aspect. Like a class, an aspect is named (in this case, TraceAspect) and can be defined in a package (in this case, aop.aspectj). An aspect can also be extended through inheritance, as you will see in the "Aspect Inheritance" section later in this chapter.

In the philosophy held by the AspectJ creators, an aspect is a software entity that is largely similar to a class—in that both define a piece of code that abstracts and modularizes a concern. Although the concern is crosscutting in the case of an aspect, classes and aspects belong to the same level and must obey—as often as possible—the same rules.

In the examples that are distributed with AspectJ, the similarities go so far that classes and aspects[1] use the same .java extension.

Aspects define pointcuts and advice code; the following sections describe these elements.

A First Pointcut Descriptor

In an aspect, the pointcut keyword is used to define a *pointcut descriptor*. Pointcut descriptors can be named. In the example of the TraceAspect aspect, the pointcut descriptor is named toBeTraced.

Each pointcut descriptor is an expression (see line 6 in Listing 3-5) that denotes the set of associated joinpoints. Several different types of joinpoints can be used. However, this is not the case in the example of the toBeTraced pointcut descriptor, in which call is the only type of joinpoint.

The call joinpoint designates the points where a method is called. The signature of the called method is given in parentheses. The signature refers to the addItem method, which is defined in the Order class, has two parameters of type String and int, returns void, and is public. This signature is so precise that only one method fits this pointcut. In the "Wildcards" section later in this chapter, you will see that wildcards can be used to match several methods with the same pointcut descriptor.

The toBeTraced pointcut is associated with the addItem method; however, this does not mean that only one joinpoint exists for this pointcut. In fact, all the locations where the method is called match the pointcut. In the example in Listing 3-1, when addItem is called two times in the run method of the Customer class, both locations match the pointcut.

In general, the number of joinpoints associated with a pointcut is not predetermined—the number varies depending on the particular pointcut and its application. It is possible to write

---

1. In many applications, there is a clear difference between business functionalities and crosscutting functionalities. The former are implemented in classes and the latter in aspects. It can then be interesting to clearly state this difference by giving different extensions to file names. You could choose, for instance, .aj or .ajava for files containing aspects, and keep .java for files containing classes.

a pointcut descriptor with no associated joinpoints and, in this case, the aspect will not modify the application. Although this is possible, it is highly unlikely that such a pointcut descriptor would be useful—most of the time, this type of pointcut descriptor corresponds to an error.

Tools are available to detect these types of cases and avoid them. For example, the AJDT plug-in provides a view that gives the corresponding joinpoints of each defined pointcut. Figure 3-1 gives an illustration of this view. As shown in the advises node, the toBeTraced pointcut descriptor is associated with two joinpoints for the Customer class. If there were no associated joinpoints, the correctness of the pointcut would have been questioned.

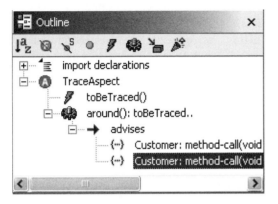

Figure 3-1. *The AJDT view of joinpoints associated with a pointcut descriptor*

A First Piece of Advice Code

The TraceAspect aspect defines only one piece of advice code. (See line 8 in Listing 3-5). Three types of advice code exist: "before," "after," and "around." For the first type, the advice code is executed before each joinpoint that is associated with the pointcut; for the second type, it is executed after; for the third type, it is executed before and after.

For any type of advice code, the joinpoints are designated by a pointcut, and each piece of advice code is associated with a pointcut. In the TraceAspect aspect, the advice code is of the "around" variety, and the associated pointcut is toBeTraced. The code is given between brackets. In this example, the "around" advice code is executed before and after the calls to the addItem method.

In the TraceAspect example, AspectJ expects the methods included in the pointcut to define the return type as void. It follows that the addItem return type is void.

Advice code is a regular block of code. Any existing Java instruction, such as a method call, a variable assignment, a for statement, a while statement, or an if statement, can be used. AspectJ adds the new keyword proceed to this list. When reached, this keyword triggers the execution of the joinpoint. The instructions prior to proceed are executed before the joinpoint, and those following proceed are executed after. Hence, proceed delimits a "before" part and an "after" part in the advice code.

The execution of a program with "around" advice code is as follows:

1. The program is started.

2. Just before a joinpoint, the "before" part is executed.

3. The proceed method is called.

4. The corresponding joinpoint is executed.

5. The "after" part is executed.

6. Program execution resuming, just after the joinpoint.

The call to proceed is optional. Certainly, it is valid for "around" advice code to not call proceed. In such a case, the code associated with the joinpoint is not executed. After the execution of the advice code, the program execution resumes directly after the joinpoint.

Advice code can call proceed in some cases and not in others. This can be seen in the case of a security aspect that controls access to a method. If the user is authenticated, the call is authorized and the aspect calls proceed. If the user does not own sufficient rights, the call is rejected and the security aspect does not call proceed. In such a case, the joinpoint is not executed.

The "before" and "after" advice code blocks do not need to call proceed. They are designed to be executed before and after joinpoints. AspectJ raises an error if proceed appears in the body of "before" or "after" advice code.

Compiling

AspectJ is a compile-time weaver (since version 1.2, AspectJ can also weave aspect at load-time). The aspect and class input files are woven together by AspectJ to produce a final application. This application can then be executed as a regular Java application.

To compile the aspect with the three classes of the order-management application, call the ajc compiler from the operating-system command shell with the following command:

```
ajc TraceAspect.aj *.java
```

This command produces a set of .class files that contain the bytecode of the aspectized application.

The first versions of AspectJ produced Java code. The output of the ajc compiler was a Java program in which instructions from aspects and classes were merged. This Java code could then be compiled by the regular javac Java compiler. The advantage of this approach was that the produced code could easily be read by developers, who could then study the way that the pointcuts and advice code blocks were implemented.

Despite these benefits, this approach had several drawbacks. The first had to do with performance. The initial translation from Java to Java was costly. In addition, a syntax analysis of the Java code was needed before the result of the weaving could be generated—and writing a Java syntax analyzer that is fast enough to manage huge amounts of code is a difficult task. Even more, this task is redundant with the one performed when the produced code is compiled. The second disadvantage had to do with the source code needed to perform the weaving. In some cases, the application was commercial or came from a developer who did not release the source code. As a result, the Java-to-Java compilation could not be applied.

To avoid these difficulties, the new versions of AspectJ can weave bytecode in .class or .jar files and do not require source code. The ajc compiler provides the option -injar to use this feature.

Running

The order-management application, which is woven with the `TraceAspect` aspect, can be run by calling the Java virtual machine with the `Customer` class.

To be run in a UNIX or Windows shell, the command is as follows:

```
java aop.aspectj.Customer
```

The output of this command is shown in Listing 3-6.

Listing 3-6. *The Output of the Order-Management Application with the Trace Aspect*

```
-> Before calling addItem
2 item(s) CD added to the order
-> After calling addItem
-> Before calling addItem
1 item(s) DVD added to the order
-> After calling addItem
Order amount: US$50.0
```

In this run, each call to the `addItem` method corresponds to a joinpoint. The execution is trapped, and the advice code defined in the `TraceAspect` aspect applies. This is "around" advice code. The message -> *Before calling addItem* is displayed, the `proceed` instruction is called, the "after" part is executed, and the message -> *After calling addItem* is displayed. Note that the call to `proceed` executes the `addItem` method.

Pointcut Descriptors

In the previous section, we introduced the basic elements of the AspectJ syntax. We showed how to write, compile, and run a first aspect-oriented application.

Although it is simplistic, the order-management application illustrates a major AOP characteristic: the separation of business from technical code. The `Customer`, `Order`, and `Catalog` classes play the role of the business code, whereas the `TraceAspect` aspect implements the technical part of the application. This separation is made possible by the use of pointcuts. Pointcuts allow you to describe where the aspects must be applied in the code. Therefore, pointcuts give you a way of "talking about" the application by designating some of the strategic locations of that application.

In the following sections, we present the syntax of the AspectJ language. We begin with the syntax of pointcuts and follow with the syntax of advice code. You will see how more-generic aspects can be written, how different types of joinpoints can be included, and how more-complex pointcuts can be defined.

Wildcards

The `toBeTraced` pointcut, which was defined in the `TraceAspect` aspect in Listing 3-5, is not generic. It captures calls exclusively to the `addItem` method. In more complex cases, it is important for you to accurately define pointcuts that contain calls to several methods.

AspectJ provides a pattern language, which allows the definition of expressions that implicitly denote several methods or classes. These symbols (*, .., and +) are called wildcards. In the following sections, we explain the principle and definition of these wildcards and give usage examples of them.

Principle

When wildcards are used jointly with the different types of joinpoints that we describe later in this chapter (in the "Joinpoint Types" section), the wildcards act as a powerful syntax capable of describing many pointcuts. In return, this flexibility can lead to pointcut descriptors that are complex and subtle.

Other AOP environments, such as JAC and JBoss AOP (see Chapters 4 and 5), have made different choices. Their pointcut languages define fewer operators and, as a consequence, their expression powers are not as flexible as that of AspectJ. On the other hand, their pointcut descriptors are simpler to write, understand, and debug.

The discussion about the trade-offs between power and simplicity remains open. Yet, in computer science and other domains, the simple solutions are often the most widely used. Similarly, the simplest pointcuts are the ones more frequently reused. Therefore, we use the simple pointcuts to illustrate and promote AOP.

The following sections define the *, .., and + wildcards. They are presented according to the element types (method, class, signature, package, and subtype) that they denote.

Method and Class Names

The asterisk (*) can be used to denote method and class names. You will see in the "Method Signatures" and "Package Names" sections, later in this chapter, that the asterisk can also be used for signatures and package names.

For methods, the asterisk designates "some or all of the methods defined in a class."

The following expression designates all the public methods in the Order class that have two parameters of type String and int and that return void:

```
public void aop.aspectj.Order.*(String,int)
```

The asterisk can be used in combination with letters to designate all the method names that contain the substring "Item", for instance. In such a case, the expression is *Item*.

As stated, the asterisk can also be used for class names. The following expression designates all the public methods of all the classes in the aop.aspectj package that have two parameters of type String and int and that return void:

```
public void aop.aspectj.*.*(String,int)
```

Method Signatures

Names, parameters, return types, and access modifiers (public, protected, and private), can be used in AspectJ pointcut descriptors.

Method parameters can be omitted and replaced by two dots (..) to indicate "any parameter." The following expression illustrates the public methods in the Order class that have any parameters and that return void:

```
public void aop.aspectj.Order.*(..)
```

Hence, the symbol of two dots handles the polymorphism of Java methods.

The return type and the access modifier can be omitted and replaced by the asterisk (*).

The following expression denotes all the methods defined in the Order class, regardless of their parameters, return types, and access modifiers:

```
* * aop.aspectj.Order.*(..)
```

In addition, the asterisk that is used to replace the access modifier can be omitted without changing the meaning of the pointcut. Therefore, the following expression is equivalent to the one just presented:

```
* aop.aspectj.Order.*(..)
```

Package Names

The two-dots symbol can also be used with package names. For example, the following expression designates all the methods of any class named Order that is in any package of the aop hierarchy, regardless of the subpackage level:

```
* aop..Order.*(..)
```

The use of the two-dots symbol between aop and Order is of great importance. Expressions such as aop.Order.*(..) and aop.*.Order.*(..) look similar but lead to completely different results. Although both expressions involve the methods defined in an Order class, they differ in the following ways:

- The aop..Order.*(..) expression denotes the entire hierarchy that starts with the aop package.

- The aop.Order.*(..) expression denotes only the class that is defined in the aop package.

- The aop.*.Order.*(..) expression denotes only the classes that are defined in the direct subpackages of the aop package.

Subtypes

The last wildcard, the plus sign (+), deals with type hierarchies and designates all the subclasses of a given class. The following expression denotes all the methods of the Order class and its subclasses:

```
* aop.Order+.*(..)
```

The plus sign can also be used after an interface name. In such a case, the pointcut designates all the methods of all the classes that implement the interface.

Because the plus sign can be used with either a class or an interface, it is referred to as a *subtyping operator*.

Wildcard-Usage Example

We will illustrate the usage of wildcards by showing a second version of the trace aspect, which is named TraceAspect2. The previous version, TraceAspect, intercepted only the calls to the addItem method. The new version is more generic and intercepts the calls to all the methods defined in the Order class.

The code of the TraceAspect2 aspect is shown in Listing 3-7.

Listing 3-7. *Using Wildcards in Pointcut Descriptors*

```
1 package aop.aspectj;
2
3 public aspect TraceAspect2 {
4
5   pointcut toBeTraced(): call(* aop.aspectj.Order.*(..));
6
7   Object around(): toBeTraced() {
8     System.out.println("-> Before the call");
9     Object ret = proceed();
10    System.out.println("<- After the call");
11    return ret;
12  }
13 }
```

The first difference between the TraceAspect and TraceAspect2 aspects is in the definition of the pointcut. (See line 5 in Listing 3-7). The pointcut descriptor is now call(* aop.aspectj. Order.*(..)). All the calls to the methods defined in the Order class are intercepted by the pointcut—whatever the methods' parameters and return types are.

A second difference can be found in the return type of the advice code block. Previously, the type was void. Now, the pointcut intercepts either a method that returns void (for example, addItem) or a method that returns double (for example, computeAmount). Strictly speaking, no common supertype exists for both void and double. As a convention, AspectJ considers that Object (see line 7 in Listing 3-7) is the common supertype for all Java primitive and object types. The result of proceed is stored in the ret variable (see line 9), which is returned at the end of the advice code block (see line 11).

Joinpoint Introspection

In the previous section, you learned that wildcards can be used to write generic pointcut descriptors. With wildcards, a pointcut can be associated with several methods. You will see in this section how to obtain some information about a joinpoint at run time. This is known as the *joinpoint-introspection mechanism.*

The term *introspection* refers to examining the inner cause of a given phenomenon and gaining information about it. In the context of AOP, the phenomenon is the joinpoint, and you want to retrieve information about the part of the actual program that allows the joinpoint to occur. A comparison can be made with the Java java.lang.reflect API that provides, for any given Java program, a description of the program's classes, fields, and methods. The program is then said to have *introspected* to obtain information about itself.

In the context of AOP, the same principle applies. The joinpoint examines itself to gain information about itself. This mechanism is useful for determining, for instance, the method call that caused the joinpoint to occur.

Introspection Syntax

The thisJoinPoint keyword implements the introspection mechanism in AspectJ. In regular Java, this is the reference to the current object. Similarly, in AspectJ, thisJoinPoint is a reference to an object describing the current joinpoint, which implements the predefined org.aspectj.lang.JoinPoint interface. Table 3-1 sums up the main methods defined in this interface. Two of them, getSignature and getSourceLocation, use predefined interfaces, which are Signature and SourceLocation, respectively. The AspectJ Javadoc documentation gives more details on the methods provided by these interfaces.

Table 3-1. *Main Methods Defined in* org.aspectj.lang.JoinPoint

Method Signature	Definition	Comment
Object[] getArgs()	Returns the joinpoint arguments	When the joinpoint deals with a method, getArgs returns the arguments of the call.
Signature getSignature()	Returns the joinpoint signature	The Signature interface gives a representation of the signature of the joinpoint. When the joinpoint deals with a method, Signature provides methods for retrieving the joinpoint method's name, access modifiers (public, private, and so on), class, and return type.
String getKind()	Returns the joinpoint type	
SourceLocation getSourceLocation()	Returns the localization of the joinpoint in the source code	SourceLocation is a predefined interface that provides access to the file name, line number, and class where the joinpoint is defined.
Object getTarget()	Returns the target object of the joinpoint	When the joinpoint deals with a method, getTarget returns the called object.
Object getThis()	Returns the source object of the joinpoint	When the joinpoint deals with a method call, getThis returns the calling object.

Usage Example

We now illustrate the joinpoint-introspection mechanism with a third version of the trace aspect, which is named TraceAspect3. In comparison to TraceAspect2, TraceAspect3 now displays the following for each joinpoint:

- The name of the intercepted method call
- The parameters of the call
- The current object—in other words, the calling object
- The target object—in other words, the called object

The code of the TraceAspect3 aspect that performs this introspection and displays these four pieces of information is shown in Listing 3-8.

Listing 3-8. *An AspectJ Program for Joinpoint Introspection*

```
package aop.aspectj;

public aspect TraceAspect3 {

pointcut toBeTraced(): call(* aop.aspectj.Order.*(..));

  Object around(): toBeTraced() {
    String methodName = thisJoinPoint.getSignature().getName();
    Object[] args = thisJoinPoint.getArgs();
    Object caller  = thisJoinPoint.getThis();
    Object callee = thisJoinPoint.getTarget();

    System.out.println("-> Method "+methodName+" begins");
    System.out.print("-> "+args.length+" parameter(s) ");
    for (int i = 0; i < args.length; i++)
      System.out.print( args[i]+" " );
    System.out.println();
    System.out.println("-> "+caller+" to "+callee);

    Object ret = proceed();
    System.out.println("<- Method "+methodName+"ends");
    return ret;
  }
}
```

The output of the order-management application with the TraceAspect3 aspect is shown in Listing 3-9. Before each call to a method from class Order, three lines display respectively: the name of the called method, the parameters of the call, and the caller and the called object.

Listing 3-9. *The Output of the AspectJ Program for Joinpoint Introspection*

```
-> Method addItem begins
-> 2 parameter(s) CD 2
-> aop.aspectj.Customer@1cd2e5f to aop.aspectj.Order@19f953d
2 item(s) CD added to the order
-> Method addItem ends
-> Method addItem begins
-> 2 parameter(s) DVD 1
-> aop.aspectj.Customer@1cd2e5f to aop.aspectj.Order@19f953d
1 item(s) DVD added to the order
-> Method addItem ends
-> Method computeAmount begins
-> 0 parameter(s)
-> aop.aspectj.Customer@1cd2e5f to aop.aspectj.Order@19f953d
-> Method computeAmount ends
Order amount: US$50.0
```

Defining Joinpoints

In the previous sections, you learned that wildcards and introspection can be used to write generic pointcuts. Up until this point, we have shown joinpoints that deal only with method calls. In this section, we will present other types of joinpoints.

Joinpoint Types

The joinpoint types provided by AspectJ can deal with methods, fields, exceptions, constructors, static blocks and, finally, advice-code executions.

Methods

For methods, AspectJ defines two types of joinpoints: method calls (defined by the `call` keyword) and method executions (defined by the `execution` keyword). In both cases, an expression must be provided to designate the methods to be called or executed.

The first difference between the `call` and `execution` types concerns the context that the joinpoint occurs in. In the former case, the joinpoint occurs in the context of the calling code, whereas in the latter case, the joinpoint occurs in the context of the called code.

A second difference, which is a direct consequence of the first, is that the values returned by the `getThis` and `getTarget` introspection methods differ. For the `call` type, `getThis` returns a reference to the caller, and `getTarget` returns a reference to the callee. For `execution`, both `getThis` and `getTarget` return a reference to the callee. The `call` type can thus be seen as more general because both the caller and the callee are available.

A method can be associated with a `call` joinpoint and an `execution` joinpoint at the same time. In such a case, the code is executed in the following order:

1. The "before" part of the advice code that is associated with the `call` joinpoint

2. The "before" part of the advice code that is associated with the `execution` joinpoint

3. The method

4. The "after" part of the advice code that is associated with the `execution` joinpoint

5. The "after" part of the advice code that is associated with the `call` joinpoint

Fields

The `get` and `set` joinpoint types intercept the instructions that read and write a field, respectively. These types are useful when you want to implement aspects that manipulate the state of an object. For instance, in the case of a persistence aspect, the state of an object needs to be stored in a file or a database. When intercepted, the read and write operations can be easily redirected to the file or the database.

The `get` and `set` types take an expression as a parameter that denotes the set of fields included in the pointcut. The definition of this expression contains three parts for each field: its type, the class that defines it, and its name. All of these parts can contain wildcards.

The following expression intercepts all the read operations on the `items` field of type `Map` that is defined in the `Order` class:

```
get( Map Order.items )
```

As for method calls and executions, the full class names (in other words, those including package names) as well as the wildcards (*, .., and +) can be used when writing the expressions for get and set.

Exceptions

The handler type corresponds to a joinpoint that occurs when a catch block of instructions begins. This type allows you to define aspects that perform compensation treatments when exceptions are thrown.

For example, this type of joinpoint can be used to log the messages that are generated by the thrown exceptions in a running application. Another usage example is defining a common treatment for all the exceptions of a given type. However implemented, the handling of exceptions with an aspect usually lightens the application—making it far more readable and maintainable.

The handler type is associated with an exception name. A name can contain the wildcards (*, .., and +). For example, the following expression intercepts the executions of the blocks that catch the java.io.IOException exception or one of its subtypes:

```
handler( java.io.Exception+ )
```

With the current version of AspectJ, only "before" advice code can be defined for pointcuts that use the handler type. Hence, some code can be executed at the beginning of a catch block but not at the end.

Constructors

AspectJ can define pointcuts that include class constructors. To achieve this, two joinpoint types are available: initialization and preinitialization. The initialization joinpoint corresponds to the actual execution of the declared constructor, excluding a possible call to an inherited constructor. The preinitialization joinpoint corresponds to the initialization code that is executed before the execution of the constructor, including any default field initializations and any field initializations that have been declared within the class body.

As for the call and execution types, the initialization type takes an expression as a parameter that denotes the constructor or the set of constructors to be intercepted. This expression contains a class name, the new keyword, and a signature, and it can contain the usual wildcards (*, .., and +).

For example, the following expression intercepts the executions of all the constructors, regardless of their signatures, that are defined in the Customer class:

```
initialization( Customer.new(..) )
```

With AspectJ, "before" and "after" advice code is valid with initialization pointcuts, but "around" advice code is not.

Static Code Blocks

In Java, static code blocks define the instructions that are executed while a class is being initialized—in other words, when the class is loaded in the virtual machine. These blocks are often used to initialize static fields.

Several static code blocks can be associated with a single class. In such a case, the order they are executed in corresponds to the order of their definition. The `staticinitialization` joinpoints correspond to the executions of these static blocks.

With `staticinitialization`, advice code can be executed before and after a static block. For instance, the following expression intercepts the execution of all static blocks that are defined in the `Catalog` class:

```
staticinitialization( Catalog )
```

As for other pointcut descriptors, class names can be associated with package names and wildcards.

Advice-Code Execution

The last existing variety of AspectJ joinpoint, `adviceexecution`, corresponds, as its name suggests, to the execution of advice code. Therefore, you can define an aspect that modifies the execution of another aspect. However, the `adviceexecution` type should be used with caution. If it is used carelessly, there is a high risk of obtaining endless loops during the execution of the application.

All the joinpoint types we have previously presented accept an expression as a parameter; this is not the case for `adviceexecution`. This joinpoint occurs when advice code, including advice code that will be associated with the joinpoint itself, is executed.

Consider the following pointcut descriptor and advice code:

```
pointcut aa(): adviceexecution();
Object before(): aa() { ... }
```

Before each execution of an advice code block, the aa pointcut launches the advice code that is given in the example. However, this advice code does not differ from any others—its execution triggers the occurrence of the pointcut, then the execution of the advice code, and so on. To avoid this endless loop, the `adviceexecution` type must be used with the filtering operators that the next section presents.

Filtering Operators

The joinpoints presented previously offer a rich syntax and can be used to define many different pointcut descriptors. You will learn in this section that they can also be combined with logical operators and that filtering operators allow you to restrict the set of caught joinpoints.

Logical Operations

Each defined pointcut descriptor can be compared to a Boolean function. For a given joinpoint, if the pointcut applies, the function returns `true`; if it does not apply, the function returns `false`.

With this logical reasoning in mind, the use of the Boolean operations AND, OR, and NOT is intuitive. They correspond to the conjunction, disjunction, and negation of the occurrence of a joinpoint, respectively. AspectJ supports these three operations with their Java syntax: && for AND, || for OR, and ! for NOT.

The following expression encompasses the executions of the `computeAmount` method and of the `getPrice` method:

```
execution( * Order.computeAmount(..) ) || execution( * Catalog.getPrice(..) )
```

The evaluation of a pointcut descriptor is computed for every existing joinpoint. A given joinpoint can be either the execution of `computeAmount` or the execution of `getPrice` but never both at the same time. Consequently, the use of && instead of || in the previous pointcut descriptor will not intercept any joinpoint.

The use of && instead of || in a pointcut descriptor is a frequent mistake. However, since the syntax of the expression is correct, the AspectJ compiler does not report an error. Only by using a tool such as the AJDT Eclipse plug-in for AspectJ (see Figure 3-1), which allows you to check the joinpoints that are associated with the pointcut, can you detect that no such points exist and that the pointcut descriptors are erroneous.

In general, combining different joinpoint types in a pointcut descriptor must be done with the || operator.

Pointcut descriptors can include tests. An expression containing `if` is followed by a Boolean expression and can be combined with any other pointcut expression.

For instance, the expression

```
if( thisJoinPoint.getArgs().length() == 1 )
```

returns `true` when the current joinpoint defines only one parameter, and it returns `false` in the other cases.

Filtering

A pointcut descriptor such as `get( * aop..*.items )` intercepts all the read operations on the `items` field. For the order-management application, two such joinpoints are included:

- The joinpoint in the `addItem` method where `items` is read in order to call the `put` method.

- The joinpoint in the `computeAmount` method where `items` is read in order to call `get`.

In certain situations, it can be useful to restrict this set to contain only one joinpoint. The `withincode` keyword, associated with a method name, can be used for this purpose. The method name can contain wildcards (*, .., and +).

The expression `withincode(expr)` will return `true` if the name of the method containing the joinpoint matches `expr`.

The expression

```
get( * aop..*.items ) && !withincode( * aop..*.computeAmount(..) )
```

designates all the read operations for the `items` field that are not defined in the `computeAmount` method.

The use of || instead of && in the previous expression does not lead to the expected result. Indeed, `!withincode(* aop..*.computeAmount(..))` is `true` for any joinpoint that is not in the `computeAmount` method. The evaluation of the expression with the logical OR operator is thus `true` for these joinpoints, and the pointcut intercepts more joinpoints than expected. In sum, no truly useful situation requires the joint usage of || and `withincode`.

The second keyword, within, exists for filtering joinpoints. This keyword is associated with a class or interface name and can contain wildcards. The within keyword allows you to retain joinpoints that are defined in a given class or set of classes.

Two keywords, this and target, allow you to perform filtering depending on object references. You previously learned that getThis and getTarget return the current object and the target object of a call or execution joinpoint, respectively. For instance, for the call type, getThis returns the reference to the caller, and getTarget returns the reference to the called object. The this and target keywords play the same role for pointcut descriptors, and they apply filtering depending on the class of the current object or target object. Each is associated with a class or interface name and can contain wildcards.

The expression

```
call( * aop..*.addItem(..) ) && this(aop.aspectj.Order)
```

is true for all the calls made to the addItem method by the Order class. This expression excludes any calls to addItem made by other classes.

Control-Flow Filtering

The filtering operators presented previously are static. They do not depend on the dynamics of the program or the way the program is run but only on its structure. Therefore, all the previous joinpoints can be statically computed without the program needing to be run.

AspectJ defines two additional filtering operators, cflow and cflowbelow. These are referred to as *control-flow operators*. Intuitively, the control flow of a program encompasses all the methods that are visited during the program's execution.

To illustrate the way that cflow and cflowbelow work, take the example of a simple program that calls the Foo.foo and Bar.bar methods from the main method. The Foo.foo method also calls Bar.bar. This last method does not perform any calls.

The following pointcut descriptors intercept the calls to the bar method only if bar is called from foo, so calls to bar from main are ignored:

```
pointcut foopcd(): call( * Foo.foo(..) );
pointcut callToBarInFoo(): call( * Bar.bar(..) ) && cflow( foopcd() );
```

The callToBarInFoo pointcut descriptor specifies that calls to bar only in the control flow of the foopcd pointcut descriptor are considered. The foopcd pointcut descriptor designates all the calls to the foo method.

Intuitively, you can consider that the control flow of the program enters the foopcd pointcut when foo is called and exits the pointcut when the call returns. The expression cflow(foopcd()) designates all the joinpoints located between this entry point and exit point.

More formally, the cflow operator is associated with a pointcut named p. All the joinpoints that occur between the moment the program encounters one of the joinpoints included in p and the moment the program exits this joinpoint are denoted by cflow(p()).

The cflowbelow operator is similar to cflow except that the joinpoints belonging to p are not returned by cflowbelow.

Pointcut Parameterization

In the previous sections, you learned about the keywords, operators, and symbols that can be used with AspectJ to define pointcuts. You learned that each pointcut descriptor is named and defined in an aspect, and that the advice code defines the treatment to be executed before and after the joinpoints that are denoted by their associated pointcuts.

In OOP languages, the methods can be parameterized. In AOP, the parameterization also applies to pointcut descriptors. The parameters contain the information that is passed from the pointcut to the utilizing advice code.

The parameters of a pointcut, like those of a method, are defined in parentheses after the name of the pointcut. Each parameter has a name and a type.

The following toBeTraced pointcut descriptor defines four parameters (src, dst, ref, and qty):

```
pointcut toBeTraced( Customer src, Order dst, String ref, int qty )
```

Pointcut parameters can pass three kinds of information: the source of the joinpoints that are included in the pointcut, the target of those joinpoints, and the parameters of those join-points. The goal is to expose the information from the joinpoint so the advice code can access that information.

The source and target of the joinpoints are accessed with a modified version of the this and target operators, which we previously presented. Instead of being associated with a class name, the operators here use an identifier. The arguments of the joinpoints are accessed with the args operator followed by a list of identifiers.

As an example, consider the following toBeTraced2 pointcut descriptor:

```
pointcut toBeTraced2( Customer src, Order dst, String ref, int qty ) :
 call(* *.*(..)) && this(src) && target(dst) && args(ref,qty);
```

This example denotes all the calls (by the call(* *.*(..)) subexpression, specifies that the source must be bound to the src parameter (by the this(src) subexpression), that the target must be bound to dst (by the target(dst) subexpression), and that the arguments must be bound to the ref and qty variables (by the args(ref,qty) subexpression).

Thanks to the type information that is given in the signature of the pointcut, you can deduce that the pointcut deals with calls to methods that the Order class defines, that take parameters of type String and int, and that are made from the Customer class.

You previously saw that the source, target, and arguments could be accessed through the joinpoint-introspection mechanism and the thisJoinPoint keyword. As you have seen in this section, pointcut parameterization is an alternative means to achieve this end—but in a typed way. Furthermore, parameterizing a pointcut generally brings more-efficient run-time performances than introspection. The only drawback of parameterization is that the types need to be available at compile time, which is not always the case when programming generic pointcuts.

Summary of Pointcut Descriptors

The AspectJ pointcut language provides a rich syntax and many keywords. Compared to JAC, JBoss AOP, and AspectWerkz, which are presented in the following chapters, AspectJ can define pointcut descriptors that are more precise—although more complex to learn.

To conclude the discussion of joinpoints, we present Table 3-2, which gives a summary of all the existing types of joinpoints in AspectJ. We classify them by their function into the following categories:

- Methods (`call` and `execution`)

- Fields (`get` and `set`)

- Exceptions (`handler`)

- Constructors (`initialization` and `preinitialization`)

- Static code blocks (`staticinitialization`)

- Advice code (`adviceexecution`)

Table 3-2. *AspectJ Joinpoint Types*

Type	Definition
`call(methexpr)`	A call to a method that matches `methexpr`
`execution(methexpr)`	An execution of a method that matches `methexpr`
`get(fieldexpr)`	A read operation on a field that matches `fieldexpr`
`set(fieldexpr)`	A write operation on a field that matches `fieldexpr`
`handler(exceptexpr)`	An execution of a `catch` block for an exception that matches `exceptexpr`
`initialization(constexpr)`	An execution of a constructor that matches `constexpr`
`preinitialization(constexpr)`	An execution of an inherited constructor that matches `constexpr`
`staticinitialization(classexpr)`	An execution of a static block in a class that matches `classexpr`
`adviceexecution()`	An execution of an advice code block

In addition to these joinpoint types, AspectJ pointcut descriptors can also include the operators that are illustrated in Table 3-3. These operators can be grouped into the following categories:

- Logical (`&&`, `||`, `!`, `if`)

- Joinpoint location in the code (`withincode` and `within`)

- Joinpoint source and target (`this` and `target`)

- Control-flow (`cflow` and `cflowbelow`)

Table 3-3. *AspectJ Operators in Pointcut Descriptors*

Keyword	Definition
&&	Logical AND
||	Logical OR
!	Logical NOT
if(expr)	Evaluation of the Boolean expression expr
withincode(methexpr)	true when the joinpoint is defined in a method with a signature that matches methexpr
within(typeexpr)	true when the joinpoint is defined in a class with a name that matches typeexpr
this(typeexpr)	true when the source-object type for the joinpoint matches typeexpr
target(typeexpr)	true when the target-object type for the joinpoint matches typeexpr
cflow(pcd)	true for any joinpoint located from the entry of the given pointcut descriptor (pcd) to the exit, inclusive
cflowbelow(pcd)	true for any joinpoint located from the entry of the given pointcut descriptor (pcd) to the exit, exclusive

Advice Code

You learned that pointcut descriptors define the areas where the instructions from an aspect need to be inserted. These instructions are defined in advice code blocks.

In object-oriented languages, the behavior of a class is defined in its methods. In contrast, in AOP, this behavior is defined in advice code. In an aspect, there may be several advice code blocks, with each one containing a set of instructions. In addition, each advice code block has a type and is associated with a pointcut descriptor.

The Code of an Advice Code Block

The code of an advice code block can contain any valid Java instruction, such as a method call, a variable assignment, an object creation (using new), a loop (using for, while, or do/while), a test (using if), and an exception-handling block (using try/catch).

Two additional instructions, proceed and thisJoinPoint, are also valid in AspectJ. These instructions are used exclusively for advice code; in any other context, they generate compiler errors. The proceed keyword executes the joinpoint and can be used only in "around" advice code. The thisJoinPoint keyword can be used for any kind of advice code. As mentioned previously, thisJoinPoint is a reference to an object that describes the current joinpoint.

The Different Types of Advice Code

AspectJ defines five types of advice code. Of these five, "before," "after," and "around" are the more-commonly encountered ones. The last two types, "after returning" and "after throwing," can be seen as refinements of the "after" type.

The "Before" Type

"Before" advice code is executed before the joinpoints that are included in the pointcut associated with the advice code.

The following example illustrates the usage of "before" advice code:

```
before(): toBeTraced() {
  System.out.println("... before the joinpoints included in toBeTraced ...");
}
```

The syntax for the definition of "before" advice code consists of the type of advice code (here, before), the name of the pointcut descriptor that is associated with the advice code (here, toBeTraced), and the code itself between curly brackets.

The second part, the name of the pointcut descriptor, is not mandatory. You can provide the code of the pointcut descriptor right after the type. In this case, the pointcut is said to be *anonymous*. An example of anonymous pointcut is the following:

```
before(): call( * Order.addItem(..) ) { ... }
```

However, the use of a named pointcut descriptor is preferred because this produces programs that are clearer and easier to maintain. Furthermore, when a pointcut descriptor is reused in several advice code blocks, the use of a name avoids useless, error-prone repetitions.

In the previous section, you learned that pointcut descriptors can accept parameters. Hence, when used, the associated advice code must also be parameterized.

The example in Listing 3-10 reuses the toBeTraced2 pointcut descriptor with four parameters and associates the pointcut with "before" advice.

Listing 3-10. *Defining Parameterized Pointcuts*

```
 1 pointcut
 2   toBeTraced2( Customer src, Order dst, String ref, int qty ):
 3     call( * *.*(..) ) &&
 4     this(src) && target(dst) && args(ref,qty);
 5 before( Customer src, Order dst, String ref, int qty ):
 6   toBeTraced2(src,dst,ref,qty) {
 7     System.out.println(
 8       "... before the joinpoints included in toBeTraced2 ...");
 9     System.out.println( src + " " + dst + " " + ref + " " + qty );
10 }
```

The four parameters that are defined in the pointcut descriptor are also used for the definition of the advice code. (See line 6 in Listing 3-10). These parameters are then available for any instruction that is defined in the body of the advice code block.

The "After" Type

"After" advice is executed after each associated joinpoint. Its code uses the same syntax rules as "before" advice. The previous examples of the toBeTraced and toBeTraced2 pointcut descriptors would be valid simply by replacing the before keyword with after.

The last two types of advice code that are defined by AspectJ are "after returning" and "after throwing." These types ensue from the idea that the execution of a joinpoint—for instance, a method-execution joinpoint—ends normally or with the raising of an exception. The former case is handled by the "after returning" type, whereas the latter case is handled by the "after throwing" type.

The "After Returning" Type

"After returning" advice code is executed after each normal execution of the joinpoints that are associated with the pointcut descriptor.

The following code illustrates the usage of the "after returning" type:

```
after() returning (double d): ... {
  System.out.println("The returned value is: "+d);
}
```

The value that is returned by the joinpoint can be accessed with the variable found in parentheses after the after returning keywords. The variable is either the exact type (here, double) of the value returned by the joinpoint or a valid supertype (for example, Object for all Java types, including primitive types).

The "After Throwing" Type

"After throwing" advice code is executed when a given joinpoint that is associated with a pointcut descriptor ends its execution by raising an exception.

The following code illustrates the usage of the "after throwing" type:

```
after() throwing (Exception e): ... {
 System.out.println("The raised exception is: "+e);
}
```

The exception that is raised by the joinpoint can be accessed with the variable defined in parentheses following the after throwing keywords. In the previous example, the variable is e. This variable can be used anywhere in the body of the advice code.

The "Around" Type

"Around" advice code is executed before and after each associated joinpoint. The proceed keyword executes the joinpoint, which is bound by the "before" and "after" parts of the advice code. Specifically, this keyword executes the joinpoint in the following way:

1. The "before" part is executed.

2. The joinpoint is executed when the proceed keyword is used.

3. The "after" part is executed.

In "around" advice code, the "before" or "after" part can be empty; then, the "around" advice code is equivalent to "before" or "after" advice code. The proceed keyword is optional in "around" advice code. If proceed is not used, the joinpoint is not executed. This behavior could correspond to a security aspect in which calls from unauthorized users are rejected, for instance. The proceed keyword can be used several times in the same "around" advice code block. However, this situation is infrequent and corresponds to cases in which several attempts at executing the application are needed—for instance, after an unexpected error.

Unlike "before" and "after" advice code, the return type of "around" advice code is associated with the return type of the joinpoints. If the "around" advice code is not a supertype of the return type that is defined for the joinpoints, the AspectJ compiler raises an error. When other return types (including the void return type) appear for the joinpoints in a given pointcut, the Object type must be used as the return type of the advice code. (In Java, Object is considered the supertype of all types.)

Listing 3-11 illustrates the use of "around" advice code.

Listing 3-11. *"Around" Advice-Code Example*

```
Object around(): ... {
  System.out.println("before");
  Object ret = proceed();
  System.out.println("before");
  return ret;
}
```

In Listing 3-11, the call to proceed returns a value that is stored in the ret variable. This is the value that is returned by the joinpoint. This value and, in fact, all other values, must be returned by the advice code (as is done here by the return ret instruction).

When the advice code is associated with a parameterized pointcut descriptor, all the parameters must be passed when proceed is called. This is illustrated by Listing 3-12.

Listing 3-12. *"Around" Advice Code with Parameters*

```
Object around( Customer src, Order dst, String ref, int qty ):
  toBeTraced2(src,dst,ref,qty) {
    System.out.println("before");
    Object ret = proceed(src,dst,ref,qty);
    System.out.println("after");
    return ret;
}
```

Advice Code and Exceptions

Advice code has the ability to raise an exception when needed. In such cases, the type of the exception must be specified in the signature of the advice code. For methods, the throws keyword must be used to specify the exception.

The following piece of code defines "around" advice code that possibly throws an exception:

```
Object around() throws Exception: ... {
  /* ... */
  if( /*condition*/ )
    throw new Exception();
  /* ... */
}
```

When an exception is declared by advice code, the type of the exception must also be specified in the signature of the joinpoint. For instance, a method-execution joinpoint must list the exception in the throws clause. This is a limitation that obliges the application code to be aware of the exceptions thrown by the aspects. In practice, this limitation can be solved by specifying that the advice code raises an exception of type RuntimeException. In Java, run-time exceptions are unchecked; therefore, the signatures of the program methods can be left unchanged.

The Introduction Mechanism

In the previous sections, you learned that pointcut descriptors and advice code blocks allow an aspect to extend or modify the behavior of an application. Pointcut descriptors designate joinpoints (method calls, method executions, read operations, write operations, and so on) in the execution flow of a program, and advice code blocks add instructions before or after these joinpoints. In all cases, if no joinpoints are activated, the advice code will not be executed either.

The introduction mechanism is used in AspectJ to extend the structure of an application. The term *introduction* refers to the process of the aspect adding code elements to the application. AspectJ can introduce, or add, six categories of these elements: fields, methods, constructors, inherited classes, implemented interfaces, and exceptions. The following sections will explain these categories in detail.

Contrary to advice code, which extends the behavior of an application only when the joinpoints are executed, the introduction mechanism is unconditional—the extended code is always added.

AspectJ uses the term *intertype declaration* to refer to the introduction mechanism. The concept behind this is that an aspect, which is considered a type, declares elements (for example, fields, methods, inherited classes, and implemented interfaces) on behalf of other types—in other words, on behalf of the classes of the application.

No special keyword is defined in AspectJ for introduced elements, which are defined declaratively.

Fields, Methods, and Constructors

An aspect that introduces fields, methods, or constructors in a class performs a declaration on behalf of this class. This declaration follows the same rules as a regular Java declaration. The name of the field or method is preceded by the name of the class that the introduction is to be performed in. Constructors are designated with the new keyword.

The aspect in Listing 3-13 introduces the date field, two methods named getDate and setDate, and a constructor in the Order class.

Listing 3-13. *Intertype Declaration*

```
import java.util.Date;

public aspect AddDate {

  private Date Order.date;
  public Date Order.getDate() { return date; }
  public void Order.setDate(Date date) { this.date=date; }
```

```
public Order.new(Date date) { this.date=date; }

after(): initialization(Order.new(..)) {
  Order myOrder = (Order) thisJoinPoint.getTarget();
  myOrder.date = new Date();
}
}
```

In the `AddDate` aspect in Listing 3-13, "after" advice code is defined after the instantiations of the `Order` class. This advice code collects the references of the instantiated orders and sets the current date to the introduced `date` field.

Although these introductions are simplistic, they should be dealt with cautiously. Accordingly, the elements defined in the application must not conflict with the elements introduced by the aspect. For instance, if a `date` field already exists in the `Order` class, a compiler error occurs.

AspectJ does not provide an option to check whether a field or method name already exists before it performs the introduction. The existence of conflicting elements is revealed only during compile time when the error occurs. Therefore, it is up to you to manually correct the program or the aspect when this occurs.

Inherited Classes and Implemented Interfaces

In addition to fields and methods, the introduction mechanism provided by AspectJ allows you to modify the inheritance and implementation hierarchies defined in an application. The `declare parents` keyword combination permits this.

The following aspect adds the `AddDateItf` interface to the `Order` class and creates an inheritance link between `AddDateImpl` and `Order`:

```
public aspect AddDate2 {
  declare parents: Order implements AddDateItf;
  declare parents: Order extends AddDateImpl;
}
```

The addition of a new interface is always possible since there are no constraints in Java on the number of interfaces implemented by a class. This is not the case for inheritance because only a single inheritance is supported in Java.

In the previous example, if the `Order` class was already a subclass of the `Document` class, the modification of the inheritance link by the `AddDate2` aspect would have produced a compiler error.

The names of the classes to be modified can contain wildcards. Logical expressions created with the Boolean OR operator (||) can be written to modify several classes with a single declaration.

Exceptions

The last element that can be introduced performs the function of catching the exceptions that are raised by an application.

The exceptions raised by the application are wrapped in a special exception called `org.aspectj.lang.SoftException`.

The `declare soft` keyword combination is provided to implement this introduction mechanism. A type and a pointcut descriptor must be provided. The type designates the type of exceptions to be caught, and the pointcut descriptor designates the joinpoints where the exceptions are to be caught.

For instance, the following line of code

```
declare soft: IOException+: call( * InputStream.*(..) )
```

declares that the subclasses of a certain exception—the `IOException` exception that is thrown when a method defined in the `InputStream` class is called—must be wrapped in the `org.aspectj.lang.SoftException` exception.

Advanced Features

The previous sections introduced the many features offered by AspectJ for programming aspects. As with other languages, advanced functionalities—apart from the mainstream features—that complement the language exist. In AspectJ, these are the concepts of the abstract aspect, aspect inheritance, aspect instantiation, aspect ordering, and the privileged aspect.

The Abstract Aspect

The aim of the *abstract aspect* in AspectJ is to define an aspect that has some undefined elements (pointcuts or methods). These elements are then said to be *abstract*. This concept is similar to that of an abstract class. The precise definition of these elements will be given in a subaspect.

Abstract aspects allow you to factor definitions that are shared by several aspects. As with abstract classes, abstract aspects cannot be instantiated.

The `abstract` keyword is used to define abstract aspects. It can be written before the `aspect` or `pointcut` keyword (for defining pointcut descriptors) and before the method that is abstract in the aspect. The following section illustrates the precise definition of an abstract aspect.

Aspect Inheritance

Inheritance can be used with aspects like it is used with classes. The goal is to extend an aspect without rewriting it completely. Only single inheritance is supported.

As with classes, the `extends` keyword provides the inheritance feature. In the following line of code, the `TraceAspect2` aspect extends the `TraceAspect` aspect:

```
public aspect TraceApect2 extends TraceAspect { ... }
```

However, aspect inheritance does not follow the same exact rules as class inheritance. An aspect can extend only abstract aspects, whereas a class can extend both abstract and nonabstract classes.

A pointcut can be redefined in a subaspect. If a pointcut is redefined, the redefined version will always be used. Pointcut redefinition with aspect inheritance follows the same rules as method redefinition with class inheritance.

Conversely, advice code cannot be redefined. Inherited advice code is thus always available in a subaspect.

The code in Listing 3-14 defines the abstract `TraceAspect` aspect with the abstract `toBeTraced` pointcut descriptor. `TraceAspect2` extends `TraceAspect` and defines the `toBeTraced` pointcut descriptor.

Listing 3-14. *The Definition of an Abstract Aspect*

```
public abstract aspect TraceAspect {
  abstract pointcut toBeTraced();
  before(): toBeTraced() { ... }
}

public aspect TraceAspect2 extends TraceAspect {
  pointcut toBeTraced(): call(* Order.*(..));
}
```

Aspect Instantiation

By default, a unique instance of an aspect is created when the application is launched. The aspect is then said to be a *singleton*. The same aspect instance is shared by all the application objects.

In special cases, it can be useful to create several instances of a given aspect. Different application objects are then aspectized by the different instances. For example, this feature can be used to dedicate different pieces of data to each part of the application.

The three following cases can occur:

- The aspect is a singleton, and only one instance of the aspect exists at run time. This is the default case.

- The aspect is instantiated several times, and the instances are associated with different application objects.

- The aspect is instantiated several times, and the instances are associated with different control-flow sequences of the application.

No keyword exists for the first case because this is the default behavior when the `aspect` keyword is used.

For the second case, two keywords are available: `perthis` and `pertarget`. The aspects can then be written as follows:

```
aspect <name> perthis( <poincut> ) { ... }
aspect <name> pertarget( <poincut> ) { ... }
```

When `perthis` is used, an instance of the aspect is created for every object that is an executing object of the given pointcut. The other objects (those that are not executing objects of the pointcut) are not aspectized. When `pertarget` is used, an instance of the aspect is created for every object that is the target object of the given pointcut.

For the third case, two keywords are available: `percflow` and `percflowbelow`. The aspects can then be written as follows:

```
aspect <name> percflow( <poincut> ) { ... }
aspect <name> perclfowbelow( <poincut> ) { ... }
```

When `percflow` is used, an aspect instance is created each time the application enters the control-flow sequence that is designated by the pointcut. As for the `cflow` operator in pointcut definitions, the joinpoints belongs to the control flow. When `percflowbelow` is used, an aspect instance is created each time the application enters the control-flow sequence that is designated by the pointcut, but the joinpoints are not included in the control flow.

The static `aspectOf` method is defined for each aspect and returns the aspect instance that is currently in use. For example, in the singleton `TraceAspect` aspect, the call `TraceAspect.aspectOf()` returns the reference to the singleton. For the `perthis` and `pertarget` types, a parameter must be passed when `aspectOf` is called; this parameter gives the source or the target object that is associated with the requested instance. For the `percflow` and `percflowbelow` types, no parameters are needed. The method returns the aspect instance or `null`, depending on whether the current run is included in the control-flow sequences that are defined for the aspects.

Aspect Ordering

When two or more aspects apply to the same joinpoint, the execution order of these aspects must be determined.

AspectJ allows you to define explicit ordering rules. This is called *explicit ordering*. If the rules are undefined, the compiler automatically orders the aspects. This is called *implicit ordering*.

Explicit Ordering

The `declare precedence` keyword combination allows you to declare the execution order of different aspects.

The following code illustrates the usage of this keyword combination:

```
aspect GlobalOrder {
  declare precedence: Authentication, Trace;
}
aspect Authentication { ... }
aspect Trace { ... }
```

In the previous code, the `Authentication` aspect is always executed before `Trace` is. Wildcards can be used in the aspect names that are associated with `declare precedence`.

Despite the location of the definition, the order is valid for the whole program. The `declare precedence` keyword combination can be used several times in a program. If the given orders are inconsistent, the AspectJ compiler raises an error.

Implicit Ordering

When no order is defined, or when the order is defined for some aspects but not for others, AspectJ applies the following rules:

- The subaspects are applied before the inherited aspects.

- No order is guaranteed for aspects that are not linked by an inheritance relationship.

- If several advice code blocks apply to the same joinpoint for a given aspect, the following rules apply:

  - "After" advice code blocks are executed last.

  - Advice code blocks are executed in the order in which they are defined in the aspect.

These rules can lead to inconsistencies which are raised by the AspectJ compiler.

It is recommended that the aspect order be defined explicitly and as often as possible with the declare precedence keyword combination. When you write an aspect, it is favorable to first write all the "before" advice code and then the "after" advice code.

The Privileged Aspect

For accessing fields or methods, the same rules apply to aspects as Java classes. For example, aspects cannot read or write a private or protected field. The purpose of this particular rule is to guarantee the integrity of the program and to avoid the accidental and erroneous altering of objects.

Nevertheless, some cases require a bypass of this limitation. AspectJ provides for these cases the concept of a privileged aspect:

```
privileged aspect <name> { ... }
```

A privileged aspect can access all the fields and methods defined in a class—regardless of their access modifiers. This feature must be used cautiously as it may corrupt the normal behavior of the program.

Declaring Warnings and Errors

AspectJ offers a mechanism that raises compile-time warnings or errors whenever a given pointcut expression is matched by a program. In this way, you can be notified if your program defines unwanted code elements.

For example, the aspect in Listing 3-15 raises a warning if the Remote interface is implemented in the bank.ejb package.

Listing 3-15. *Declaring Warnings with an Aspect*

```
public aspect Foo {
  declare warning:
    execution(* Remote+.*(..)) && within(bank.ejb.*):
      " Remote may interfere with EJBs in bank.ejb";
}
```

A message can be associated with each raised warning.

The declare error keyword combination works similarly.

Load-Time Weaving

By default, AspectJ is a compile-time weaver. Given a set of `.java` source files and a set of aspects, the `ajc` command-line tool produces a set of `.class` files in which the aspects are woven to the classes.

Since version 1.2, AspectJ can weave code at load time. The source code of the program is no longer required, and AspectJ can weave any class that can be obtained with the class-loading mechanism of the Java language.

New Features in AspectJ 5

During the writing of this book, AspectJ 1.2.1, which was released on November 5, 2004, was the latest stable version of AspectJ. However, a newer version, numbered 1.5.0 and officially called AspectJ 5, is under preparation. The first major developments of AspectJ 1.5.0M1 were made available to the developing community in December 2004. The main purpose of this evolution was to incorporate the changes brought to the Java language by Java 5.

The features described in the remainder of this section can be found in the developer release of AspectJ 1.5.0, which is available at the time of the writing of this book. By the time AspectJ 5 is final, these features may have slightly changed according to user's feedback, design choices, or error corrections.

Most of the changes brought by AspectJ 5 deal with *annotations* (also known as *metadata*). First, an aspect can deal with an annotated Java program. The annotations defined for classes or methods can be taken into account when defining a pointcut. Also, annotations can be introduced into a Java program. Second, annotations have an impact on the syntax of the AspectJ language itself. Instead of using dedicated keywords such as `aspect` and `pointcut`, you can write annotated Java classes that will be understood by the AspectJ weaver as aspects. These two categories of features are presented in the remainder of this section.

Working with Annotations in Aspects

The handling of annotations in Java programs brings several changes to the AspectJ language. The changes concern the definition of an aspect, the pointcut-definition language, and the introduction of annotations.

Annotations and Pointcut Definitions

You learned in the previous sections that a pointcut can capture elements of a Java program, such as methods and fields, and link them together in order to aspectize them. In this process, the writing of a pointcut relies heavily on the elements that define a field or method, such as the name, type, or signature. It then seems natural to incorporate annotations for fields or methods in the writing of a pointcut.

With AspectJ 5, the pattern language for a pointcut descriptor is extended with the at-sign symbol (@) followed by an annotation name. For instance, the following expression

```
execution( @Transaction * *.*(..) )
```

designates all the joinpoints that are executions of a method annotated with `@Transaction`, regardless of the method's return type, declaring class, name, or signature.

Several annotations can be specified, in which case all of them are required for the element to be included in the pointcut.

The Boolean OR operator (||) can be used between annotations to signify that at least one of the annotations must be present. For instance, @(Foo || Bar) means that either @Foo or @Bar is required as an annotation.

The Boolean NOT operator (!) is used in front of an annotation. For instance, !@Foo means that all elements that are not annotated with @Foo are included in the definition.

Joinpoints can be filtered according to the annotations available to the source and target objects of a method call. The @this and @target operators are defined for this purpose. For instance, the following expression

```
call( * *.*(..) ) && @target( @Transaction )
```

designates all the calls to a method that is annotated with @Transaction.

At the time this book was written, it was not possible to match joinpoints based on their annotation values. This facility may be supported in future releases of AspectJ.

Introducing Annotations

In AspectJ 5, the declare keyword is associated with four new forms that allow you to introduce annotations in Java programs.

Introducing annotations consists of defining a pattern that refers to program elements (classes, interfaces, fields, methods, or constructors) and giving the annotations that must be introduced for all the program elements that match the pattern.

For instance, the following instruction

```
declare @type: bank.* : @EJBean;
```

introduces the annotation @EJBean for all the types (classes and interfaces) that are defined in the bank package.

Similarly, annotations can be introduced for methods. The keyword combination is then declare @method and the pattern refers to method names. For example, the following instruction

```
declare @method: bank.*.deposit(..): @Transaction(value="required");
```

introduces the annotation @Transaction(value="required") for all the deposit methods that are defined in the bank package.

The declare @field and declare @constructor keywords follow the same principle.

Defining Aspects with Annotations

Using the previously presented features, you can write aspects that deal with a Java program containing annotations, or you can write aspects that introduce annotations.

The annotations that are presented in this section are very different. Their purpose is to replace the current syntax of the AspectJ language and to allow you to write annotated Java classes. These classes are understood by the AspectJ weaver not as regular Java classes but as aspects. This approach creates an entirely new development style in which there are no more syntax extensions, but instead there are a set of annotations available for AOP.

The first annotation is @Aspect. A Java class annotated with @Aspect is understood as an aspect. The following code snippet defines the TraceAspect4 aspect:

```
@Aspect
public class TraceAspect4 {
  // ...
}
```

You learned in the "Advanced Features" section earlier in this chapter that aspects can be qualified, either with an instantiation clause (using perthis, pertarget, percflow, or percflowbelow) or with the privileged keyword. These qualifiers still exist with the @Aspect annotation style. For example, the following annotation

```
@Aspect(
  instantiationModel=AspectInstantiationModel.PERTARGET,
  perClausePattern="aPointcutDefinition()",
  isPrivileged=true )
```

defines a privileged aspect with a PERTARGET instantiation model.

Pointcut Definition

With the annotation-based development style, a pointcut is a method with an empty body that is annotated with @Pointcut. This annotation takes the pointcut expression as a parameter. For example, the following code snippet defines the pointcut toBeTraced:

```
@Pointcut( "call(* aop.aspectj.Order.*(..))" )
void toBeTraced() {}
```

With this new style, the parameters that would have been defined for a pointcut are now defined as parameters of the annotated method.

Advice-Code Definition

Advice code blocks are already blocks of instructions, so it is quite natural that advice code blocks are now methods. Five new annotations are available, one for each different type of advice code: @Before, @After, @AfterReturning, @AfterThrowing, and @Around.

In all five cases, the annotation takes the associated pointcut expression as a parameter.

"Before" Advice Code

The following code snippet illustrates the definition of "before" advice:

```
@Before( "toBeTraced()" )
public void beforeTrace() { ... }
```

Note that with this new development style, advice code blocks now share the same name as the method.

If the "before" advice code needs to access the joinpoint, a parameter of type JoinPoint is added to the method signature, as shown here:

```
@Before( "toBeTraced()" )
public void beforeTrace( JoinPoint jp ) { ... }
```

If the pointcut expression defines parameters, these parameters will also be made available as method parameters. The following code lines, for example, define "before" advice code for method calls in which the src and dst parameters are bound to the source and target, respectively, of the call:

```
@Before( "toBeTraced() && this(src) && target(dst)" )
public void beforeTrace( Object src, Object dst ) { ... }
```

This principle of appending the joinpoint and the pointcut parameters to the signature of the advice-code method also applies to other types of advice code.

"Around" Advice Code

"Around" advice code is similar to "before" advice code. The only issue here is raised by the annotation development style, which is linked to proceed. If you do not change the old syntax, the call to proceed will lead to a compiler error. (Keep in mind that aspects are now regular Java classes.)

To solve this problem, AspectJ 5 defines proceed as a method of the ProceedingJoinPoint interface, which extends the existing JoinPoint interface and allows the joinpoint to be visible as a parameter of the "around" advice-code method.

The following lines of code illustrate the definition of "around" advice code:

```
@Around( "toBeTraced()" )
public Object trace( ProceedingJoinPoint jp ) {
  // ... Before code
  Object ret = jp.proceed();
  // ... After code
  return ret;
}
```

"After" Advice Code

The definition of "after" advice code does not differ from the definition of "before" advice code except that the annotation is @After.

The situation is slightly different for @AfterReturning and @AfterThrowing. The returned value or the thrown exception must be made visible in the advice-code method.

In the case of @AfterReturning, a new parameter named returning is added to the annotation. Its value identifies the method parameter that will contain the returned value. The following lines define "after returning" advice code:

```
@AfterReturning( value="toBeTraced()", returning="ret" )
public void afterTrace( Object ret ) { ... }
```

The value returned by the intercepted joinpoints is assigned to the ret parameter.

The principle is the same for "after throwing" advice code, except that the annotation defines a parameter named throwing for holding the thrown exception.

Declare Statements

The `declare` statement is available in various forms in AspectJ:

- `declare parents ... implements` and `declare parents ... extends`: These are the two most current forms, which allow you to introduce a new interface and a new superclass, respectively.

- `declare error` and `declare warning`: These forms raise errors and warnings.

- `declare @...`: Annotations can be introduced with this form.

- `declare precedence`: Aspect ordering can be defined with this form.

- `declare soft`: This form can be used to soften exceptions.

At the time of the writing this book, all the previous forms of `declare` statements, except `declare parents ... extends` and `declare soft`, were available with the new annotation-based development style. The two exceptions may be added in a future release.

The aspect in Listing 3-16 illustrates the definition of the following:

- A precedence rule between all the aspects that have a name starting with `Authentication` and the `Trace` aspect

- The declaration to raise a warning whenever the `Remote` interface is implemented in the `bank.ejb` package

- The introduction of the annotation `@EJBean` for the types defined in the `bank.ejb` package

- The introduction of the annotation `@Transaction(value="required")` for the `deposit` methods defined in the `bank.ejb` package

Listing 3-16. *AnnotationBased Declare Statements*

```
@Aspect
@DeclarePrecedence( "Authentication*,Trace" )
public class GlobalOrder {

  @DeclareWarning( "execution(* Remote+.*(..)) && within(bank.ejb.*)" )
  final static String message = "Remote may interfere with EJBs in bank.ejb";

  @DeclareAnnotation( "bank.*" )
  @EJBean
  Object beans;

  @DeclareAnnotation( "bank.*.deposit(..)" )
  @Transaction(value="required")
  void depositMethods() {}
}
```

Aspect Instantiation in AspectJ 5

AspectJ 5 supports the five aspect-instantiation modes—the default singleton mode, `perthis`, `pertarget`, `percflow`, and `percflowbelow`—that are available in the previous version. (See the "Aspect Instantiation" section earlier in this chapter for further details.)

AspectJ 5 introduces a sixth mode: `PERTYPEWITHIN`. With this mode, a new aspect instance is created for each new type that is designated in the pointcut expression associated with `PERTYPEWITHIN`.

The following aspect illustrates the `PERTYPEWITHIN` mode:

```
@Aspect(
  instantiationModel=AspectInstantiationModel.PERTYPEWITHIN,
  perClausePattern="aop.aspectj.*")
public class FooBarAspect { ... }
```

This aspect will be instantiated for each different class that is defined in the `aop.aspectj` package.

Other Java 5 Features

Autoboxing does not impose any changes on the AspectJ language. The fact that primitive types (`int`, `float`, `double`, and so on) are equivalent to their class-based ones (`Integer`, `Float`, `Double`, and so on) simply means that when the AspectJ compiler computes the joinpoints that match a given pointcut, the compiler does not distinguish between a primitive type and its class-based counterpart.

Variable-length argument lists can be used when you write a pointcut descriptor. For instance, the following pointcut descriptor

```
call( * *.*( double, Object... ) )
```

designates all the calls to all the methods that take at least a `double` argument and a variable-length list of `Object` arguments as parameters.

Summary

This chapter presented the syntax of the AspectJ language. AspectJ extends the Java language with keywords for writing aspects, pointcuts, advice code, and intertype declarations. An aspect-oriented application in AspectJ contains Java classes that implement the core logic of the application and AspectJ aspects that implement the crosscutting functionalities.

The classes and the aspects are woven together to produce the final application. Most of the time, the weaving occurs at compile time. AspectJ provides a compiler (named `ajc`) for that. With newer versions of AspectJ, the weaving can also be done at load time—when the application is loaded into the Java virtual machine.

The pointcut language provided by AspectJ allows you to define where an aspect applies in an application. A pointcut descriptor denotes a set of joinpoints. Several types of joinpoints are supported by AspectJ. The two that are most frequently used are the `call` and `execution` joinpoints. These are the points in the execution flow of a program where a method is called or executed, respectively. Several other types of joinpoints exist in AspectJ: `get` and `set` for read and write operations, `handler` for exceptions, `initialization` and `preinitialization` for constructors, `staticinitialization` for static code blocks, and `adviceexecution` for executions of advice code.

Advice code defines the modifications that are brought to an application by an aspect. Each advice code block is associated with a pointcut that defines where these modifications apply. Three main types of advice code are provided by AspectJ: "before," "after," and "around." Advice code applies either before the executions of its associated joinpoints, after the executions, or both. In the latter case, the advice code is called "around" advice code. Two other types of advice code are provided by AspectJ: "after returning," and "after throwing." The former applies for to that return normally, whereas the latter applies to joinpoints that end their executions by raising an exception. The behavior of an aspect is provided by the advice code blocks that are attached to the aspect. Any Java instructions are valid in those blocks. AspectJ provides two additional instructions: `thisJoinPoint` and `proceed`. The former provides information (method name, class name, parameters, and so on) about the current joinpoint. The latter, which can be used exclusively with "around" advice code, allows you to execute the joinpoint.

The mechanism known by the term *intertype declaration* provides a way for AspectJ to extend an application with additional features, such as fields, methods, constructors, interfaces, and superclasses.

Finally, AspectJ 5 takes advantage of the many new features of the Java 5 language, and it introduces a whole new development style that is based on annotations. Instead of using keywords such as `aspect` and `pointcut`, you can write aspects as annotated Java classes.

■ ■ ■

CHAPTER 4

Java Aspect Components

Chapter 3 presented the syntax and usage of one AOP environment: the AspectJ language. This chapter presents a second AOP environment: Java Aspect Components (JAC).

Like AspectJ, JAC allows you to develop aspect-oriented programs. However, these environments differ in two significant ways. First, AspectJ is a language that defines new keywords, whereas JAC is a framework and, as such, is a regular Java program. JAC provides an API that allows you to define aspects, pointcuts, and pieces of advice code.

Second, the two environments differ in their aspect-weaving mechanisms. AspectJ weaves aspects at compile time or at load time. JAC weaves aspects at run time, which leads to more adaptable programs because aspects can be dynamically added and removed.

A research team led by Renaud Pawlak, with Laurent Martelli and Lionel Seinturier, designed JAC in 1999. The first versions were released in 2000, but the ideas behind JAC were rooted in research that began in 1998 by the aforementioned team and several computer-science research laboratories: the CEDRIC laboratory at CNAM (Conservatoire National des Arts et Métiers), Paris; the LIP6 laboratory at University Paris 6; and the LIFL laboratory at the University of Lille, France. Other contributors included Laurence Duchien and Gérard Florin.

JAC is open-source software that is freely released under the terms of the GNU Lesser General Public License (LGPL). This license allows JAC to be incorporated into business products. In 2003, JAC joined the ObjectWeb community for open-source middleware. For up-to-date information about JAC, see `http://jac.objectweb.org`. For general information about the ObjectWeb community, see `http://www.objectweb.org`.

Creating a First JAC Application

This section presents a simple example of an aspect-oriented application that uses JAC. The example introduces the syntax for aspects, pointcuts, and advice code.

The example reuses the order-management application, which manages client orders, that Chapter 3 presented. However, the code in this chapter uses JAC to implement the same trace aspect as the one that was programmed in Chapter 3. This aspect traces the execution of the application, thus determining the methods that are called and the order that they are called in.

Creating a First Aspect

The first JAC aspect monitors each ordered item by displaying a message before and after the `addItem` method, which the `Order` class defines.

This aspect is defined by two classes: TraceAspect and TraceWrapper. The TraceAspect class defines the pointcut. The TraceWrapper class defines the advice code, which JAC calls a *wrapper*. Listing 4-1 presents the TraceAspect code, and Listing 4-2 (later in this chapter) presents the TraceWrapper code.

Listing 4-1. *A Trace Aspect Component*

```
 1 package aop.jac;
 2
 3 import org.objectweb.jac.core.AspectComponent;
 4
 5 public class TraceAspect extends AspectComponent {
 6
 7   public TraceAspect() {
 8     pointcut(
 9       ".*",
10       "aop.jac.Order",
11       "addItem(java.lang.String,int):void",
12       "aop.jac.TraceWrapper",
13       null, false );
14   }
15 }
```

Notice that the TraceAspect class defines an aspect by extending the AspectComponent class, which is defined by the JAC API as the root class of all aspects. Consequently, JAC aspects are often called *aspect components*.

Creating a First Pointcut

As you can see in Listing 4-1, the call to the pointcut method, which is inherited from AspectComponent, declares a pointcut in the TraceAspect class. The method takes six parameters. The first three designate the joinpoints that match the pointcut. The fourth, which is shown on line 12, defines the wrapper that is associated with the pointcut. The last two parameters define an exception handler and the way that the aspect is instantiated. (See the "Introducing Exception Handlers" and "Aspect Instantiation" sections later in this chapter.)

The methods that match a pointcut are defined by three parameters: the method names (on line 11), the class names (on line 10), and the object names (on line 9). As you will see in the "Pointcuts" section later in this chapter, these parameters are strings that can contain wildcards.

The pointcut that TraceAspect defines includes the addItem method, which takes a String and an int as parameters for all the objects that are instances of the aop.jac.Order class.

JAC allows you to include only selected instances of a class in a pointcut. This feature can be useful when programming distributed applications, for example. In such a case, some server objects that are instances of the same class commonly need to be aspectized differently. Object names in pointcut definitions allow this, as you will see in the "Object Naming" section later in this chapter.

Creating a First Wrapper

As stated earlier, JAC uses the term *wrapper* instead of the term *advice code*. No difference exists between an advice code block in AspectJ and a wrapper in JAC. Both are code blocks that define the behavior of an aspect. The code that a wrapper defines can be executed before or after the joinpoint.

JAC requires you to define wrappers and aspects in distinct classes. This feature allows you to reuse wrappers independently from aspects. As you can see on line 12 of Listing 4-1, the definition of a pointcut links a wrapper to an aspect.

Listing 4-2 presents the `TraceWrapper` code.

Listing 4-2. *A Trace Wrapper*

```
1 package aop.jac;
2
3 import org.aopalliance.intercept.ConstructorInvocation;
4 import org.aopalliance.intercept.MethodInvocation;
5 import org.objectweb.jac.core.AspectComponent;
6 import org.objectweb.jac.core.Wrapper;
7
8 public class TraceWrapper extends Wrapper {
9
10   public TraceWrapper(AspectComponent ac) {
11     super(ac);
12   }
13
14   public Object invoke(MethodInvocation mi) throws Throwable {
15     System.out.println("-> Before addItem");
16     Object ret = proceed(mi);
17     System.out.println("-> After addItem");
18     return ret;
19   }
20
21   public Object construct(ConstructorInvocation ci) throws Throwable {
22     return proceed(ci);
23   }
24 }
```

Notice that you define JAC wrappers by extending the `Wrapper` class. These are always "around" wrappers; no special definition exists for "before" or "after" wrappers. You can define the latter two types by omitting the "after" or "before" part in an "around" wrapper.

JAC wrappers implement the AOP Alliance API.

A wrapper must define a constructor with a parameter of type `AspectComponent`, and the wrapper must call the corresponding inherited constructor. (See line 11 of Listing 4-2). This constructor is called by the JAC runtime when the wrapper is instantiated. The parameter then becomes the reference to the aspect that is associated with the wrapper.

The existing JAC joinpoints are method executions and constructor executions. The `invoke` and `construct` methods are called by the JAC runtime when these joinpoints occur. The methods return an `Object` and can throw an exception of type `Throwable`, which is the root class for all exceptions and errors in Java. The `invoke` method takes a parameter of type `MethodInvocation`. This parameter reifies the joinpoint with information such as the method name or the parameters of the call. The `ConstructorInvocation` parameter plays the same role for constructor executions.

The `proceed` method delimits the "before" and "after" parts of a wrapper. This method executes the joinpoint, or it calls the next wrapper if several wrappers are woven for the same joinpoint. The call to `proceed` is optional. Conversely, `proceed` can be called several times.

The `invoke` and `construct` methods are mandatory—even if they define no instructions.

Creating an Aspect-Configuration File

Aspect configuration is an essential task when programming with JAC. This feature is not often provided by other AOP environments, such as AspectJ, although it is a key factor when reusing aspects.

Each aspect that is defined with JAC is associated with an aspect-configuration file. You choose the parameters that are to be configured in the aspect. The end user defines the aspect-configuration file and the values that are associated with these parameters. For example, when using a transaction-demarcation aspect, you must indicate the methods that are to be executed in the transaction. When using a persistence aspect, you must designate the attributes that are to be saved in a database.

The principle of an aspect-configuration file exists in other approaches, such as that of J2EE. The idea is to separate the code from the initialization values that are used by the code. The code can then be reused without any modifications or recompilations, whereas the initialization values will depend on the execution context.

J2EE and JAC share the same principle—however, the way that they deal with the configuration process differs. In both cases, a set of parameters is associated with the persistence, transaction, naming, and access-control services. With J2EE, these parameters are provided by the servers, are fixed, and cannot be changed. With JAC, you choose precisely the configuration parameters that you want to provide.

The Syntax of an Aspect-Configuration File

Each aspect defined with JAC is associated with an aspect-configuration file that ends with the .acc extension. This file is loaded at run time when the aspect is instantiated. The file can be modified and reloaded while the program is running or between two runs of the same program. The configuration of the program is then dynamically adapted.

Each line in an aspect-configuration file is a call to a public method that is defined in the aspect class. A line begins with the name of the method, continues with a space-separated list of parameters, and ends with a semicolon. (The "Creating an Aspect–Configuration File" section later in this chapter defines the syntax of aspect-configuration files in more detail.)

An Example of Aspect Configuration

Listing 4-3 shows the TraceAspect2 aspect, which rewrites TraceAspect so that the pointcut is made configurable through the trace method.

Listing 4-3. *A Configurable Aspect Component for Tracing*

```
package aop.jac;
import org.objectweb.jac.core.AspectComponent;

public class TraceAspect2 extends AspectComponent {

  public void trace( String objectPE, String classPE, String methodPE ) {
      pointcut(
        objectPE, classPE, methodPE,
        "aop.jac.TraceWrapper",
        null, false );
  }
}
```

The trace method takes three parameters: objectPE, classPE, and methodPE. To define a pointcut, the trace method calls the pointcut method with these three parameters. To obtain a program similar to the one that is defined by TraceAspect, the aspect-configuration file named traceaspect2.acc can be written as follows:

```
trace ".*" "aop.jac.Order" "addItem(java.lang.String,int):void"
```

The aspect-configuration file provides the current value for the definition of the pointcut. These values can be changed without recompiling the aspect. Reloading the aspect-configuration file into JAC at run time causes the pointcut that is associated with the aspect and the traced joinpoints to change.

In the preceding example, we made the three parameters that define the pointcut configurable. We could have extended the example by adding parameters to the trace method for the wrapper class or for the remaining parameters. It is up to the aspect programmer to make such choices.

Creating an Application-Descriptor File

Each JAC application is associated with a `.jac` file. This file provides information about the entry point of the application and the aspects that need to be initially woven. (See the "Configuring JAC Applications" section later in this chapter for more details on this application-descriptor file.)

An Example of an Application-Descriptor File

Listing 4-4 show the `customer.jac` file, which is a valid application-descriptor file for the order-management application.

Listing 4-4. *The Application-Descriptor File for the Order-Management Application*

```
applicationName: Order management
launchingClass: aop.jac.Customer
aspects: traceid traceaspect2.acc true
jac.acs: traceid aop.jac.TraceAspect2
```

An application-descriptor file consists of property names and property values. In this type of file, each line begins with a property name followed by a colon and ends with a property value. In Listing 4-4, the `applicationName` property defines a string that identifies the application, and the `launchingClass` property defines the fully qualified name of the class to be loaded to launch the application.

The `aspects` and `jac.acs` properties deal with the aspects to be woven when the application starts. For the `aspects` property, each aspect is defined by three values: an identifier (here, `traceid`) that is chosen by the application–descriptor-file writer; the name of the aspect-descriptor file (here, `traceaspect2.acc`); and a Boolean value (here, `true`) that indicates whether the aspect is initially woven. For each identifier declared in an aspect, the `jac.acs` property defines the class that implements the aspect. In our example, the `traceid` identifier corresponds to the `aop.jac.TraceAspect2` aspect.

Compiling a JAC Application

Five categories of files are to be included when programming with JAC:

- The `.java` files of the application—in this case, `Customer.java`, `Order.java`, and `Catalog.java`.

- The aspect files—here, just `TraceAspect2.java`.

- The wrapper files—here, just `TraceWrapper.java`.

- The aspect-configuration files—here, just `traceaspect2.jac`.

- The application–descriptor file—here, `customer.jac`.

The first three categories of files can be compiled by calling the regular Java compiler, `javac` or `jikes`, with the `jac.jar` JAC library referenced in the class path. The last two categories contain text files that will be loaded and parsed by the JAC runtime.

If JAC was installed in the c:\jac directory, and all the application files were in the src directory, you would run the Java compiler with the following command:

```
javac -d classes -classpath c:\jac\jac.jar src\*.java
```

The resulting .class files would then be stored in the classes directory.

Running a JAC Application

An aspect-oriented application with JAC can be run by launching the framework with an application-descriptor file. The jac.jar library contains all the classes that are needed to launch the framework.

To run the order-management application, the command is as follows:

```
java -jar c:\jac\jac.jar -R c:\jac -C src;classes customer.jac
```

The -R option indicates the JAC installation directory (c:\jac in our example). The -C option specifies the path-like structure (here, the src and classes directories) that JAC can load files from. The last parameter in the command line is the name of the application-descriptor file.

Output from a JAC Application

The previous command gives the output that is shown in Listing 4-5.

Listing 4-5. *The Output of the Order-Management Application*

```
JAC version 0.12.1
--- Launching Application Order management ---
--- configuring traceid aspect ---
-> Before addItem
2 item(s) CD added to the order
-> After addItem
-> Before addItem
1 item(s) DVD added to the order
-> After addItem
Order amount: US$50.0
JAC system shutdown: notifying all ACs...
Bye bye.
```

The first three lines of Listing 4-5 are automatically displayed by JAC. They contain a welcome message with the JAC version number, the name of the application that was launched, and a line for each woven aspect. The output of the application follows, showing each execution of the addItem method, which is wrapped by a message. The last two lines of output are displayed by JAC.

Creating Pointcuts

The previous section introduced the basic elements of JAC. We showed how to write, compile, and run a first aspect-oriented application. This section studies the definition of a pointcut.

The `pointcut` method, which is defined in the `AspectComponent` class, allows you to define pointcuts. Three categories of parameters can be passed when you define a pointcut:

- *Pointcut expression*: This expression defines the joinpoints that are included in the pointcut.

- *Wrapper class*: This class defines the code that will be executed before and after the join-points.

- *Exception handler*: The exception handler that is associated with the pointcut provides a method to catch and treat the exceptions that the joinpoints and the wrapper can throw. The exception handler is a method with a given signature that is implemented in the wrapper class. Exception handlers are optional.

The following sections explain these three categories in detail.

Pointcut Expressions

Pointcut expressions in JAC are composed of three subexpressions. A fourth is added when programming distributed applications.

The joinpoints that are included in a pointcut are either method executions or constructor executions. JAC also performs an automatic bytecode analysis to classify the methods that are defined in an application. The purpose of this analysis is to detect whether the methods access or modify the object state. This information is made available in the pointcut definition language, and you can define pointcuts that include all the methods that perform read or write operations on designated fields, for example.

The three subexpressions that are contained in a pointcut definition deal with the names of classes, objects, and methods, respectively. The subexpressions are referred to as class expressions, object expressions, and method expressions. These expressions can be thought of as filters. Their purpose is to filter a set of classes, objects, or methods and retain only those that match the expressions.

The roles of the three expressions can be defined as follows:

Class expression: A class expression defines a filter for class names. The filtering is performed on fully qualified class names—for example, names that include the package and class identifiers.

Object expression: An object expression defines a filter for object names. All business objects that are instantiated by JAC are automatically associated with a name. This name plays a role largely similar to that of a regular Java reference. The purpose is to uniquely identify each created object so that you can aspectize certain objects of a class (to customize their behaviors) while leaving others unchanged. The object names are automatically created by appending instance numbers to the class name. For example, the name `order#0` identifies the first instance of the `Order` class.

Method expression: A method expression defines a filter for method signatures. A signature contains a name, a comma-separated list of parameter types, and a return type. For example, the expression addItem(java.lang.String,int):void designates the addItem method that takes a String and an int as parameters and returns void.

The previous expressions are regular expressions that follow the syntax defined by the GNU regexp library.

Regular Expressions

JAC uses the GNU regexp library (see http://www.cacas.org/java/gnu/regexp) to deal with regular expressions. This library defines a syntax for regular expressions and provides an API to check whether a string matches a given regular expression.

Operators

The GNU regexp library defines several operators for writing pattern expressions. However, this section focuses only on the main operators. For additional information, see the documentation on the GNU regexp Library web site.

The dot (.) operator provides a shortcut for designating any character. The * and + operators allow you to designate repetitions of a given expression. The * operator matches zero or *n* repetitions of an expression, whereas + matches at least one repetition of an expression. The .* expression is widely used; it matches any sequence of characters.

The [ ] operator is used to designate a set of characters. For example, the expression [abc] matches any of the characters *a*, *b*, or *c*. The ^ operator is equivalent to a Boolean NOT operator. The expression [^abc] matches any character except *a*, *b*, or *c*. Intervals can be defined in sets by using the minus operator (-). For example, the expression [d-m] matches any lowercase letter between *d* and *m*, inclusive.

JAC Operators

In addition to the operators provided by the GNU regexp library, JAC defines four operators that can be used in pointcut expressions: ALL, &&, ||, and !. The ALL operator is a shortcut for .*, and the three remaining operators correspond to the Boolean AND, OR, and NOT operators, respectively.

Examples of Regular Expressions

This section illustrates how to use GNU regular expressions with JAC.

The method expression set.*:void selects all the methods that have a signature starting with set and ending with :void (the method returns void), regardless of the parameters.

The method expression set.*(java.lang.String):void selects all the methods that have a name starting with set, that take a String as a parameter, and that have a return type of void.

The method expression get.*():.* selects all the methods that have a name starting with get and that take no parameters, regardless of the return type.

The class expression ALL selects all the existing classes.

Method-Type Operators

The purpose of method-type operators is to classify and select methods according to their impact on the object state. For example, the you might want to select all the methods that modify the object state by setting the value of a given field. (Such methods are called *setters*.)

In approaches such as that of JavaBeans, the definition of a setter relies on naming conventions. In other words, the names of all setters must start with *set*. Whatever the body of such a method is, the method is considered a setter. Conversely, a method with a name that does not start with *set* is not considered a setter—even if the method sets a field. This can lead to counterintuitive naming schemes. For example, a method that computes and sets the amount of an order must be named setAmount if you want JavaBeans to consider the method a setter—even if computeAmount would be more intuitive and logical.

To detect setters and getters, JAC relies on a bytecode analysis performed with the Byte Code Engineering Library (BCEL). (See http://jakarta.apache.org/bcel.) When a class is loaded, its bytecode is immediately analyzed. For example, when the opcode for reading a field is present in a method body, metadata is attached to the method to classify it as a getter. This metadata is made available when you write a pointcut.

The following method-type operators are defined by JAC:

- ACCESSORS: This operator selects each method that reads one or more fields defined in its class.

- MODIFIERS: This operator selects each method that writes one or more fields defined in its class.

- GETTERS(list): This operator selects each method that returns the value of any of the fields mentioned in the given list. The list is a comma-separated list of fields, as in GETTERS(name,address).

- SETTERS(list): This operator selects each method that sets the value of any of the fields mentioned in the given list. The value must have been passed to the method as a parameter.

All the previously listed operators can be combined with those defined by the GNU regexp library.

The following expression selects the methods that perform a write operation on a field, the methods that return the value of the age field, and the methods that have a name starting with *compute*:

```
MODIFIERS || GETTERS(age) || compute.*
```

To further illustrate these operators, consider the Person class that is shown in Listing 4-6.

Listing 4-6. *An Illustration of Method-Type Operators with the Person Class*

```
public class Person {
  private String name;
  private int age;
  public void birthday() { age++; }
  public String whatIsYourNamePlease() { return name; }
  public void foo(String first,String last) { name=first+last; }
  public void bar(String name) { this.name=name; }
}
```

The four previously listed operators define the following selections:

ACCESSORS selects the whatIsYourNamePlease and birthday methods. The birthday method reads the age field before incrementing it, and the whatIsYourNamePlease method reads the name field before returning it.

MODIFIERS selects the birthday, foo, and bar methods. These methods modify one of the fields that is defined in the Person class.

GETTERS(name) selects the whatIsYourNamePlease method, which returns the value of the name field.

SETTERS(name) selects the bar method, which sets the name field with a value that is passed as a parameter. This last condition is important for qualifying the method as a setter. Indeed, the foo method also sets the field name, but it does so with a value that is "passed" indirectly as a parameter. (In other words, the value is obtained through string concatenation.) Therefore, the foo method is considered not a setter but a modifier.

Two additional operators exist that classify methods depending on their behavior with collections (for example, with fields that implement the java.util.Collection interface):

ADDERS(list): This operator selects the methods that add an element to a collection. The added element must have been passed to the method as a parameter. The given list is a comma-separated list of collection fields.

REMOVERS(list): This operator selects the methods that remove an element from a collection. The removed element must have been passed to the method as a parameter.

Associating a Wrapper with a Pointcut

In the examples of the TraceAspect and TraceAspect2 aspects, you learned that the pointcut method defines pointcuts. The first parameters passed to this method are expressions that deal with the definitions of the classes, objects, and methods included in the pointcut. In this section, we present the three cases in which a wrapper can be associated with a pointcut.

In the first and most frequent case, defining the wrapper requires two parameters: wrapperClassName, which is a string that defines the wrapper class name; and one2one, which is a Boolean value. The wrapper class must be a subclass of org.objectweb.jac.core.Wrapper. In all cases, JAC dynamically instantiates the specified wrapperClassName class. When this instantiation occurs, it depends on the value of one2one:

- A value of false causes all the joinpoints included in the pointcut to share the same wrapper. In this case, the wrapper is a singleton.

- A value of true causes each joinpoint included in the pointcut to be associated with a dedicated instance of the wrapper class.

The value false generates fewer objects and thus saves memory. However, if the wrapper is stateful and the state depends on the joinpoint, the sharing can lead to inconsistencies. In such a case, it is easier to have one dedicated instance of a wrapper for each joinpoint and use the value true for one2one.

The second case is rather similar to the first. Three parameters instead of two must be passed to define the wrapper. They are the wrapper class name; the Boolean one2one; and initParameters, which is an array of objects. This last parameter contains the initial values that must be passed when instantiating the wrapper.

With the last case, you pass a unique parameter named wrappee. This parameter must implement the org.objectweb.jac.core.Wrapper type. The instance will be used to wrap all the joinpoints included in the pointcut. This case is useful when the wrapper cannot be easily created by the framework, or when you want to use a customized instance of a wrapper.

Creating Wrappers

In the previous section, you learned how to define a pointcut with JAC. In this section, you will learn how to write wrappers.

Programming an aspect with JAC consists of writing at least two classes: one (such as TraceAspect2) for the definition of pointcuts, and one for each wrapper associated with a pointcut. This allows you to easily reuse pointcut definitions independently from wrappers and vice versa.

Wrapper classes with JAC must extend the org.objectweb.jac.core.Wrapper class, which is the root class of all existing wrappers. All wrappers are "around" wrappers.

Wrapper instances are created either by JAC or by you when you define the pointcuts. In all cases, a link is maintained between the aspect and the wrapper instances. This link comes into existence when a wrapper is instantiated; the wrapper provides a constructor that takes the instance of the associated aspect as a parameter. This parameter implements the org.objectweb.jac.core.AspectComponent type, which is the root class of all JAC aspects.

A typical definition of a wrapper class starts with the following lines of code:

```
import org.objectweb.jac.core.AspectComponent;
import org.objectweb.jac.core.Wrapper;

public class MyWrapper extends Wrapper {
  public MyWrapper(AspectComponent ac) { super(ac); }
```

With JAC, two types of joinpoints exist: method executions and constructor executions. The "before" and "after" code that is executed around these joinpoints is defined in the invoke and construct methods, which are presented in the following sections.

Methods

The code that is executed before and after a method-execution joinpoint is defined in the invoke method. This method takes a unique parameter that implements the MethodInvocation type, returns an Object, and throws the Throwable type. The definition of MethodInvocation is detailed in the "Joinpoint Introspection" section later in this chapter. The declaration of the invoke method is shown here:

```
public Object invoke( MethodInvocation mi ) throws Throwable;
```

The proceed method can be called by the invoke method to execute the intercepted method. Several aspects can be woven around the same joinpoint. In such a case, a chain of wrappers is created around the joinpoint. The proceed method executes the next wrapper in the chain or, if the end of the chain is reached, the intercepted method.

The proceed method can be called several times in the same invoke method. In such a case, several executions of the same method are performed. This can be useful when you need to rerun a method that previously failed.

On the other hand, the proceed method might never be called. In such a case, the intercepted method is not executed, and the call is returned to the caller.

The general format of the invoke method is shown in Listing 4-7.

Listing 4-7. *The General Format of the invoke Method*

```
public Object invoke( MethodInvocation mi ) throws Throwable {
  // before code
  Object ret = proceed(mi);
  // after code
  return ret;
}
```

The invoke method is mandatory—even if no code is defined.

Constructors

Like method executions, constructor executions can be aspectized with the construct method. The signature of this method is as follows:

```
public Object construct( ConstructorInvocation ci ) throws Throwable;
```

The proceed method plays the same role for construct as for invoke. No particular characteristics distinguish invoke from construct, except the difference in their names.

Joinpoint Introspection

The term *introspection* refers to examining the inner cause of a given phenomenon and gaining information about it. In the context of AOP, the phenomenon is the joinpoint, and you want to retrieve information about the part of the actual program that allows the joinpoint to occur.

With JAC, the introspection mechanism is made available by the MethodInvocation and ConstructorInvocation parameters that are passed when the invoke and construct methods are called. These types are defined in the AOP Alliance API, which is included in JAC.

Figure 4-1 illustrates the interface hierarchy that defines MethodInvocation and ConstructorInvocation.

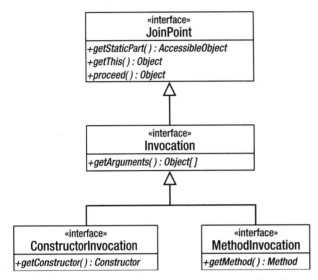

Figure 4-1. *The* org.aopalliance.intercept *interface hierarchy*

The JoinPoint interface is the root type for all interceptions. For each joinpoint, three methods are defined: proceed, which executes the joinpoint; getThis, which returns the object where the joinpoint occurred; and getStaticPart, which returns the code element defining the joinpoint. This code element can be either a method or a constructor. It is represented by the java.lang.reflect.AccessibleObject class which, in the J2SE reflection API, is the superclass of all the code elements where reflection applies.

The Invocation interface extends JoinPoint with the getArguments method to manipulate the arguments of the intercepted execution. These arguments are returned as an array of objects that can be read or written.

The last two interfaces, ConstructorInvocation and MethodInvocation, correspond to constructor executions and method executions. Each provides a method that returns the intercepted constructor (as a parameter of type java.lang.reflect.Constructor) or the intercepted method (as a parameter of type java.lang.reflect.Method).

Wrapper Chains

Several wrappers can be attached to the same joinpoint. These wrappers are referred to as *chained*. In a wrapper, the call to proceed executes the next wrapper in the chain. When the end of the chain has been reached, the joinpoint will be executed.

Figure 4-2 illustrates this mechanism with a chain of three wrappers. Each arrow represents either a method call or a method return. The arrows are numbered to indicate the execution-flow order.

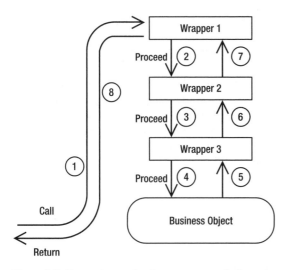

Figure 4-2. *Execution order in a wrapper chain*

The initial call is passed to the first wrapper in the chain which, in turn, executes the "before" code. The first and second calls to proceed (arrows 2 and 3) execute the next wrapper in the chain. When the execution flow reaches the third wrapper, the call to proceed executes the joinpoint (arrow 4). After the execution of the joinpoint, the execution flow returns to the third wrapper (arrow 5) which, in turn, executes the "after" code. Next, the "after" code for the second and first wrappers is executed and, last, the call is returned.

Configuring Aspects and JAC Applications

·Configuration is another key mechanism of JAC. This feature allows aspects to be reused efficiently. This section presents the syntax of both aspect-configuration files and application-descriptor files.

Configuring Aspects

Each aspect that is defined with JAC is associated with a text-based aspect-configuration file. The extension for this type of file is .acc.

An aspect-configuration file provides the parameters that are required to adapt the aspect to a new application. For example, the purpose of this file for a transaction aspect is to define which methods in the application are to be executed in a transactional context.

The notion of an aspect-configuration file exists in other approaches, such as that of J2EE. In J2EE, aspect-configuration files provide certain parameter values that tailor the system services to the specific needs of the application. By configuring the services that are provided by the application server, it is possible to reuse them with different applications. Although the syntax of aspect-configuration files differs between J2EE and JAC (in the case of J2EE, the files are XML files), the purpose is the same: allowing you to customize the aspects for the application and later modify the customization without having to recompile the application.

The purpose of an aspect-configuration file is to define a list of method calls. These calls are passed from JAC to the aspect just after the aspect's instantiation. You choose the steps that are required to configure the aspect, and the calls perform any configuration treatment that you define.

Many possibilities are available when configuring aspects. For example, it is possible to configure complex aspects, such as the GUI aspect, that would not be possible with an approach based only on parameters and values. The power of the GUI aspect lies in its configuration methods which, when called from the configuration file, construct the graphical appearance of an application. (For more information on the GUI aspect, see the "Using the JAC Aspects Library" section later in this chapter.)

The Syntax of Aspect-Configuration Files

An aspect-configuration file defines the aspect methods that must be called when the aspect is instantiated.

Each line in the file begins with the name of the method to call, continues with the values of the given parameters, and ends with a semicolon. The parameters are specified in a space-separated list. String parameters must be written between double quotes, and arrays must be written between brackets.

Comments in aspect-configuration files follow the same syntactic rules that Java does.

You can include other files in an aspect-configuration file by using the `include` keyword.

An Example of an Aspect-Configuration File

Consider the `PresentationAC` aspect that is shown in Listing 4-8.

Listing 4-8. *The PresentationAC Aspect Component*

```
package aop.jac;
import org.objectweb.jac.core.AspectComponent;

public class PresentationAC extends AspectComponent {
  public void display() { /* ... */ }
  public void setAttributesOrder(
            String className,
            String[] attributeNames ) { /* ... */ }
  public void setCategory(
            String className,
            String[] attributeNames,
            String value ) { /* ... */ }
}
```

`PresentationAC` defines the `setAttributesOrder` method to specify the display order for the attributes of the given `classname` class. This order is defined by the `attributeNames` array, which contains the attribute names.

The aspect-configuration file, named `presentation.acc`, contains the following lines:

```
setAttributesOrder Customer { lastName, firstName, phone, email };
setCategory Customer { lastName, firstName } main;
display ;
```

This aspect-configuration file calls the setAttributesOrder method and then calls the display method. The first call takes the value Customer for the classname parameter, and it takes the values lastName, firstName, phone, and email for the attributeNames array. No parameters are defined for the call to the display method.

Grouping Parameters in Aspect-Configuration Files

Grouping parameters introduces some so-called "syntactic sugar" into aspect-configuration files.

The syntax for grouping parameters is as follows:

```
group <value> {
   <method> [ <parameter> ... ] ;
   ...
}
```

When a group is used, the given value is added as the first parameter for every call that is specified between the curly brackets. Grouping parameters can be used to avoid redundancies—especially in cases that use the same value for several successive calls.

The following configuration file, named presentation2.acc, is equivalent to presentation.acc:

```
group Customer {
  setAttributesOrder { lastName, firstName, phone, email };
  setCategory { lastName, firstName } main;
}
display ;
```

Strictly speaking, group is not a keyword; it is an identifier that you can freely choose. Any identifier that is not a method name and that is defined in the aspect can be chosen for defining a group.

Definitions that use the grouping mechanism can be nested. For example, the aspect-configuration file

```
group Customer {
  attribute lastName {
    setCategory General ;
  }
}
```

is equivalent to

```
setCategory Customer lastName General ;
```

Definitions that use the grouping mechanism can be factored. For example, the aspect-configuration file

```
group Customer,Employee {
  setAttributesOrder { lastName, firstName, phone, email };
}
```

is equivalent to

```
setAttributesOrder Customer { lastName, firstName, phone, email };
setAttributesOrder Employee { lastName, firstName, phone, email
```

Configuring JAC Applications

A JAC application-descriptor file is a text file that provides information about launching the application. It defines a set of property names and values that is loaded by JAC when the end user starts the application. The extension .jac is commonly used for application-descriptor files.

Each line in an application-descriptor file starts with the name of a property followed by a colon and ends with the property value. The backslash character (\) can be used to continue the definition of the value to next line.

For example, the application-descriptor file

```
applicationName: Order management
launchingClass: \
        aop.jac.Customer
```

defines the values "Order management" and "aop.jac.Customer" for the applicationName and launchingClass properties, respectively.

Lines starting with the pound-sign character (#) are interpreted as comments.

Table 4-1 presents the list of properties that can be used in an application-descriptor file.

Table 4-1. *JAC Application-Descriptor Properties*

Property	Definition
applicationName	The application name
launchingClass	The main class name
aspects	A series of three values for defining the aspect identifiers, the aspect-configuration files, and the Boolean values that specify whether the aspects are initially woven
jac.acs	A series of two values for defining the aspect identifiers and the classes that implement those aspects
jac.comp.wrappingOrder	The weaving order when several wrappers apply to the same joinpoint
jac.topology	For distributed applications, the names of the hosts where the application is deployed

Using the Introduction Feature

You can extend the structure of an application by using the *introduction* feature to add new code elements. JAC can *introduce*, or add, two categories of these elements: role methods and exception handlers.

Role Methods

You introduce a *role method* to define new behaviors.

A role method is defined in a wrapper class. You can choose the name, signature, and return type of the method. However, the first parameter must be org.objectweb.jac.core.Wrappee. This parameter corresponds to the application object where the method will be introduced.

The wrapper shown in Listing 4-9 illustrates the definition of a role method.

Listing 4-9. *The Definition of a Role Method*

```
package aop.jac;

import org.aopalliance.intercept.ConstructorInvocation;
import org.aopalliance.intercept.MethodInvocation;
import org.objectweb.jac.core.AspectComponent;
import org.objectweb.jac.core.Wrappee;
import org.objectweb.jac.core.Wrapper;

public class TraceWrapper4 extends Wrapper {

  public TraceWrapper4(AspectComponent ac) { super(ac); }

  public void computeAmountAndPrint( Wrappee o, String header ) {
    double amount = ((Order)o).computeAmount();
    System.out.println(header+amount);
  }

  public Object construct(ConstructorInvocation ci) throws Throwable {
      return proceed(ci);
  }
  public Object invoke(MethodInvocation mi) throws Throwable {
      return proceed(mi);
  }
}
```

The computeAmountAndPrint method can be introduced in the Order class to compute and print the amount of an order. The first parameter, o, is the instance of the Order class where the role method is invoked. The second parameter, header, is a string that is printed before the amount.

A role method can be called by the invokeRoleMethod method, which is defined in the org.objectweb.jac.core.Wrappee class. This method takes three parameters: the instance that receives the call, the name of the role method, and the array of objects to pass as parameters to the method.

For example, the code block

```
Wrapping.invokeRoleMethod(
      (Wrappee)o, "computeAmountAndPrint", new Object[]{">> "});
```

corresponds to calling the computeAmountAndPrint method for the object o with the string ">>" as a parameter.

Exception Handlers

Exception handlers enable you to modularize the treatments that are attached to exceptions. Rather than scattering several versions of a try/catch block in the application code, you can usually write the code that is defined in the catch block in a unique and well-defined entity: the exception handler.

The exception handler is defined in a wrapper and catches exceptions that are generated by joinpoints or wrappers. The handler is declared when you call the pointcut method to define a pointcut. The signature of the pointcut method is imposed, a unique parameter of type Exception must be defined, and the return type must be Object. The name of the exception handler can be freely chosen.

Each defined exception handler can be dedicated to handling a particular type of exception. For example, one handler can treat the IOException, whereas another handles network exceptions.

The TraceAspect5 aspect, which is shown in Listing 4-10, illustrates the definition of an exception handler.

Listing 4-10. *An Example of a Role Method and an Exception Handler*

```
package aop.jac;
```

```
import org.aopalliance.intercept.ConstructorInvocation;
import org.aopalliance.intercept.MethodInvocation;
import org.objectweb.jac.core.AspectComponent;
import org.objectweb.jac.core.Wrapper;

public class TraceAspect5 extends AspectComponent {
  public TraceAspect5() {
    pointcut(
      "ALL","ALL","ALL", "aop.jac.TraceWrapper4",
      "myIOExceptionHandler", false );
  }
}

public class TraceWrapper5 extends Wrapper {

  public TraceWrapper5(AspectComponent ac) { super(ac); }

  public Object myIOExceptionHandler(Exception e) throws Exception {
    System.out.println( "Exception "+e.getMessage()+"raised" );
    if ( ! (e instanceof java.io.IOException) )
      throw e;
    return null;
  }
```

```
    public Object construct(ConstructorInvocation ci) throws Throwable {
        return proceed(ci);
    }
    public Object invoke(MethodInvocation mi) throws Throwable {
        return proceed(mi);
    }
}
```

The call to `pointcut` specifies that the `myIOExceptionHandler` method, which is defined in the `aop.jac.TraceWrapper5` class, will handle exceptions for the joinpoints and wrappers that are included in the pointcut. This pointcut includes all the methods, classes, and objects that are defined in the application. If the type is not `IOException`, the `myIOExceptionHandler` method displays a message and propagates the exception.

Several exception handlers can be defined for a given joinpoint; in such a case, they are chained. If a handler propagates the exception, the next handler in the chain is executed. If all the handlers propagate the exception, the application exits.

Using the JAC Aspects Library

A library containing 16 different aspects is distributed with JAC. The purpose of this library is to aid application developers by providing ready-to-use solutions for commonly encountered problems. Several aspects are provided with the library to demonstrate that AOP can be applied to the development of many different types of applications. The aspects provided in the library permit you to quickly program a prototype or a demonstration. When used in an operational context, however, you must improve and complete these aspects.

Among the 16 available aspects, the following are mature enough to be used in an operational context:

- GUI aspect

- Authentication aspect

- User-profile aspect

- Confirmation aspect

- Persistence aspect

- Integrity aspect

The following sections present the 16 aspects grouped into 4 categories: user-interface aspects, persistence and transaction aspects, distribution aspects, and other aspects.

Using the User-Interface Aspects

The GUI aspect is one of the most original aspects provided by JAC. The purpose of this aspect is to define the graphical user interface of the application.

Two versions of the GUI aspect are provided: Swing and HTML/servlet. They both support the same configuration methods. Therefore, the end user can interact with the application through a Swing interface or a web browser.

The `org.objectweb.jac.aspects.gui.GuiAC` class implements the GUI aspect.

Overview of the GUI Aspect

Figures 4-3 and 4-4 illustrate the GUI aspect. The sample application manages invoices and clients. Invoices and clients can be added and removed. Each invoice is linked to a client. The application can list either the existing clients with their corresponding invoices or the current invoices with their associated clients. (For more details on this application, see the JAC web site at http://jac.objectweb.org. Click Documentation, and then click JAC Tutorial.)

Figure 4-3 is a snapshot of the Swing version of the application, whereas Figure 4-4 is a snapshot of the HTML/servlet version. Both versions contain the same Java code and aspect-configuration file. The only difference lies in the launching option that is passed to JAC and that starts either the Swing GUI aspect or the HTML/servlet one.

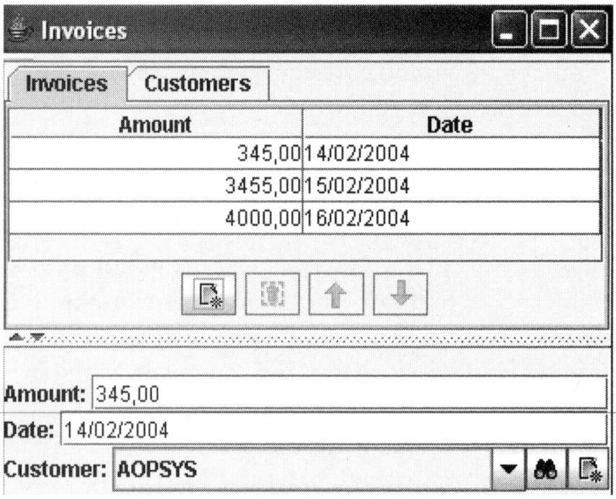

Figure 4-3. *Swing version of the GUI aspect*

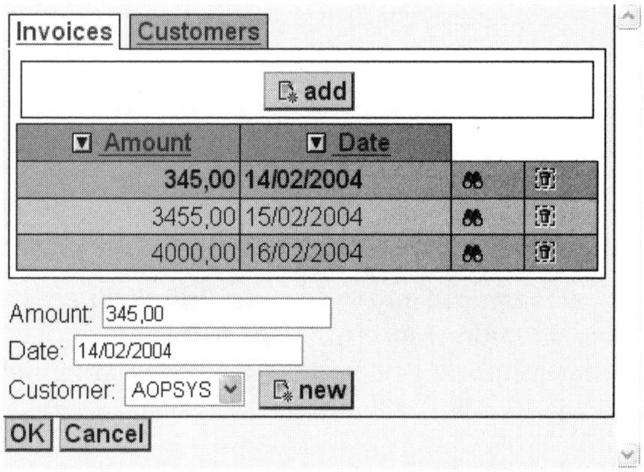

Figure 4-4. *HTML/servlet version of the GUI aspect*

Overview of Other User-Interface Aspects

In addition to the GuiAC aspect, the following aspects are available to handle interactions between the user and the application:

- *Authentication aspect*: The AuthenticationAC aspect manages access control lists. Method executions can be restricted to authorized users.

- *User-profile aspect*: The UserAC aspect manages user profiles.

- *Session-management aspect*: The SessionAC aspect manages user sessions. Data that is dedicated to each individual user of the application can be stored and kept in memory while the user is connected to the application.

- *Confirmation aspect*: The ConfirmationAC aspect displays dialog boxes that ask for confirmation from the user.

Using the Persistence and Transaction Aspects

The persistence aspect permits the saving of data in files or databases. This aspect is used to safely store any critical data that is used by an application.

The transaction aspect provides a way to safely execute an action or a group of actions. A typical example of a *transaction* is a transfer between two bank accounts. In this case, the transfer must be completed or the part of the transaction that was already performed will be canceled.

Both the persistence and transaction aspects use databases. The persistence aspect uses databases to safely save data; the transaction aspect uses databases to guarantee the properties of atomicity, coherence, isolation, and durability.

JAC provides two versions of the persistence aspect: PersistenceAC and HibernateAC. PersistenceAC uses JDBC to save data in a file or database; HibernateAC uses the Hibernate (http://hibernate.bluemars.net) persistence framework.

JAC provides two versions of the transaction aspect: TransactionAC and DisTransAC. TransactionAC performs simple transactions on objects that are stored in memory. This aspect does not manage data locking; hence, concurrent executions may give inconsistent results. DisTransAC uses the ObjectWeb Java Open Transaction Monitor (JOTM) transaction monitor. JOTM implements a two-phase validation protocol on data that is stored in databases and that can be distributed on different hosts of a network. (For more information about JOTM, see http://jotm.objectweb.org.)

Using the Distribution Aspects

JAC provides a set of aspects for executions that occur on hosts distributed over a network and for data that exists on such hosts. In this case, the application objects interact remotely with an aspect that implements communications based on the Java Remote Method Invocation (RMI) protocol. A prototype implementation of this aspect that is based on Common Object Request Broker Architecture (CORBA) Internet Inter-ORB Protocol (IIOP) is also available.

Prior to the execution of a distributed application, JAC daemon servers must be launched on all the hosts that will take part in the application. Then, the following aspects can be used to implement distributed applications:

- *Deployment aspect*: The DeploymentAC aspect deploys an application on a set of remote hosts. Starting from a reference host, the deployment process consists of uploading the bytecode of the classes onto selected hosts and then copying or instantiating the application objects on these hosts. Alternatively, DeploymentAC can install replicas of given objects onto different hosts. This feature constitutes the basic mechanism for providing fault-tolerant applications—whenever a host holding one of the replicas fails, any of the other hosts that are still running can replace the faulty host.

- *Consistency aspect*: The ConsistencyAC aspect implements a memory-consistency protocol among replicas. The chosen protocol provides strong consistency—as soon as one of the replicas is modified, the modification is propagated to all the other replicas. The goal is to keep all the replicas synchronized with the same data.

- *Broadcasting aspect*: The BroadcastingAC aspect broadcasts a method call to a set of distributed replicas.

- *Load-balancing aspect*: The LoadBalancingAC aspect distributes requests to a set of replicas. By using this aspect, you take advantage of the computing power of several hosts. This aspect implements a simple round-robin algorithm for the load balancing.

The distribution aspects can be used to distribute both application objects and aspect objects. Indeed, when managed by JAC, these types of objects contain no fundamental differences. Hence, aspect objects can be remotely deployed or replicated with DeploymentAC, and the different replicas can be managed by ConsistencyAC.

Implementing a distributed application with JAC is not limited to using the four distribution aspects but also involves defining pointcuts. In the "Creating Pointcuts" section earlier in this chapter, you learned that you must provide three expressions to define a pointcut. These expressions define the objects, classes, and methods that are included in the pointcut. A fourth expression, called a *host expression*, comes into play when you program distributed applications.

The host expression is a regular expression that specifies the hosts that are included in the pointcut. The joinpoints are filtered according to the objects, classes, methods, and hosts where the joinpoints occur. Pointcuts are then distributed and can include joinpoints located on different hosts.

Using Other Aspects

To conclude this presentation of the JAC aspects library, we present the following general-purpose aspects that are useful in several application contexts:

- *Cache aspect*: The CacheAC aspect caches method results. When cached, the results can be reused without the re-execution of the methods. This speeds up the execution time of the application by avoiding unnecessary executions.

- *Integrity aspect*: The IntegrityAC aspect implements referential-integrity constraints between sets of data. This aspect prevents the accidental deletion of data that is linked by a logical constraint. For example, when managing clients and invoices, the end user must not accidentally delete a client if invoices are still associated with the client. The IntegrityAC aspect performs checks that enforce such constraints.

- *Synchronization aspect*: The SynchronizationAC aspect manages locks to synchronize the access to methods. For example, this aspect ensures that a method is not executed by more than one method at a time.

Programming in UMLAF

UML Aspectual Factory (UMLAF) is the standard IDE that is distributed with JAC. This IDE is a rapid application development (RAD) environment that allows you to easily and rapidly develop applications with JAC. UMLAF uses the Unified Modeling Language (UML) notation to design applications.

UMLAF implements only the class diagrams that are defined in UML. Although this is far from a full implementation of UML, class diagrams are nevertheless the most widely used diagrams at this time. These diagrams are sufficient in many cases—especially when aspects come into play.

UMLAF extends the UML notation by adding the notions of an aspect and a pointcut. Aspects in UMLAF are considered to be a new kind of modeling element (much like classes); pointcuts define a new kind of relationship.

Figure 4-5 displays a snapshot of UMLAF. Three classes (Invoices, Invoice, and Client), an aspect (TraceAspect), and a pointcut are defined.

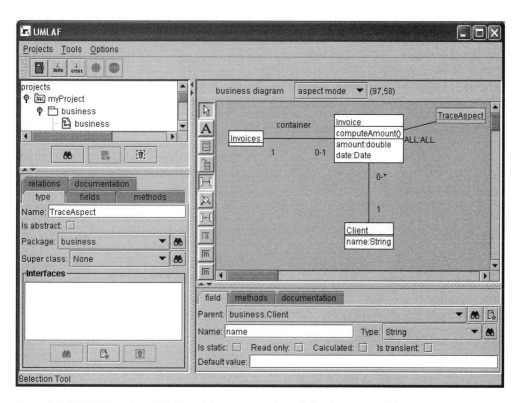

Figure 4-5. *UMLAF—a UML RAD tool for aspect-oriented development with JAC*

UMLAF covers the entire developmental life cycle of an application. The business core of the application can be designed, new aspects can be added, and aspects that are defined in the library can be reused. UMLAF automates the writing of aspect-configuration files and application descriptors. A code-editing facility is provided. UMLAF generates JAC-specific code, compiles applications, and launches applications.

UMLAF is an application that was written with JAC. Nine aspects were used for writing UMLAF. The most important ones are GuiAC, SessionAC, PersistenceAC, ConfirmationAC, and IntegrityAC.

Advanced Features

This section presents the advanced features of JAC.

Aspect Instantiation

When programming aspects with JAC, you must define two varieties of classes: one for the aspects and another for the wrappers. One variety extends org.objectweb.jac.core.AspectComponent, and the other extends org.objectweb.jac.core.Wrapper.

The cardinality of the aspect class is always one. Each aspect is represented by only one instance per Virtual Machine (VM). An aspect manager (org.objectweb.jac.core.ACManager) manages all the aspect instances used by an application and provides features to weave aspects into the application.

The cardinality of the wrapper class is somewhat more complex. First, a wrapper can be used in several pointcuts. Second, the cardinality varies for each pointcut depending on the value of the one2one parameter, which is given when you define a pointcut.

When one2one is false, only one instance of a wrapper class is created for the pointcut. This instance is shared by all the joinpoints that are included in the pointcut. When several pointcuts use the same wrapper, each pointcut uses its own instance of the wrapper.

When one2one is true, each joinpoint owns an instance of the wrapper class.

When the application is distributed, these two rules are applied on each host. For example, when one2one is false, one instance of a wrapper class exists per pointcut and per host.

Aspect Ordering

When several aspects apply to the same joinpoint, you must define the execution order of the aspects. This order can be specified in the application-descriptor file with the jac.comp.wrappingOrder property, which is an ordered list of wrapper-class names. Whenever two wrappers specified in the list apply to the same joinpoint, their execution order is the one defined by the list.

For example, the following definition specifies that AuthenticationWrapper must be executed before VerboseWrapper:

```
jac.comp.wrappingOrder: \
    org.objectweb.jac.aspects.authentication.AuthenticationWrapper \
    org.objectweb.jac.wrappers.VerboseWrapper
```

There is no automatic rule that defines which wrapper must be executed before another; this decision is up to you. In the previous example, we chose to first authenticate calls and then log them. Therefore, only the calls that are successfully authenticated will be logged. In a different context, we might choose to log every call—even those that are not successfully authenticated. Hence, the reverse order would be defined.

When the `jac.comp.wrappingOrder` property is omitted, no ordering rule is enforced, and the execution order is not guaranteed for two wrappers that apply to the same joinpoint.

RTTI

Run-time type identification (RTTI) can be thought of as an extension of reflection. The purpose is to construct a data structure that represents the code elements of a Java program. The elements taken into account are classes, methods, and fields. RTTI offers the ability to define annotations for these elements. An API is provided to set and get these annotations. RTTI is, then, very similar to the annotation mechanism introduced by J2SE 5.0—except that annotation can be dynamically modified at run time.

You learned in the "Method-Type Operators" section earlier in this chapter that pointcut expressions can contain keywords, such as `SETTERS` and `REMOVERS`, that select methods according to their behaviors. These behaviors, which are determined by a bytecode analysis, are stored as annotations in the RTTI API.

The method-type operators are not the only annotations that can be stored in the RTTI API—any programmer-defined property can be stored. For example, the `persistent` annotation can be attached to every field that needs to be saved in persistent storage. Values can also be stored with the properties. For example, the `authorizedUsers` property together with the value 10 can be attached to a method to declare that, at most, ten users can concurrently execute this method.

Object Naming

Every application object created by JAC is assigned a unique name to identify it. By default, this name is constructed by appending the pound-sign character (#) and an instance number to the lowercase name of the class. The instance number starts at 0 and is incremented each time a new instance is created. For example, `order#0` is assigned to the first instance of the `Order` class.

Pointcut expressions can select objects depending on their names.

The `org.objectweb.jac.core.NameRepository` class provides a repository for all the object names that exist in the application.

The code block in Listing 4-11 displays the name and the reference of every existing object in an application programmed with JAC.

Listing 4-11. *Using the JAC Naming Repository*

```
Repository rep = NameRepository.get();
Object[] objects = rep.getObjects();
for (int i = 0; i < objects.length; i++) {
  String name = rep.getName(objects[i]);
  System.out.println(name+" "+objects[i]);
}
```

The repository can be queried to find the reference associated with a name, and vice versa.

Run Options

Every application developed with JAC must be launched with the org.objectweb.jac.core.Jac class, which is defined in the jac.jar file. Given the name of the application–descriptor file, this class launches an application and the associated aspects.

The Jac class accepts a number of command-line parameters, which are presented in Table 4-2.

Table 4-2. *JAC Command-Line Parameters*

Category	Option	Comment
Main	-R directory	Specifies the root directory of the JAC installation
Main	-C classpath	Specifies the class path for launching the application
Information	-r	Displays the version number of JAC
Information	-v	Displays information messages on the behavior of JAC
Information	-d	Displays debugging information
Information	-L file	Redirects messages to the specified file
Information	-h	Displays a help message
GUI	-G name	Launches the Swing version of the GUI that has the given name
GUI	-W name[:port]	Launches the HTML/servlet version of the GUI that has the given name and, if specified, uses the given port number for the web server

Summary

In this chapter, we presented the JAC framework for dynamic aspect-oriented programming. JAC does not introduce any new keywords nor a compiler, but it provides a framework and an API for programming aspects. In JAC, aspects are run-time entities that can be woven and unwoven while an application is running.

Aspects are defined by extending the AspectComponent class which, in JAC, is the root class for all aspects. Among other things, this class defines the pointcut method for defining pointcuts.

Pointcuts include two types of joinpoints: method executions and constructor executions. These joinpoints are selected by regular expressions that filter the set of all classes, methods, objects and, when the application is run in distributed mode, hosts. The granularity of a pointcut is the object. Hence, some instances of a class can be included in a pointcut but others cannot.

The code executed before and after a joinpoint is defined in a wrapper. Wrappers are classes that implement the AOP Alliance API. They provide methods for the interception and introspection of joinpoints.

In a JAC application, you can introduce two kinds of code elements: role methods and exception handlers. Both are defined as methods in a wrapper class.

JAC is distributed with a library of 16 ready-to-use aspects. These aspects cover a wide range of commonly encountered needs—from maintaining persistent data to implementing a GUI. The aspect that carries out the latter functionality may be the most original, and it provides a way of displaying an application through Swing or a web browser.

The key mechanism for reusing a JAC aspect is aspect configuration. Configuring an aspect consists of defining which parameters tailor the aspect to a specific application context. Any parameter can be configured; it is up to you to define which part of the aspect to make configurable. The configuration can be changed without recompiling the aspect or the application. It can even be reloaded while the application is running, in which case it dynamically reconfigures the aspects.

JAC is distributed with an IDE named UMLAF. You can design, program, compile, and execute a JAC application with this RAD tool. This tool provides a class-diagram view of the application that allows you to graphically design classes and aspects and their relationships.

■■■

CHAPTER 5

JBoss AOP

This chapter illustrates a third environment for aspect-oriented programming: JBoss AOP. The syntax and concepts presented in this chapter correspond to version 1.1.1 of JBoss AOP, which is the latest version available at the time of the writing of this book.

JBoss AOP, like JAC, is a framework for AOP. Aspects and advice code blocks are written in regular Java, without any new keywords. However, in JBoss AOP, pointcuts are defined in XML—unlike JAC, where they are defined in Java. In addition, the weaving is dynamic and performed at run time, similar to that in JAC.

JBoss AOP was designed and developed by Bill Burke. The JBoss Group—in particular, Marc Fleury, the CEO—contributed to the ideas that led to the implementation of JBoss AOP. JBoss AOP can be used as a stand-alone framework, or it can be included in the JBoss 4.x J2EE application server.

JBoss AOP is open-source software released freely under the terms of the GNU Lesser General Public License (LGPL). While JBoss AOP is open source, this license allows for the incorporation of the software into business products. The JBoss AOP web site is `http://www.jboss.org/products/aop`.

Using JBoss AOP: An Introduction

This section presents an example of an aspect-oriented application with JBoss AOP. This example introduces the syntax for writing aspects, pointcuts, and advice code.

We will reuse the order-management application that was presented in Chapter 3. The application manages client orders. We will implement the same trace aspect that was programmed in Chapter 3, but with JBoss AOP. This aspect traces the execution of the application and determines the called methods and the order that they are called in.

A First Trace Aspect

The first aspect written with JBoss AOP monitors each ordered item by displaying a message before and after the `addItem` method as defined in the `Order` class.

This aspect is defined by two files: `jboss-aop.xml` and `TraceInterceptor.java`. The former is an XML file that defines a pointcut; the latter is a Java file that defines the advice code associated with this pointcut.

JBoss AOP uses the term *interceptor* instead of *advice code*; however, there are no differences between the two. Both define code that will be run before and after the joinpoints included in the pointcut.

A First Pointcut

JBoss AOP pointcuts are defined in an XML file. The preferred file name is `jboss-aop.xml`, although this name can be changed.

Two main XML tags are available: `<bind>` to define a pointcut, and `<interceptor>` to define the interceptor associated with the pointcut. The "Pointcuts" section later in this chapter defines the syntax of these tags in more detail.

We illustrate the mechanism for defining pointcuts with the `jboss-aop.xml` file that is shown in Listing 5-1.

Listing 5-1. *The XML Definition of a Pointcut with JBoss AOP*

```
1 <?xml version="1.0" encoding="UTF-8"?>
2 <aop>
3   <bind
4    pointcut="execution(
5       public void aop.jboss.Order->addItem(java.lang.String,int))"
6   >
7       <interceptor class="aop.jboss.TraceInterceptor" />
8   </bind>
9 </aop>
```

After the regular header for all XML documents (shown on line 1 of Listing 5-1), the `<aop>` tag starts the definition of the aspects.

The tag for defining a pointcut is `<bind>`. The `pointcut` attribute (shown on line 4 of Listing 5-1) provides the pointcut expression. In the given value, the expression contains the `execution` keyword and a method signature. The `execution` keyword denotes the joinpoints where the methods that are associated to the given signature are executed. In Listing 5-1, the signature designates the `addItem` method defined in the `Order` class. Although not the case in this example, the signature can contain wildcards.

The `<interceptor>` tag (shown on line 7 of Listing 5-1) defines the interceptor that is associated with the pointcut. In the listing, the corresponding class is `org.jboss.TraceInterceptor`.

A First Interceptor

With JBoss AOP, an interceptor class must implement the `org.jboss.aop.advice.Interceptor` interface. This interface defines two methods: `getName`, which returns the name of the interceptor, and `invoke`, which defines the code to be run before and after the joinpoints.

The class in Listing 5-2 defines the `TraceInterceptor` interceptor that was mentioned in the previous pointcut definition.

Listing 5-2. *A JBoss AOP Trace Interceptor*

```
package aop.jboss;

import org.jboss.aop.advice.Interceptor;
import org.jboss.aop.joinpoint.Invocation;
import org.jboss.aop.joinpoint.MethodInvocation;
```

```java
public class TraceInterceptor implements Interceptor {
    public String getName() { return "TraceInterceptor"; }

    public Object invoke(Invocation invocation) throws Throwable {

        MethodInvocation mi = (MethodInvocation) invocation;
        String methodName = mi.getMethod().getName();

        System.out.println("-> Before "+methodName);
        Object rsp = invocation.invokeNext();
        System.out.println("-> After "+methodName);
        return rsp;
} }
```

The invoke method is called by the JBoss AOP framework just before the occurrence of a joinpoint. The only argument of this call contains information about the joinpoint. The return type corresponds to the value returned by the aspect.

Several types of joinpoints exist with JBoss AOP. In the previous pointcut definition, the only type mentioned was that of method executions. In the example in Listing 5-2, the invocation parameter in the call to invoke can only denote method executions. The first line in the body of invoke performs a cast operation to assign invocation to the mi variable, which is of type MethodInvocation. The interceptor displays a message, calls the invokeNext method, displays another message, and returns. The invokeNext method plays the same role that proceed does with AspectJ or JAC—when called, invokeNext executes the joinpoint.

Compiling

The two most convenient ways of compiling an application written with JBoss AOP are with the JBoss AOP IDE or with Ant.

The JBoss AOP IDE, which is a plug-in for Eclipse, allows you to write, compile, and run JBoss AOP applications inside Eclipse. Instructions for installing the JBoss AOP IDE can be found on the JBoss AOP web site at http://www.jboss.org/products/aop. This plug-in adds the notion of a JBoss AOP project to Eclipse. You define a pointcut either by modifying the jbossaop.xml file, which is automatically added when the project is created, or by interactively selecting the methods in Eclipse that need to be included in the pointcut.

The second solution for compiling a JBoss AOP application is using Ant. Suppose that JBoss AOP is installed in the c:\jboss-aop-1.1.1 directory. The file that is shown in Listing 5-3 and that is named build.xml allows you to compile and run the order-management application.

Listing 5-3. *An Ant File for Compiling a JBoss AOP Application*

```xml
<?xml version="1.0" encoding="UTF-8"?>
<project default="run" name="Gestion de commandes">

    <property name="jboss-aop.root" value="c:\jboss-aop-1.1.1"/>
```

```
<target name="prepare">
  <path id="classpath">
    <pathelement path="." />
    <fileset dir="${jboss-aop.root}/lib">
      <include name="*.jar" />
    </fileset>
  </path>
  <taskdef name="aopc" classname="org.jboss.aop.ant.AopC"
           classpathref="classpath"/>
</target>

<target name="compile" depends="prepare">
  <javac srcdir="src" destdir="." debug="on" deprecation="on"
         optimize="off" includes="**">
    <classpath refid="classpath"/>
  </javac>
  <aopc compilerclasspathref="classpath" classpathref="classpath"
        verbose="true">
    <classpath path="."/>
    <src path="."/>
    <aoppath path="jboss-aop.xml"/>
  </aopc>
</target>
```

```
<target name="run" depends="compile">
  <java fork="yes" failOnError="true" className="aop.jboss.Customer">
    <sysproperty key="jboss.aop.path" value="jboss-aop.xml"/>
    <classpath refid="classpath"/>
  </java>
</target>

</project>
```

The build.xml file defines three tasks: compile, run, and prepare. Each task is also called a *target* and is defined by a <target> tag. The first target compiles the application by compiling the .java files with the regular Java compiler (see the <javac> tag), and then it prepares the compiled classes for weaving with the JBoss AOP compiler (see the <aopc> tag). Note that <aopc> is a custom Ant task that is defined in the prepare target (see the <taskdef> tag). The run target launches the application by running the Java virtual machine (see the <java> tag). Finally, prepare is a utility target, which is run before compile to set the Java class path and to declare the custom aopc Ant task.

To compile the order-management application, call Ant from the operating-system command shell with the following command:

```
ant compile
```

Running

To run the order-management application, call Ant from the operating-system command shell with the following command:

```
ant run
```

The output of this command is shown in Listing 5-4.

Listing 5-4. *The Output of the Order-Management Application with a JBoss AOP Trace Aspect*

```
Buildfile: build.xml
prepare:
compile:
run:
       [java] -> Before addItem
       [java] 2 item(s) CD added to the order
       [java] -> After addItem
       [java] -> Before addItem
       [java] 1 item(s) DVD added to the order
       [java] -> After addItem
       [java] Order amount: US$50.0
BUILD SUCCESSFUL
Total time: 1 second
```

The two executions of the addItem method have been trapped, and the messages of the TraceInterceptor interceptor are displayed before and after these joinpoints.

Pointcuts

This section presents, in detail, the syntax of the XML file for defining pointcuts with JBoss AOP.

The default name for this file is jboss-aop.xml, but the name can be changed if necessary. The corresponding XML Document Type Definition (DTD) defines the <aop> tag as the root tag. Several pointcuts can be defined in the same file. Each pointcut is defined by the <bind> tag and associated with an interceptor by the <interceptor> tag.

The general structure of a jboss-aop.xml file is as follows:

```xml
<?xml version="1.0" encoding="UTF-8"?>
<aop>
  <bind pointcut=" ... pointcut expression ... " >
    <interceptor class=" ... interceptor class ... " />
  </bind>
  ...
</aop>
```

The Different Types of Pointcuts

JBoss AOP allows you to define five types of pointcuts: method, constructor, field, all, and method call. Each of these types is associated with a specific keyword, which is used when you write a pointcut expression.

In this section, we explain the common rules concerning the wildcards that are used to write pointcut expressions, we define the five types of pointcuts, and we give the rules for filtering joinpoints.

Wildcards

When defining a pointcut, you write an expression to declare the elements that must be included in the pointcut. In the previous example of the order-management application, the pointcut expression was as follows:

```
<bind pointcut="execution(
    public void aop.jboss.Order->addItem(java.lang.String,int))" >
```

Only the addItem method was included in the pointcut, with its fully qualified signature provided. In more general cases, you want to include more than one method per pointcut. In such cases, the asterisk (*) and two-dots symbol (..) can be used as wildcard characters to replace any part of the signature. Additionally, annotations can be used in place of method names and class names. Table 5-1 illustrates the usage of wildcards in method signatures.

Table 5-1. *Examples of Wildcard Usage with JBoss AOP*

Expression	Definition
public void aop.jboss. Order->addItem(*,int,*)	All public methods named addItem that are defined in the aop.jboss.Order class and that take three parameters, the second being an int
public void aop.jboss.Order- >add*(..)	All public methods with a name starting with add that are defined in the aop.jboss.Order class, whatever their parameters are
private * aop.jboss.Order- >*(..)	All private methods that are defined in the aop.jboss.Order class
* aop.*.O*->getX()	The getX methods defined in any class that has a name starting with the letter O and that is a subpackage of the aop package
* *->@Remote(..)	All methods that are associated with the @Remote annotation
* @Persistent->*(..)	All methods defined in a class that is associated with the @Persistent annotation

When you write pointcut expressions, the $instanceof keyword can be used in place of class names. This keyword is associated with a type name (class or interface) and designates all the classes that either implement the given type (if the type is an interface) or are subclasses of the given type (if the type is a class). For example, * $instanceof(Remote)->*(..) designates all the methods defined in classes that implement the Remote interface.

Pointcut expressions can be combined with the logical AND, OR, and NOT operators (AND, OR, and !). For example, the following expression

```
<bind pointcut="execution(* Foo->foo()) OR execution(* Bar->bar())" >
```

includes all the joinpoints where the foo method is executed and all the joinpoints where the bar method is executed.

The pointcut-naming mechanism allows you to factor expressions that are used in several pointcut definitions. For this, the <pointcut> tag assigns a name to an expression. You can then reuse this name when writing a pointcut. For example, the two lines

```
<pointcut name="foo" expr="execution(* Foo->foo())" />
<pointcut name="bar" expr="execution(* Bar->bar())" />
```

define the expressions foo and bar, which can then be used in pointcut expression such as the following:

```
<bind pointcut="foo OR bar" />
```

Method-Execution and Constructor-Execution Pointcuts

The execution keyword designates method and constructor executions in pointcut definitions. You have already seen several examples of pointcut definitions that include method executions. The principle is the same for constructor executions, except that the new keyword replaces the method name in the definition. For example, the following pointcut

```
<bind pointcut="execution(public aop.jboss.Order->new(..))" >
```

includes the executions of all the public constructors defined for the Order class.

Field Pointcuts

Operations on fields can be included in pointcut definitions. For these actions, three keywords are available: get, set, and field. The get keyword designates read operations. The set keyword designates write operations. Finally, the field keyword designates read and write operations. These keywords are associated with the names of the fields that are to be included in the pointcut. For method signatures, these names can contain the asterisk (*) wildcard character. For example, the expression

```
<bind pointcut="set(private * aop.jboss.Order->articles*)" >
```

designates the write operations on all the fields that have a name starting with *articles* and that are defined in the Order class.

The all Pointcut Type

The all pointcut type encompasses all the previously described types—method, constructor, and field. For example, the definition

```
<bind pointcut="all(aop.jboss.O*)" >
```

includes all the joinpoints where a method or constructor is executed, where a field is read or written, and where the location is a class that both belongs to the aop.jboss package and has a name starting with the letter *O*.

Method-Call Pointcuts

The last type of pointcut defined by JBoss AOP handles method calls. The following expression illustrates the usage of the call type:

```
<bind pointcut="call(* aop.jboss.Order->*(..))" >
```

This expression includes all the joinpoints where a method that is defined in the Order class is called.

Filtering Joinpoints

The previous keywords allowed you to select joinpoints based on their types. In many situations, you must also select joinpoints based on where the code corresponding to the joinpoint is defined (using the within and withincode keywords) and on whether the declaring class defines any given methods or fields (using the has and hasfield keywords).

The within keyword is associated with a class expression, such as within(aop.jboss.*.). This pointcut-definition snippet includes only the joinpoints that are defined in the corresponding classes. In the example, the classes belong to the aop.jboss package.

The withincode keyword plays the same role for method and constructor expressions. For example, the expression withincode(public *->*(..)) includes the joinpoints that are defined in a public method or constructor.

A pointcut expression containing the has keyword includes only the joinpoints defined in a class that contain the given method (or methods, if the expression contains wildcards). For instance, the expression has(void *->foo(..)) selects the joinpoints declared in any class that contains a method named foo.

The hasfield keyword plays the same role for field expressions.

Note that these filtering operators are seldom used alone. Usually they are combined with logical operators and with keywords for selecting joinpoint types. For example, the expression

```
<bind pointcut="call(* aop.jboss.Order->addItem(..)) AND
    withincode(* aop.jboss.Customer->run())" >
```

selects the joinpoints that are located in the run method of the Customer class and where the addItem method of the Order class is called.

Associating an Interceptor with a Pointcut

In the previous section, we presented the definition of a pointcut expression with the <bind> tag. In this section, we will present the mechanism that associates a pointcut with an interceptor.

Declaring an Interceptor

You can attach an interceptor to a pointcut with the `<interceptor>` tag. The only mandatory information is the name of the class that implements the interceptor. For example, the following declaration

```
<bind pointcut="execution(* aop.jboss.Order->*(..))">
  <interceptor class="aop.jboss.MyInterceptor" />
</bind>
```

associates the `aop.jboss.MyInterceptor` interceptor to the pointcut that includes the executions of all the methods defined in the `Order` class.

Optionally, interceptors can be named. The assigned name can be referenced in the `jboss-aop.xml` file whenever the corresponding interceptor needs to be reused. This feature avoids copy-and-paste errors by removing useless, redundant declarations of an interceptor-class name. The following lines of code illustrate the usage of a named interceptor:

```
<interceptor class="aop.jboss.MyInterceptor" name="myInter" />
<bind pointcut="execution(* aop.jboss.Order->*(..))">
  <interceptor-ref name="myInter" />
</bind>
```

In this example, the interceptor `aop.jboss.MyInterceptor` interceptor is named `myInter`. This name is used in the pointcut definition (see the `<interceptor-ref>` tag).

Interceptor Stacks

The mechanism of an interceptor stack provides a way to group interceptors. The stack is named and can be used to define a pointcut. All the interceptors grouped in the stack will be executed around the joinpoints included in the pointcut. The stack is ordered, and the interceptors are executed in the order of their definition in the stack.

The `<stack>` tag is used to define an interceptor stack. Interceptors can be added to the stack by giving either their class (using the `<interceptor>` tag) or their name (using the `<interceptor-ref>` tag). For example, the following code

```
  <stack name="myStack">
    <interceptor-ref name="myInter" />
    <interceptor class="aop.jboss.Interceptor2" />
  </stack>
```

defines the `myStack` stack, which contains two interceptors: `myInter`, and the anonymous interceptor implemented by the `aop.jboss.Interceptor2` class.

The `<stack-ref>` tag is available for associating a pointcut definition with an interceptor stack, and it can be used when defining a pointcut:

```
<bind pointcut="execution(* aop.jboss.Order->*(..))">
  <stack-ref name="myStack" />
</bind>
```

Note that stacks can also include other stacks.

Interceptors

The previous section presented the XML syntax provided by JBoss AOP for defining pointcuts. This section presents the way that interceptor classes are written.

JBoss AOP interceptors are equivalent to AspectJ advice code and JAC wrappers—they define code that can be run before and after joinpoints.

Implementing an Interceptor

A JBoss AOP interceptor class must implement the `org.jboss.aop.advice.Interceptor` interface. Two methods are defined in this interface:

- `getName`: This method must return an identifier, which you have chosen, for the interceptor.

- `invoke`: This method defines the code that must be run before and after the joinpoint.

The signature of the `invoke` method is:

```
Object invoke(Invocation invocation) throws Throwable;
```

This method's unique parameter, `invocation`, reifies the joinpoint and provides information about its parameters and location. In the next section, we will present the methods available for joinpoint introspection in detail.

The `invoke` method is invoked by the JBoss AOP framework whenever a joinpoint is met that matches the pointcut definition associated to the interceptor. The value for invocation is provided by the framework.

In the body of the `invoke` method, the call to `invokeNext` executes either the joinpoint or, if a stack is defined, the next interceptor in the stack. The `invokeNext` method is implemented by the `Invocation` type and plays the same role as `proceed` does for AspectJ and JAC.

In regular cases, `invokeNext` is invoked one time by the interceptor. However, the call to `invokeNext` is optional. Conversely, an interceptor can attempt to call `invokeNext` several times.

The general pattern of an interceptor definition is shown in Listing 5-5.

Listing 5-5. *A JBoss AOP Interceptor*

```
import org.jboss.aop.advice.Interceptor;
import org.jboss.aop.joinpoint.Invocation;

public class MyInterceptor implements Interceptor {
    public String getName() { return "aName"; }
    public Object invoke(Invocation invocation) throws Throwable {
        System.out.println("Before code ");
        Object rsp = invocation.invokeNext();
        System.out.println("After code");
        return rsp;
    } }
```

Joinpoint Introspection

The term *introspection* refers to examining the inner cause of a given phenomenon and gaining information about it. In the context of JBoss AOP, you want to retrieve information about the part of the program that lets the joinpoint occur.

The Invocation interface is the root type for the introspection mechanism. This interface is implemented by the InvocationBase class. Each type of a joinpoint is represented by a subclass of InvocationBase. Figure 5-1 illustrates this hierarchy. For clarity, only the main methods are given. You should refer to the Javadoc documentation provided with JBoss AOP for a list of all the methods that are defined in this hierarchy.

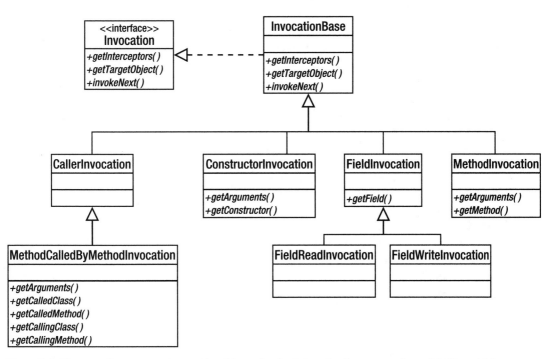

Figure 5-1. *The* org.jboss.aop.Invocation *hierarchy for joinpoint introspection with JBoss AOP*

The InvocationBase class provides some common methods that are shared by all the joinpoint types. The getTargetObject and getInterceptors methods return the object where the current joinpoint occurred and the array of interceptors associated to the current joinpoint, respectively. The invokeNext method executes the joinpoint.

Each class that implements Invocation corresponds to a type of a joinpoint:

- The CallerInvocation class reifies method and constructor calls. Four direct subclasses are defined (only the first one is represented on the figure): MethodCalledByMethodInvocation, MethodCalledByConstructorInvocation, ConstructorCalledByMethodInvocation, and ConstructorCalledByConstructorInvocation. These classes represent method and constructor calls that come from either a method or a constructor.

- The MethodCalledByMethodInvocation class reifies a method called from another method. The parameters of the call can be retrieved with the getArguments method. The getCalledClass and getCalledMethod methods return the class and the method called, respectively. The getCallingClass and getCallingMethod methods return the same pieces of information for the caller side.

- The ConstructorInvocation class corresponds to the executions of a constructor. The getArguments and getConstructor methods retrieve the arguments and the constructor that was executed, respectively.

- The FieldInvocation class corresponds to operations on fields. Two subclasses, FieldReadInvocation and FieldWriteInvocation, are defined to reify read and write operations, respectively.

- The MethodInvocation class reifies method executions. The getArguments method returns the array of the arguments of the execution. The getMethod method returns the method where the execution occurred.

Aspect Classes

With the Interceptor interface provided by JBoss AOP, you can use the invoke method to write the code that would be written in an advice code block with AspectJ. This mechanism is limited because you can only write one piece of advice code per interceptor class. To suppress this limitation, JBoss AOP proposes the notion of the aspect class.

An aspect class in JBoss AOP is a regular Java class that groups several interception methods together. Each method has the same signature as the invoke method in an interceptor class. However, you can freely choose the method name. (The name invoke is no longer mandatory.) Thus, several different interception methods can be written in the same class.

The MyJBossAOPAspect class, shown in Listing 5-6, illustrates the notion of the aspect class.

Listing 5-6. *A JBoss AOP Aspect Class*

```
package aop.jboss;
import org.jboss.aop.joinpoint.Invocation;

public class MyJBossAOPAspect {
    public Object methInterceptor(Invocation invocation) throws Throwable {
        System.out.println("Before code");
        Object rsp = invocation.invokeNext();
        System.out.println("After code");
        return rsp;
    } }
```

As with interceptors, the association between a pointcut and an advice class is declared in the jboss-aop.xml file. The <advice> tag must be used. The XML file in Listing 5-7 gives an example.

Listing 5-7. *An XML File for Associating a Pointcut with an Aspect Class*

```
1 <?xml version="1.0" encoding="UTF-8"?>
2 <aop>
3    <aspect class="aop.jboss.MyJBossAOPAspect" />
4    <bind pointcut="execution(void *->addItem(..))">
5       <advice name="methInterceptor"
6             aspect="aop.jboss.MyJBossAOPAspect" />
7    </bind>
8 </aop>
```

The XML file declares that the `aop.jboss.MyJBossAOPAspect` class is an advice class (see line 2 in Listing 5-7), and it binds this class to the pointcut that includes all the executions of the `addItem` method.

Using the Mix-In Mechanism

With the *mix-in mechanism* provided by JBoss AOP, you can extend the behavior of an application. This mechanism is similar to the mechanism known as *intertype declaration* in AspectJ.

With the mix-in mechanism, you can introduce interfaces, fields, and methods to the existing classes of an application.

Definition

Like pointcuts and interceptors, a mix-in is defined in the `jboss-aop.xml` file with the `<introduction>` and `<mixin>` tags. The basic code for defining a mix-in is as follows:

```
<introduction class="aop.jboss.Order">
<mixin>
  ...
</mixin>
</introduction>
```

In this example, the mix-in mechanism is applied to the `Order` class.

Within the tags `<mixin>` and `</mixin>` tags, three other tags can be used:

- `<class>`: This tag provides the class that will be "mixed in" with the class of the application (in the previous example, the `Order` class.) The mix-in class contains the code elements (fields and methods) that are to be added to the application class.

- `<interfaces>`: This tag defines the interface implemented by the class that is "mixed in" with the application. The class can implement several interfaces; in this case, a comma-separated list of interface names is given.

- `<construction>`: This tag provides the constructor call, which must be used to instantiate the mix-in class. We will illustrate its usage in the following section. Conceptually, the mix-in mechanism introduces the code element of the mix-in class in an application class. Concretely, two objects exist in the Java virtual machine: one for the application class and one for the mix-in class. The `<construction>` tag defines the way this mix-in instance is created.

Example

To illustrate the mix-in mechanism, we will extend the order-management application by adding a date to all the orders that are created. We will begin by defining the interface and the class that will be mixed in with the application.

The `CalendarItf` interface defines methods for setting and retrieving a date. The `Calendar` class, which is shown in Listing 5-8, provides an implementation for this interface.

Listing 5-8. *The Implementation of the Calendar Class*

```
package aop.jboss;
import java.util.Date;

public interface CalendarItf {
  public void setDate(Date date);
  public Date getDate();
}

public class Calendar implements CalendarItf {
  private Object initial;
  private Date date;
  public Calendar( Object initial ) {
    this.initial = initial;
    date = new Date();
  }
  public void setDate(Date date) {
    this.date = date;
  }
  public Date getDate() {
    return date;
  }
}
```

In addition to the `setDate` and `getDate` methods, the `Calendar` class defines a constructor that takes an `Object` as a parameter. This is the constructor that will be called by JBoss AOP when this mix-in class is instantiated.

The XML file in Listing 5-9 associates the `Calendar` mix-in class with the `Order` application class.

Listing 5-9. *Defining a Mix-In with JBoss AOP*

```
<?xml version="1.0" encoding="UTF-8"?>
<aop>
  <introduction class="aop.jboss.Order">
  <mixin>
    <interfaces> aop.jboss.CalendarItf </interfaces>
    <class> aop.jboss.Calendar </class>
    <construction> new aop.jboss.Calendar(this) </construction>
```

```
    </mixin>
    </introduction>
</aop>
```

An application class that is extended with the mix-in mechanism can be cast to the types of the interfaces specified in the `<interfaces>` tag. In the example in Listing 5-9, every instance of `Order` can be converted to `CalendarItf`.

Annotations

Annotations are a new feature introduced by Java 5. Annotations provide a way of extending the definition of a Java program element, such as a method or a class. For example, a method can be associated with annotations that reveal additional characteristics, such as the fact that the access to the method is restricted to given users or the fact that the method must be executed within the context of a transaction.

There are two ways of working with annotations in JBoss AOP. First, you can define annotations in your application and use these annotations when writing pointcuts. Second, annotations can be used to write aspects. In this last case, annotations replace the declarations that are usually written in the `jboss-aop.xml` XML file.

Annotations in Pointcut Definitions

When you write a pointcut, an annotation can be used in place of a type name (class or interface), method name, or parameter name. All the code elements that are associated with the given annotations will match the pointcut.

For example, the following pointcut

```
<bind pointcut="execution(* *->@Transaction(..))" >
```

includes the executions of all the methods that are annotated with `@Transaction`.

As a second example, consider the following definition:

```
<bind pointcut="execution(* $instanceof{@Bean}->*(int,@Key))" >
```

Such a pointcut includes the executions of all the methods defined in a class that implements an interface annotated with `@Bean`. As an additional condition, only the methods that take two parameters, the first being an `int` and the second one being annotated with `@Key`, are included.

Annotations for Writing Aspects

The second use of annotations is for writing aspects. You can write annotated Java code to define classes or pointcuts, for example. With annotations, the `jboss-aop.xml` XML file, which was previously required with JBoss AOP, is suppressed. Every definition that could be written in XML can now be replaced by an annotation in a Java file.

Annotated Aspects

The first useful annotation is @Aspect. As its name suggests, this annotation defines an aspect class. You learned in the previous sections that an aspect class is a collection of interception methods. The same definition applies here, except that the class is preceded by the @Aspect annotation. In the following example, the MyJBossAOPAspect class is declared as an aspect class:

```
import org.jboss.aop.Aspect;

@Aspect
public class MyJBossAOPAspect {
  ...
}
```

Annotated Pointcut Definitions

Within an aspect class, you define interception methods. Two additional actions must be performed. First, you must define pointcuts. Second, you must associate a pointcut to each defined interception method.

With JBoss AOP, pointcuts are defined as public static fields of type Pointcut and are annotated with @PointcutDef, and interception methods are annotated with @Bind. The @PointcutDef pointcut takes a string that contains the pointcut expression as a parameter. The @Bind pointcut takes a string that references the field defining the pointcut as a parameter.

The aspect class that is shown in Listing 5-10 sums up these notions.

Listing 5-10. *The JBoss AOP Annotation Style for Defining Pointcuts*

```
package aop.jboss;
import org.jboss.aop.Aspect;
import org.jboss.aop.PointcutDef;
import org.jboss.aop.pointcut.Pointcut;

@Aspect
public class MyJBossAOPAspect {

  @PointcutDef( "call(* Foo->Bar(..))" )
  public static Pointcut pcd;

  @Bind( pointcut="aop.jboss.MyJBossAOPAspect.pcd" )
  public Object myInterceptor( Invocation invocation ) {
    // ... Before code
    Object ret = invocation.invokeNext();
    // ... After code
    return ret;
  }
}
```

The pcd field defines a pointcut that includes the calls to the Bar method defined in the Foo class. The myInterceptor method is an interception method that is bound to the pcd pointcut.

Annotated Mix-In

You learned in the previous section that the mix-in mechanism allows you to extend the application classes. With this mechanism, mix-in classes define code elements that will be introduced in target application classes.

The annotation for defining a mix-in is @Mixin. Two parameters must be defined: target is the class where the mix-in must be applied, and interfaces is the list of interfaces that are introduced in the target class and that are implemented by the mix-in class.

The @Mixin annotation must be associated with a static method defined in an aspect class (in other words, a class annotated with @Aspect) or an interceptor class. The method annotated by @Mixin acts as a constructor for mix-in objects. Given a parameter that is an application object, this method must return the mix-in object, which will be introduced in the application object.

The AnnotatedMixIn aspect class, which is shown in Listing 5-11, illustrates the usage of annotated mix-in.

Listing 5-11. *The JBoss AOP Annotation Style for Defining Mix-Ins*

```
package aop.jboss;
import org.jboss.aop.Aspect;
import org.jboss.aop.Mixin;

@Aspect
public class AnnotatedMixIn {

  @Mixin( target=Order.class, interfaces={CalendarItf.class} )
  public static Calendar createCalendar( Order myOrder ) {
    return new Calendar(myOrder);
} }
```

In Listing 5-11, the createCalendar method creates an instance of the Calendar class. This instance is introduced in the target Order class, and it implements the CalendarItf interface.

Annotated Interceptors

The @InterceptorDef annotation can be used to define interceptor classes. A second annotation, @Bind, must be provided. As for pointcut definitions, this annotation binds the interceptor to a given pointcut.

The interceptor class in Listing 5-12 illustrates the usage of @InterceptorDef.

Listing 5-12. *The JBoss AOP Annotation Style for Defining Interceptors*

```
package aop.jboss;

import org.jboss.aop.advice.Interceptor;
import org.jboss.aop.joinpoint.Invocation;

@InterceptorDef
@Bind( pointcut="execution(public aop.jboss.Order->*(..))" )
```

```
public class TraceInterceptor implements Interceptor {

    public String getName() { return "TraceInterceptor"; }

    public Object invoke(Invocation invocation) throws Throwable {
        // ... Before code
        Object ret = invocation.invokeNext();
        // ... After code
        return ret;
} }
```

Advanced Features

This section presents the advanced features of JBoss AOP.

Dynamic AOP

Besides the ability to declare pointcuts in XML files or with annotations, JBoss AOP offers the possibility of dynamically declaring and weaving a pointcut.

The code snippet in Listing 5-13 illustrates this feature.

Listing 5-13. *Dynamic Weaving*

```
1 import org.jboss.aop.AspectManager;
2 import org.jboss.aop.advice.AdviceBinding;
3
4 AdviceBinding ab = new AdviceBinding( "execution(* *->foo(..)" );
5 ab.addInterceptor( myInterceptor.class );
6 AspectManager.instance().addBinding( ab );
```

A new pointcut (here, called an *advice binding*) is declared (see line 4 in Listing 5-13). An interceptor class (myInterceptor) is associated with this pointcut (see line 5). Finally, the advice binding is registered with the aspect manager (see line 6).

This functionality requires you to perform a so-called *preparation phase*. For JBoss AOP, this phase consists of transforming some selected application objects. These objects will then be ready to be aspectized in the future through the addBinding method.

There are two ways of preparing application objects:

- You can use the <prepare> tag in an XML file. The tag takes a pointcut expression as a parameter. All the objects included in the pointcut will be prepared.

- You can associate the @Prepare annotation with a public static field of type Pointcut. As with the tag, a parameter for denoting the objects to be prepared is required.

For example, the following XML code snippet

```
<prepare expr="execution( Foo->*(..) )" />
```

prepares all the objects of the Foo class.

Instantiating an Aspect

By default, every aspect or interceptor class defined with JBoss AOP is a singleton. This means that only one instance of each class can exist when the application is run. This mode is called PER_VM.

The advantage of the PER_VM mode is to limit memory consumption and avoid unnecessary creations of the aspect class. The drawback is that any field defined in the class will be shared by all the advice-code executions; hence, if these executions are concurrent, access to the field may need to be synchronized.

Three other modes are available for aspects and interceptors: PER_CLASS, PER_INSTANCE, and PER_JOINPOINT. In the first case, an instance of the aspect class is created for every class that is included in a pointcut associated to this aspect. With PER_INSTANCE, an instance of the aspect class is created for each object included in the pointcut. Finally, with PER_JOINPOINT, an instance is created for every encountered joinpoint.

These modes are declared either in XML or with annotations. In XML, the <aspect> tag for declaring an aspect takes scope as a parameter; scope contains the chosen mode. The same parameter is available for the @Aspect annotation.

If none of these four modes fits your needs, you can decide to provide your own factory class. This class will be responsible for creating instances of aspects or interceptors. A factory class must implement the org.jboss.aop.advice.AspectFactory interface. Aspect factory classes are declared either in XML or with annotations.

Configuring an Aspect

The purpose of the configuration mechanism is to separate the definition of application parameters from the definition of the initial values assigned to these parameters. The parameters are usually defined as fields in Java classes. The values are defined in an external file (for instance, a text file or XML file.) You can then modify the values without recompiling the code where the parameters are defined.

JBoss AOP offers a mechanism for configuring aspect classes with parameters. The type of each parameter must be either a primitive type, such as int, double, or boolean, or one of the following:

- String

- String[]

- Class

- Class[]

- BigDecimal

- File

- Document

- InetAddress

- URL

Aspect classes must provide methods that set their configuration parameters. Parameter values are defined in the jboss-aop.xml file. The <attribute> tag can be included in each <aspect> tag that defines an aspect. The attribute's name and value associated with <attribute> define the value for the corresponding parameter name.

For example, the following aspect class defines two parameters named header and count:

```
public class MyAspect {
  public void setHeader( String value ) { /* ... */ }
  public void setCount( int value ) { /* ... */ }
}
```

The following XML code snippet defines the values "->" and "3" for header and count:

```
<aspect class="MyAspect">
  <attribute name="header" value="->" />
  <attribute name="count" value="3" />
</aspect
```

Introducing Annotations

With the mix-in mechanism, you can introduce new methods into existing application classes. In addition, JBoss AOP allows you to introduce annotations into a class, method, field, or constructor.

There are two ways of introducing annotations: in the jboss-aop.xml XML file or with annotations. The latter case may be somewhat confusing, but you will see that annotations are written to introduce other annotations into an application.

Introducing Annotations with XML

In a jboss-aop.xml file, the <annotation-introduction> tag can be used to introduce annotations. This tag is associated with a pointcut expression. The annotation will be added to each joinpoint included in the pointcut.

For example, the following XML code snippet

```
<annotation-introduction expr="execution(*->foo(..))">
    @Release(production=false,version=1)
</annotation-introduction>
```

introduces the @Release(production=false,version=1) annotation into every foo method defined in the application.

Introducing Annotations with Annotations

In the "Annotations" section earlier in this chapter, you learned that every part of a declaration (aspect, pointcut, mix-in, and so on) that can be written in an XML file can also be written as an annotation. Therefore, instead of using the previously mentioned XML <annotation-introduction> tag, you can write an annotation that will perform the same job.

The annotation for introducing another annotation is @AnnotationIntroductionDef. Three parameters must be provided:

- expr: This parameter is a string that contains a pointcut expression. Every joinpoint included in the pointcut will be annotated.

- invisible: When set to false, this Boolean parameter allows the introduced annotation to be visible at run time. When set to true, the introduced annotation is visible only at compile time.

- annotation: This parameter is a string that introduces an annotation.

For example, the same annotation introduction that the previous section illustrated can be written as shown in Listing 5-14.

Listing 5-14. *The JBoss AOP Annotation Style for Defining Annotations*

```
package aop.jboss;
import org.jboss.aop.Aspect;
import org.jboss.aop.AnnotationIntroductionDef;
import org.jboss.aop.annotation.AnnotationIntroduction;

@Aspect
public class AnnotatedAnnotationIntroduction {

  @AnnotationIntroductionDef(
      expr = "execution(*->foo(..))",
      invisible = false,
      annotation="@Release(production=false,version=1)" )
  public static AnnotationIntroduction a;
}
```

The @AnnotationIntroductionDef annotation must be associated with a public static field that is of type AnnotationIntroduction and that is defined in an aspect class or interceptor class.

Summary

In this chapter, you learned to write an application with the JBoss AOP framework. JBoss AOP can be used alone, or it can be embedded in the JBoss application server. As with other AOP languages and frameworks, a JBoss AOP aspect is composed of pointcuts and advice code.

JBoss AOP advice code blocks are defined in either interceptor classes or so-called aspect classes. With interceptors, you have the possibility of defining just one advice code block per class, whereas several advice code blocks can be defined in the same aspect class. In both cases, the advice code block is a method, and in the case of interceptors, it is named invoke. These methods define the code that must be executed before and after joinpoints. Just as AspectJ and JAC provide the proceed method for executing the joinpoint, JBoss AOP provides the invokeNext method.

Pointcuts can be defined either in XML files or with annotations added to the aspect and interceptor classes. In the former case, the definition of the pointcuts is clearly separated from that of the interceptors and aspect classes. Hence, these classes are independent of any pointcut and can be reused more easily. With annotations, pointcuts and aspects are defined in the same location. The advantage of this situation is that it allows the beginner AOP programmer to be more intuitive. Annotations are defined next to the aspect classes, so they are easier to understand. The other advantage of annotations is that they are natively supported by modern IDEs, such as the recent versions of Eclipse, which include Java 5.

Like JAC, JBoss AOP is a framework that supports dynamic AOP. In other words, aspects can be woven and unwoven at run time without stopping the application.

Finally, the recent versions of JBoss AOP are distributed with a library of ready-to-use aspects for transaction management (specifically, demarcation, injection, and locking), security, remote interactions, clustering, and cache management.

CHAPTER 6

■■■

Spring AOP

This chapter presents a fourth environment for aspect-oriented programming: Spring AOP.

Spring AOP is part of the Spring Framework Open Source project (http:// www.springframework.org), which aims to simplify the development of J2EE applications. Spring was initially created by Rod Johnson, and has been Open Source since February 2003. The architectural concepts, however, go back to early 2000, and emerged from its creator's experience on J2EE commercial developments, which have been published in Rod Johnson's book, *Expert One-on-One J2EE Design and Development* (Wrox Press, 2002). Spring is now a successful Open Source project with a very active community, and is licensed under the terms of the Apache 2.0 license.

Although AOP is not the primary goal of the Spring Framework, the support that AOP provides, though limited, is general enough to be depicted in this book. Similar to JAC, Spring AOP supports the AOP Alliance API, which is a common effort of standardization for generic interception in Java, as used by many AOP platforms. In addition, Spring AOP has been designed to be easily used in many J2EE environments and application servers (such as WebLogic, Tomcat, JBoss, Resin, and Jetty).

In this chapter, we briefly present the architecture of the Spring Framework in general. We then focus on Spring AOP and the provided AOP features.

Note that we use Spring version 1.2 only as a reference since it is the most recent and stable version available at the time of this writing.

An Overview of the Spring Framework

The Spring Framework belongs to the family of lightweight containers. The Spring container manages beans. It is simply materialized by a factory (org.springframework.beans.factory. BeanFactory) that needs to be called when instantiating new beans. More specifically, in a J2EE environment, the factory is generally an application context (org.springframework.context. ApplicationContext, subclass of BeanFactory) that supports all the operations necessary so that the beans can be initialized and run in a J2EE environment. AOP and other supports such as message resource handling, event propagation, and declarative configuration mechanisms are also implemented by the factory.

Spring and its factories implement the so-called Inversion of Control (IoC), also known as the Dependency Injection. This means that all of the configuration, especially the bean dependencies, is in charge of the factories (lightweight containers). As a direct consequence, it is not necessary for the beans to resolve other beans or to go through complex initialization processes, because the factory does it all.

Bean Factories

In order to implement the IoC and to correctly initialize the created beans, factories need to be aware of an application's environment. This is why, in most cases, factories are configured. A typical factory is org.springframework.beans.factory.xml.XmlBeanFactory, which allows the factory to be configured through some XML configuration files. The following code creates a factory configured with a file called conf.xml:

```
ClassPathResource res = new ClassPathResource("conf.xml");
XmlBeanFactory factory = new XmlBeanFactory(res);
```

In general, however, the configuration file is called applicationContext.xml. Since the application may contain several modules, it can also be divided into several parts:

```
ClassPathXmlApplicationContext appContext = new ClassPathXmlApplicationContext(
        new String[] {"applicationContext.xml", "applicationContext-part2.xml"});
BeanFactory factory = (BeanFactory) appContext;
```

In this code, we use the ClassPathXmlApplicationContext factory, which is an application context (a factory) that supports XML configuration. Of course, for the final user it can simply be seen as a BeanFactory.

Creating and Configuring Beans

In order to be created, beans require the following:

- A Java class definition

- A configuration

The Java class definition is usually a regular Java class following bean conventions: properties should be accessible through getter/setter pairs. Spring, however, allows any class to become a bean, and therefore any kind of Java object can be managed by the container and referenced by other beans, exactly like regular beans. Spring also allows the beans to define a constructor with some parameters, so that the bean properties are initialized in a more straightforward way.

As previously indicated, a typical bean configuration is written in an XML file, which contains bean definition entries. (Note that configurations can also be achieved programmatically, but we will not enter into this level of detail in this book.) Each bean entry defines the name (or id) and the Java class of the bean. At this point, the bean can be referenced by other bean definition entries. In addition, several configuration parameters can be added to the entries such as the values of the properties, the values of the constructor's parameters, lifecycle management configurations, etc.

A First Bean Definition

As a simple example, we write the class in Listing 6-1.

Listing 6-1. *A First Bean Definition*

```
package aop.spring;

public class ExampleBean {

    private AnotherBean beanOne;
    private YetAnotherBean beanTwo;
    private int i;

    public void setBeanOne(AnotherBean beanOne) {
        this.beanOne = beanOne;
    }

    public void setBeanTwo(YetAnotherBean beanTwo) {
        this.beanTwo = beanTwo;
    }

    public void setIntegerProperty(int i) {
        this.i = i;
    }
}
```

This class contains two references towards AnotherBean and YetAnotherBean, and an integer property i. It also defines setters for all of them. In order to make this class recognized as a bean by a Spring bean factory or application context, we must write the XML configuration in Listing 6-2.

Listing 6-2. *A First Configuration*

```
1   <bean id="exampleBean" class="aop.spring.ExampleBean">
2       <property name="beanOne"><ref bean="anotherExampleBean"/></property>
3       <property name="beanTwo"><ref bean="yetAnotherBean"/></property>
4       <property name="integerProperty"><value>1</value></property>
5   </bean>
```

In this configuration, we create a new bean named exampleBean (id attribute of the bean element), which is an instance of the class aop.spring.ExampleBean (class attribute of the bean element) defined previously. The initialization of the properties is done through the property elements. For primary properties, the value element will be used to create a primitive value (line 4). For references, a ref element will be used to reference another bean (lines 2 and 3). Of course, the referenced beans must be defined elsewhere in a similar manner. A minimal configuration is as shown in Listing 6-3.

Listing 6-3. *A First Configuration (Continued)*

```
<bean id="anotherExampleBean" class="aop.spring.AnotherBean"/>
<bean id="yetAnotherBean" class="aop.spring.YetAnotherBean"/>
```

In Spring, beans are singletons by default. In order to change this strategy, and to make the factory create a new instance each time a bean is accessed, the configuration should set the singleton attribute to false simply by changing the first line of the configuration of Listing 6-2:

```
<bean id="exampleBean" class="aop.spring.ExampleBean" singleton="false">
```

An Alternative Definition

As stated previously, an alternative to this is to use constructor initialization. In this case, the bean class is defined as shown in Listing 6-4.

Listing 6-4. *A Constructor-based Alternative Definition of Our First Bean*

```
package aop.spring;

public class ExampleBean {

    private AnotherBean beanOne;
    private YetAnotherBean beanTwo;
    private int i;

    public ExampleBean(AnotherBean anotherBean,
                    YetAnotherBean yetAnotherBean, int i) {
        this.beanOne = anotherBean;
        this.beanTwo = yetAnotherBean;
        this.i = i;
    }
}
```

And the configuration must be as shown in Listing 6-5.

Listing 6-5. *Constructor-based Configuration*

```
<bean id="exampleBean" class="aop.spring.ExampleBean">
    <constructor-arg><ref bean="anotherExampleBean"/></constructor-arg>
    <constructor-arg><ref bean="yetAnotherBean"/></constructor-arg>
    <constructor-arg type="int"><value>1</value></constructor-arg>
</bean>
```

Accessing the Bean

Once defined, a bean must be accessed through a factory. The BeanFactory class defines the following methods:

- boolean containsBean(String): Checks that the factory contains a given bean name

- Object getBean(String): Instantiates/accesses a given bean name

- Object getBean(String,Class): Instantiates/accesses a given bean name and casts it to a given class

- boolean isSingleton(String): Determines whether or not the bean that corresponds to the name is a singleton

- String[] getAliases(String): Returns the aliases for the given bean name (a bean can have several names in the configuration)

We can now write a program for retrieving a reference on a bean after having checked that it exists in the factory and that it is defined as a singleton:

```
// we assume that conf.xml contains the bean definition, and that ExampleBean
// is in the classpath
ClassPathResource res = new ClassPathResource("conf.xml");
XmlBeanFactory factory = new XmlBeanFactory(res);
ExampleBean myBean=null;
if(factory.containsBean("exampleBean") && factory.isSingleton("exampleBean")) {
    myBean=factory.getBean("exampleBean");
}
```

Bean Initialization and Dependency Injection

In the two equivalent definitions presented previously, when the program instantiates the aop.spring.ExampleBean class, it uses the factory that is parameterized by the configuration to automatically inject the values or the bean dependencies. In the first case of our example, the factory called the setters to initialize the properties: this kind of injection is called *setter-based dependency injection*. In the second case, the factory automatically called the constructor of the class with the appropriate arguments: this is called *constructor-based dependency injection*. In the case that several constructor arguments are of the same type, the ambiguity can be solved by using the index attribute in the constructor-arg element; the index then corresponds to the argument's index, as declared in the constructor's prototype.

The strength of the IoC (or Dependency Injection) model is that all the bean dependencies are handled by the factory (container). Consequently, the factory implements all the lookup, proxying, and any other tedious operations that are normally not completely transparent for the beans (as in a typical EJB/J2EE programming model). For instance, there is no need to use any locator or business delegate design patterns (see the section "Using J2EE Design Solutions" in Chapter 10) because the factory will do it for you.

The bean factory will also check the configuration after it is created, which avoids possible errors such as references to nonexisting beans or circular dependencies.

Other Bean Configuration Features

This section briefly mentions other bean configuration features.

Overview of the Supported XML Elements for Data

As you have seen, Spring allows the configuration of the bean primitive properties' data with the value XML element and the configuration of the references with the ref element.

Spring also supports collections (lists, sets, and maps) and data elements, as shown in the configuration in Listing 6-6.

Listing 6-6. *A More Complex Configuration Example*

```
<beans>
    ...
    <bean id="moreComplexObject" class="example.ComplexObject">
        <property name="someList">
            <list>
                <value>a list element </value>
                <ref bean="aReferencedBean"/>
            </list>
        </property>
        <property name="someMap">
            <map>
                <entry key="an entry key">
                    <value>some value</value>
                </entry>
                <entry key="another entry key for a reference">
                    <ref bean="myDataSource"/>
                </entry>
            </map>
        </property>
        <property name="someSet">
            <set>
                <value>some string</value>
                <ref bean="myDataSource"/>
            </set>
        </property>
    </bean>
</beans>
```

We summarize all the available data elements in the following list:

- bean: Inlines a bean definition (in this case, the bean can be anonymous and the id attribute is not needed)

- ref: Defines a reference to another bean

- idref: Defines a string value that corresponds to a bean id (in this case, the factory checks that the id exists in the application environment)

- list: Defines a list of any other elements

- set: Defines a set of any other elements

- map: Defines a map of entries (entry attribute)

- props: Defines a java.util.Properties element

- value: Defines a primitive value

- null: Defines a null value (indeed, <value\> defines an empty string and should be replaced by <null\> when needed)

All of these data elements are also recursively available within a `property`, an `entry`, a `set`, or a `list` element.

Auto-wiring Collaborators

In order to minimize the XML configuration code, Spring provides some auto-wiring capabilities. *Auto-wiring* consists of enabling the container (factory) to resolve the dependencies automatically by using some pragmatic strategies. Even though this is not encouraged (well-defined dependencies are preferred), this feature is worth mentioning since it illustrates the real benefits and possibilities of factories and, consequently, of the IoC concept advocated by Spring.

The auto-wiring mode of a bean can be configured by using the `autowire` attribute of the bean element. It can take the following values:

- `no`: No auto-wiring at all.

- `byname`: The references are automatically added by matching the names of the properties and the names of the beans.

- `byType`: The references are automatically added by matching the types of the properties and the types of the beans.

- `constructor`: The references are automatically added by matching the types of the properties and the types of the bean constructor arguments.

- `autodetect`: Chooses `constructor` or `byType` through introspection of the bean class.

Other Features

Spring provides many other configuration features, such as object life-cycle management, which specifies some bean destruction methods, as well as other features designed for beans to be aware of the container. The reader interested in further details on this subject should refer to literature that is specific to Spring, since it is not the goal of this book to enter into the non-AOP details of Spring.

Abstraction Layers

Spring aims to facilitate J2EE development; therefore, it provides a set of abstraction layers that assist with the integration of Spring bean-based applications with various technologies commonly encountered in J2EE development. These abstraction layers, listed here, cleanly integrate with the Spring bean container, especially through the IoC capabilities of Spring:

- A common abstraction layer for transaction management, which allows for pluggable transaction managers and demarcate transactions, without the disadvantage of low-level issues. Generic strategies for JTA and a single JDBC DataSource are included.

- A JDBC abstraction layer, which simplifies the writing of queries and error handling.

- Integration with Hibernate, JDO, and iBATIS SQL Maps, in terms of resource holders, DAO implementation support, and transaction strategies. First-class Hibernate support with a lot of IoC convenience features, which address many typical Hibernate integration issues.

- A flexible MVC web application framework, built on core Spring functionality. This framework is configurable via strategy interfaces, and accommodates multiple view technologies like JSP, Velocity, Tiles, iText, and POI.

Spring AOP: An Introduction

We have presented the basics of Spring and the IoC principle; in this section, we introduce Spring AOP with a simple example.

For our example, we reuse the same Order Management example as in the previous chapters (see Chapters 3, 4, and 5) and implement the same trace aspect that was programmed in these chapters, but now with Spring AOP. This aspect traced the execution of the application.

A Simple Trace Aspect

Our first aspect written with Spring AOP monitors each ordered item by displaying a message before and after the method addItem as defined in the class Order.

Defining this aspect requires us to define a Java class TraceInterceptor (similar to "around" advice), and also to define a corresponding bean in the XML bean definition file (usually applicationContext.xml). Still in a bean definition file, a pointcut must be defined and linked to the interceptor by using an *advisor*. In the Spring Framework, AOP is naturally integrated because it follows the IoC principle and is consistently defined with the bean model. Interceptor, pointcut, and advisor dependencies are implemented exactly like regular bean dependencies.

In order to enable AOP, the program must use an ApplicationContext factory (or a derivative). It is important to notice that the ApplicationContext factory will return an AOP proxy when accessing a bean. Spring uses J2SE proxies to generate the proxies when possible (when an interface is defined for the bean), and CGLIB proxies otherwise. When a method is called on a bean, it is the AOP proxy that automatically up-calls the potentially installed interceptors for this method.

A Simple Pointcut

Spring AOP pointcuts are defined in the XML bean definition entries, but they can also be defined programmatically (as you will see later in the "Pointcuts" section). A typical way to define a pointcut in XML is to use a set of regular expressions (Perl 5 syntax). When all the regular expressions of a pointcut match the method's name (including its class name), it means that the method is a joinpoint belonging to the pointcut (see Listing 6-7).

Listing 6-7. *A Pointcut Configuration Example*

```
1 <bean id="tracePointcut"
2       class="org.springframework.aop.support.Perl5RegexpMethodPointcut">
3   <property name="pattern"><value>aop.spring.Order.addItem</value></property>
4 </bean>
```

This XML code defines a new pointcut bean identified by the tracePointcut ID and instance of a RegexpMethodPointcut class (supporting regular expression). The pattern property of line 3 defines a single regular expression matching the method addItem of the Order class.

A Simple Interceptor

With Spring AOP, an interceptor class must implement the interface org.aopalliance. MethodInterceptor and provide the implementation for the invoke method, which defines the code to be run before and after the joinpoints.

The class in Listing 6-8 defines the interceptor TraceInterceptor as mentioned in the previous pointcut definition:

Listing 6-8. *A Trace Interceptor with Spring*

```
package aop.spring;

import org.aopalliance.MethodInterceptor;
import org.aopalliance.MethodInvocation;

public class TraceInterceptor implements MethodInterceptor {

    public Object invoke(Invocation invocation) throws Throwable {
        String methodName = invocation.getMethod().getName();

        System.out.println("-> Before "+methodName);
        Object rsp = invocation.proceed();
        System.out.println("-> After "+methodName);
        return rsp;
} }
```

The method invoke is called by Spring AOP just before the occurrence of a joinpoint. The only argument of this call contains information about the joinpoint. The return type corresponds to the value returned by the aspect. Here, the interceptor displays a first message, calls the method proceed, displays a second message, and then returns. The proceed method has the same semantics as usual: it executes the advised method (also *intercepted method* or *method joinpoint*).

Spring can only advise method calls: The creator of Spring considers field advising to be potentially harmful in the Spring context, since it violates the bean encapsulation principles.

A Simple Advisor

In order to attach a pointcut to an interceptor, Spring adds the concept of a pointcut *advisor*. Here, to attach the pointcut and interceptor defined previously, we add the XML definition in Listing 6-9.

Listing 6-9. *Configuring a Trace Advisor*

```
<bean id="traceAdvisor"
      class="org.springframework.aop.support.DefaultMethodPointcutAdvisor">
  <property name="advice">
        <ref local="traceInterceptor"/>
  </property>
  <property name="pointcut">
        <ref local="tracePointcut"/>
  </property>
</bean>
```

where `traceInterceptor` is the bean identifier of the trace interceptor defined as shown in Listing 6-10.

Listing 6-10. *Configuration of the Trace Interceptor*

```
<bean id="traceInterceptor"
      class="aop.spring.TraceInterceptor">
```

The pointcut definition can be integrated directly into the advisor definition. This is the case when, for example, the pointcut does not need to be reused in other aspects. In this case, the advisor definition looks as shown in Listing 6-11.

Listing 6-11. *A More Integrated Configuration of the Trace Advisor*

```
<bean id="traceAdvisor"
      class="org.springframework.aop.support.RegexpMethodPointcutAdvisor">
  <property name="advice">
        <ref local="traceInterceptor"/>
  </property>
  <property name="pattern">
        <value>aop.spring.Order.addItem</value>
  </property>
</bean>
```

Pointcuts

This section presents how to define pointcuts in Spring AOP.

Basics

In Spring, pointcuts are defined as regular beans that must implement the `org.springframeork.aop.Pointcut` interface (see Listing 6-12).

Listing 6-12. *The Pointcut Interface*

```
public interface Pointcut {
    ClassFilter getClassFilter();
```

```
    MethodMatcher getMethodMatcher();
}
```

The class filter of a pointcut is an object that defines the scope of the pointcut. It implements the interface in Listing 6-13.

Listing 6-13. *The ClassFilter Interface*

```
public interface ClassFilter {
    boolean matches(Class clazz);
}
```

The matches method returns true if the filtered class clazz belongs to the filter and, consequently, if it is part of the parent pointcut's scope.

The method matcher will then tell, for a filtered class, whether a given method is a joinpoint for the parent pointcut. The interface is as shown in Listing 6-14.

Listing 6-14. *The MethodMatcher Interface*

```
public interface MethodMatcher {
    boolean matches(Method m, Class targetClass);
    boolean isRuntime();
    boolean matches(Method m, Class targetClass, Object[] args);
}
```

The isRuntime method indicates whether this matcher should be applied at run time on an AOP proxy. In the AOP world, this kind of selection is called *dynamic shadow selection*. This operation, which will reveal whether or not a shadow is a joinpoint for a given pointcut, is performed at run time by using some contextual information. When isRuntime returns true, the three-parameter matches method is called with the values of the current invocation. If isRuntime returns false, only the two-parameter matches method is called. In the latter case, the method matcher is used only once—during the AOP proxy initialization process.

Programmatically Defined Pointcuts

By using this API, programmers can define new pointcuts programmatically. Listing 6-15, for instance, shows the definition of a pointcut that matches public void aop.spring.Order. addItem(*,int,*).

Listing 6-15. *A Programmatically Defined Pointcut*

```
package aop.spring;
public class APointcut implements Pointcut {
    public ClassFilter getClassFilter() {
        return new ClassFilter() {
            public boolean matches(Class clazz) {
                return clazz.getName().equals("aop.spring.Order");
            }
        }
    }
```

```
        public MethodMatcher getMethodMatcher() {
            return new MethodMatcher() {
                public boolean matches(Method m, Class targetClass) {
                    return Modifier.isPublic(m.getModifiers())
                        && m.getName().equals("addItem")
                        && m.getParameterTypes().length == 3
                        && m.getParameterTypes()[1] == int.class;
                }
                public boolean isRuntime() { return false; }
                public boolean matches(Method m, Class targetClass, Object[] args) {
                    return false;
                }
            }
        }
    }
}
```

Once this definition is complete, the programmer must simply define the corresponding bean, so that the application context can apply this pointcut to the beans.

```
<bean id="myPointcut" class="aop.spring.APoincut">
```

Regexp Pointcuts

Spring provides an implementation for pointcuts that uses regular expressions in the class `org.springframework.aop.support.AbstractRegexpMethodPointcut` (two implementations are available: one for Perl5 and one for JDK regexps). A regexp pointcut defines the method `setPattern(String pattern)`. The `setPatterns(String[] patterns)` method can be used to define several patterns with the or semantics. The advantage of this kind of pointcut is that it can be used in an XML configuration to define a pointcut in a declarative way. It covers most of the common cases so that programmatically defined pointcuts rarely need to be used. The regexp pointcut, however, does not match on the parameter types nor on the return type, but only on the fully qualified method name.

For instance, the code in Listing 6-16 defines a pointcut that matches all the getters and setters of the Order class:

Listing 6-16. *A Regexp Pointcut Example*

```
<bean id="tracePointcut"
      class="org.springframework.aop.support.Perl5RegexpMethodPointcut">
  <property name="patterns">
    <list>
        <value>aop.spring.Order.get* </value>
        <value>aop.spring.Order.set*</value>
    </list>
  </property>
</bean>
```

Control Flow Pointcut

In Spring, *cflows* are implemented by `org.springframework.aop.support.ControlFlowPointcut`, which defines the two properties `clazz` and `methodName`. If `methodName` is null, the cflow starts at all the methods of the class. Compared to other AOP frameworks, the Spring cflows are quite limited since they cannot be applied to other pointcuts. Also, Spring does not support the cflow-below concept. It is likely that, in the future, cflow capabilities will be enhanced if there is a strong need in the community to use them in the Spring context.

Associating an Interceptor with a Pointcut

In the previous section, we defined pointcuts in Spring. In order to associate an interceptor with a pointcut, the programmer must define a pointcut advisor. A pointcut advisor implements the `org.springframework.aop.PointcutAdvisor` interface, which is shown in Listing 6-17.

Listing 6-17. *The PointcutAdvisor Interface*

```
public interface PointcutAdvisor extends Advisor {
    Pointcut getPointcut();
}
```

And for an example of where `org.springframework.aop.Advisor` is the interface defining the advising, see Listing 6-18.

Listing 6-18. *The Advisor Interface*

```
public interface Advisor {
    boolean isPerInstance();
    Advice getAdvice();
}
```

You can see that the advisor defines the advice and the instantiation policy. If the `isPerInstance` method returns `true`, then a different advice instance will be used for each advised bean. If it returns `false`, one instance will be shared by all the advised beans in the application context. However, in Spring version 1.2 (the version used at the time of this writing), our studies showed that the `isPerInstance` feature was not supported. So, only shared instances are available at the moment.

In order to easily create new pointcut advisors, the programmer can use the `org.springframework.aop.support.DefaultPointcutAdvisor` as it comes or subclass it). With a bean configuration, we can bind an existing pointcut with an existing advice (see Listing 6-19).

Listing 6-19. *Configuring an Advisor*

```
<bean id="myAdvisor"
      class="org.springframework.aop.support.DefaultMethodPointcutAdvisor">
  <property name="advice"><ref local="myInterceptor"/></property>
  <property name="pointcut"><ref local="myPointcut"/></property>
</bean>
```

The pointcut property can be omitted from the definition. In this case, the advisor will advise all the methods of all the beans, similar to a .* pointcut.

As shown in our simple trace example, it is also possible to merge the definition of a regexp pointcut in an advisor (à la AspectJ). The advisor then automatically creates a new regexp pointcut, which is used to initialize the pointcut property.

Advice

The previous section presented the way for defining pointcuts in Spring. We now focus on writing and using advice code. Spring provides several types of advice. The most general form is the interceptor, which is similar to "around" advice.

Interceptors ("Around" Advice)

With Spring AOP, an interceptor class must implement the interface org.aopalliance. MethodInterceptor and provide the implementation for the invoke method, which defines the code to be run before and after the joinpoints.

Since Spring is compliant with the AOP Alliance API, programming "around" advice is similar to programming "around" advice in JAC, and therefore the principles are the same (refer to the section entitled "Wrappers" in Chapter 4). Also, Figure 4-1 gives the joinpoint model of AOP Alliance, which is available for introspection in Spring.

Spring does not, however, support constructor interception. Since the beans are transparently built within the factory, which implements all the mechanics for dealing with beans within a particular context, the constructor interception is not suitable for the Spring Framework anyway. Thus, only the org.aopalliance.MethodInvocation is available for introspection in Spring.

Other Types of Advice

Spring AOP also supports other kinds of advice that are not defined in the AOP Alliance and do not rely on its introspection model.

Even though using the "interceptor" advice is the most general form, using another type of advice can be beneficial because it is simpler to use, and it also can reflect better what the aspect does without having to read the advice code. In addition, it is generally slightly more efficient since it does not require the construction of the org.aopalliance.MethodInvocation instance for introspection. Thus, the following advice types are preferred and should be used if possible, unless the programmer needs the advice code to run on another AOP Alliance–compliant platform.

"Before" Advice

The main advantage of a "before" advice is that there is no need to invoke the proceed method, and therefore no possibility of inadvertently failing to proceed down the interceptor chain.

A "before" advice implements the MethodBeforeAdvice interface, which is shown in Listing 6-20. Even though this interface explicitly holds on method, Spring does not support field or constructor advising. However, the API design does leave room for such an extension.

Listing 6-20. *The BeforeAdvice Interface*

```
public interface MethodBeforeAdvice extends BeforeAdvice {
    void before(Method m, Object[] args, Object target) throws Throwable;
}
```

Note that the return type is void. The "before" advice can insert a custom behavior before the joinpoint executes, but cannot change the return value. If a "before" advice throws an exception, this will abort further execution of the interceptor chain. The exception will propagate back up the interceptor chain. If it is unchecked, or on the signature of the invoked method, it will be passed directly to the client; otherwise it will be wrapped in an unchecked exception by the AOP proxy.

Listing 6-21 provides an example of a "before" advice in Spring that counts all method invocations:

Listing 6-21. *A Counting "Before" Advice Example*

```
public class CountingBeforeAdvice implements MethodBeforeAdvice {
    private int count;
    public void before(Method m, Object[] args, Object target) throws Throwable {
        ++count;
    }

    public int getCount() {
        return count;
    }
}
```

"Throws" Advice

"Throws" advice is invoked after the return of the joinpoint if the joinpoint threw an exception. Spring offers typed "throws" advice. This means that the org.springframework.aop.ThrowsAdvice interface does not contain any methods: it is a tag interface that indicates the given object implements one or more typed "throws" advice methods. These should be of the form afterThrowing ([Method], [args], [target], subclassOfThrowable).

Only the last argument is required; therefore, there can be anything from one to four arguments, depending on whether the advice method is interested in the method and arguments. The following are examples of "throws" advice methods.

This advice will be invoked if a RemoteException is thrown (including subclasses—see Listing 6-22).

Listing 6-22. *A "Throws" Advice Example*

```
public  class RemoteThrowsAdvice implements ThrowsAdvice {
    public void afterThrowing(RemoteException ex) throws Throwable {
        // Do something with remote exception
    }
}
```

The advice in Listing 6-23 is invoked if a ServletException is thrown. Unlike the preceding advice, it declares four arguments, so that it has access to the invoked method, method arguments, and target object:

Listing 6-23. *A "Throws" Advice Example, with Arguments*

```
public static class ServletThrowsAdviceWithArguments implements ThrowsAdvice {
    public void afterThrowing(Method m, Object[] args, Object target,
                              ServletException ex) {
        // Do something with all arguments
    }
}
```

The final example, shown in Listing 6-24, illustrates how these two methods could be used in a single class, which handles both RemoteException and ServletException. Any number of "throws" advice methods can be combined in a single class.

Listing 6-24. *A Combined "Throws" Advice Example*

```
public static class CombinedThrowsAdvice implements ThrowsAdvice {
    public void afterThrowing(RemoteException ex) throws Throwable {
        // Do something with remote exception
    }

    public void afterThrowing(Method m, Object[] args, Object target,
                              ServletException ex) {
        // Do something will all arguments
    }
}
```

"After Returning" Advice

"After returning" advice in Spring implements the org.springframework.aop.
AfterReturningAdvice interface, shown in Listing 6-25.

Listing 6-25. *The AfterReturningAdvice Interface*

```
public interface AfterReturningAdvice extends Advice {
    void afterReturning(Object returnValue, Method m, Object[] args, Object target)
            throws Throwable;
}
```

"After returning" advice can access the return value but cannot modify it. Like "before" advice, it can access the invoked method, the methods arguments, and the target.

As an example, the "after returning" advice in Listing 6-26 counts all successful method invocations that have not thrown exceptions:

Listing 6-26. *A Counting "After" Advice Example*

```
public class CountingAfterReturningAdvice implements AfterReturningAdvice {
    private int count;

    public void afterReturning(Object returnValue, Method m, Object[] args, Object
                               target)
            throws Throwable {
        ++count;
    }

    public int getCount() {
        return count;
    }
}
```

This advice does not change the main execution path. If it throws an exception, this will be thrown up the interceptor chain instead of a return value.

"Introduction" Advice and Mix-Ins

In Spring, introductions are implemented as a special kind of advice: the "introduction" advice. Hence, introductions implement an `org.springframework.aop.IntroductionInterceptor` interface, which is a subclass of the `org.aopalliance.intercept.MethodInterceptor` (see Listing 6-27).

Listing 6-27. *The IntroductionInterceptor Interface*

```
public interface IntroductionInterceptor extends MethodInterceptor {
    boolean implementsInterface(Class intf);
}
```

When defining an introduction, the `invoke` method inherited from the AOP Alliance `MethodInterceptor` interface must implement the introduction: if the invoked method is part of an introduced interface, the introduction interceptor is responsible for handling the method call. Note that contrary to regular interceptors, introductions cannot invoke `proceed`.

Since introduction advice applies only at class level, rather than at method level, the "introduction" advice necessitates the use of a special kind of advisor, which is provided by an `org.springframework.aop.InterceptionIntroductionAdvisor` (see Listing 6-28).

Listing 6-28. *The InterceptionIntroductionAdvisor Interface*

```
public interface InterceptionIntroductionAdvisor extends InterceptionAdvisor {
    ClassFilter getClassFilter();
    IntroductionInterceptor getIntroductionInterceptor();
    Class[] getInterfaces();
}
```

Contrary to a regular advisor, the introduction advisor does not define any `MethodMatcher` or `Pointcut`, so that only class filtering is logical. The `getInterfaces` method returns the interfaces introduced by the advisor.

To illustrate the use of introductions, we use a simple mix-in example taken from the Spring test suite. Suppose that we want to introduce the interface in Listing 6-29 into one or more objects.

Listing 6-29. *The Lock Introduction Example: The Lockable Interface*

```
package aop.spring;

public interface Lockable {
    void lock();
    void unlock();
    boolean locked();
}
```

At the end, we want to be able to cast any advised objects to `Lockable` and call `lock` and `unlock` methods. When the `lock` method is called, the target object becomes locked, and all setter methods will throw a `LockedException`. When the `unlock` method is called, the target object behaves normally again.

To implement this example, we need an `IntroductionInterceptor`. Spring provides a default implementation that is convenient for most cases and that can be subclassed for our case: `org.springframework.aop.support.DelegatingIntroductionInterceptor`.

The `DelegatingIntroductionInterceptor` is designed to delegate an introduction to an actual implementation of the introduced interface(s), concealing the use of interception to do so. The delegate can be set to any object using a constructor argument; this is the default delegate (when the no-arg constructor is used). In our example, the delegate is the `LockMixin` subclass of `DelegatingIntroductionInterceptor`. Given a delegate (by default itself), a `DelegatingIntroductionInterceptor` instance looks for all interfaces implemented by the delegate (other than `IntroductionInterceptor`), and will support introductions against any of them. The final exposed interfaces are defined by the `IntroductionAdvisor`.

So, `LockMixin` subclasses `DelegatingIntroductionInterceptor` and implements `Lockable`. `DelegatingIntroductionInterceptor` automatically deduces that `Lockable` can be supported for introduction (see Listing 6-30).

Listing 6-30. *The Lock Mix-in Implementation*

```
package aop.spring;

import org.springframework.aop.support.DelegatingIntroductionInterceptor;

public class LockMixin extends DelegatingIntroductionInterceptor
                    implements Lockable {
    private boolean locked;

    public void lock() {
        this.locked = true;
```

```
    }

    public void unlock() {
        this.locked = false;
    }

    public boolean locked() {
        return this.locked;
    }

    public Object invoke(MethodInvocation invocation) throws Throwable {
        if (locked() && invocation.getMethod().getName().indexOf("set") == 0)
            throw new LockedException();
        return super.invoke(invocation);
    }
}
```

In this code, the `locked` instance variable adds some state to the target object. Notice that we can overload the `invoke` method of the interceptor in order to implement the locked check. This check could have been done in a separate "before" advice, but it is more concise in this way because the `invoke` method can directly access the `locked` field. Mix-ins generally do not require the redefinition of the `invoke` method. The `DelegatingIntroductionInterceptor` default implementation is usually enough: it calls the delegated method if the method is introduced, or otherwise proceeds towards the joinpoint.

The required "introduction" advisor can, for instance, subclass `DefaultIntroductionAdvisor`, as shown in Listing 6-31, which directly implements `ClassFilter`, so that the `matches` method can simply be overridden to select advised classes (by default all the classes are advised).

Listing 6-31. *The Lock Mix-in Advisor Implementation*

```
package aop.spring;

import org.springframework.aop.support.DefaultIntroductionAdvisor;

public class LockMixinAdvisor extends DefaultIntroductionAdvisor {
    public LockMixinAdvisor() {
        super(new LockMixin(), Lockable.class);
    }
    // we only apply the lock mix-in to the Order class
    public boolean matches(Class clazz) {
        return clazz.getName().equals("aop.spring.Order");
    }
}
```

The mix-in can then be activated with the simple XML definition:

```
<bean id="lockAdvisor" class="aop.spring.LockMixinAdvisor"/>
```

It is important to understand that it is impossible to use an `IntroductionInterceptor` without an `IntroductionAdvisor`. With introductions, the advisor is per-instance because it is stateful, and therefore you need a different instance of `LockMixinAdvisor` and `LockMixin` for each advised object, so that the `locked` variable is local to an advised bean.

Advanced Features

This section presents some advanced features of Spring AOP.

Ordering Aspects

By default, advice applies in the same order as constructed. At times, the programmer may want to guarantee a given order. In Spring, to make the factory automatically ensure an order, the advisor that installs the advice must implement the `org.springframework.core.Ordered` interface (see Listing 6-32).

Listing 6-32. *The Ordered Interface*

```
public interface Ordered {
    int getOrder();
}
```

In advisors, `getOrder` returns `Integer.MAX_VALUE` by default, which means that it has the lowest priority (0 being the highest). To force an order, you can configure the order property of an advisor as any other bean; for example, to ensure that the lock mix-in showed in the previous section is applied with the highest priority, you use the code in Listing 6-33.

Listing 6-33. *Ordering the Lock Advisor*

```
<bean id="lockAdvisor" class="aop.spring.LockMixinAdvisor">
    <property name="order"><value>0</value></property>
</bean>
```

Programmatically Configured Aspects

Since Spring AOP is dynamic AOP, advice can be dynamically attached or detached from a given advised object.

The Advised Interface

When using a factory that supports AOP (the `ApplicationContext` factory being the most common), the bean instances returned by the factory during a call to the `getBean` methods are actually AOP proxies. These AOP proxies implement the `org.springframework.aop.framework.Advised` interface. Consequently, any program can cast the manipulated objects into the `Advised` interface and access the AOP framework API to implement program-based dynamic aspect configuration/reconfiguration.

The (partial) `Advised` interface is shown in Listing 6-34.

Listing 6-34. *The Advised Interface*

```
public interface Advised {
    [...]
    Advisor[] getAdvisors();
    int indexOf(Advisor advisor);
    void addAdvisor(Advisor advisor) throws AopConfigException;
    void addAdvisor(int pos, Advisor advisor) throws AopConfigException;
    boolean removeAdvisor(Advisor advisor) throws AopConfigException;
    boolean replaceAdvisor(Advisor a, Advisor b) throws AopConfigException;
    void removeAdvisor(int index) throws AopConfigException;

    void addAdvice(Advice advice) throws AopConfigException;
    void addAdvice(int pos, Advice advice) throws AopConfigException;
    boolean removeAdvice(Advice advice) throws AopConfigException;

    boolean isFrozen();
}
```

The Advised interface provides all the primitives to programmatically manipulate the advisors that apply on a given AOP Proxy. It also allows for direct advising, when an Advice instance is available.

Notice the isFrozen method, which returns true if no configuration is possible on the advised instance. When isFrozen returns true, an attempt to call any configuration method will throw an AopConfigException.

Using the Proxy Factory

When a bean is accessed through a factory that does not originally support AOP, it is still possible to programmatically add some AOP features. This is done through ProxyFactory, which allows for the dynamic creation of a new proxy delegating to a new proxied bean. Listing 6-35 shows an example.

Listing 6-35. *Example of Use for the Proxy Factory*

```
// creates a new proxy factory
ProxyFactory factory = new ProxyFactory(MyBusinessInterfaceImpl);
// adds an interceptor to be added to all methods
factory.addInterceptor(myMethodInterceptor);
// adds an advisor
factory.addAdvisor(myAdvisor);
// retrieves an AOP proxy for my business interface
MyBusinessInterface tb = (MyBusinessInterface) factory.getProxy();
```

Auto-Proxying

In Spring, a factory can be configured to automatically create specific proxies for the accessed beans. This is the *auto-proxy* feature.

With this feature, the programmer sets up certain special bean definitions in the XML bean definition file for configuring the auto-proxy infrastructure. The configuration declares the targets eligible for auto-proxying.

Two configuration means are available:

- Using an auto-proxy creator that refers to specific beans in the current context

- Auto-proxy creation driven by source-level metadata attributes

Using an Auto-Proxy Creator

For the first means of configuration, several auto-proxy creators are available in the org.springframework.aop.framework.autoproxy package. For instance, the BeanNameAutoProxyCreator automatically creates AOP proxies for beans with names matching literal values or wildcards (see Listing 6-36).

Listing 6-36. *Configuration for Auto-Proxying*

```
<bean id="myBeanNameProxyCreator"
    class="org.springframework.aop.framework.autoproxy.BeanNameAutoProxyCreator">
    <property name="beanNames"><value>order*</value></property>
    <property name="interceptorNames">
        <list>
            <value>myInterceptor</value>
        </list>
    </property>
</bean>
```

Here, we ask for the creation of an AOP proxy for all the beans with names starting with order. The AOP proxies will be advised by the advisors given by the interceptorNames property.

Metadata Driven Auto-Proxying

A particularly important type of auto-proxying is driven by metadata. Instead of using XML deployment descriptors as in EJB, configuration for transaction management and other enterprise services is held in source-level attributes (similarly to the .NET model).

To implement this feature, the programmer can use the DefaultAdvisorAutoProxyCreator, which automatically creates proxies for a given bean if an advisor has to advise any of its methods. As a consequence, if the advisor is programmatically able to be metadata-aware by using the Spring API for source-level metadata, or even the Java 5 metadata facility, the auto proxying will be metadata driven. As an example, we can use the org.springframework.transaction.interceptor.TransactionAttributeSourceAdvisor, which is provided by Spring and selects the advisable method depending on source-level transactional attributes.

```
<bean id="autoProxyCreator"
    class=
    "org.springframework.aop.framework.autoproxy.DefaultAdvisorAutoProxyCreator">
</bean>

<bean id="txAdvisor"
```

```
    autowire="constructor"
    class=
    "org.springframework.transaction.interceptor.TransactionAttributeSourceAdvisor">
    <property name="order"><value>1</value></property>
</bean>
```

Summary

In this chapter, we depicted the basic features of Spring and illustrated how to use Spring AOP.

Spring provides a lightweight bean container (factory) that implements the Inversion of Control (Dependency Injection) principle. The IoC principle allows a clean separation between the bean definition and the bean dependency management and configuration. In short, when an application needs a bean, it asks the factory in charge of creating it and configuring it with the application context (usually expressed in XML bean configuration files).

A strength of Spring is that it applies the same IoC principles to AOP, which gives it two primary advantages: First, AOP is cleanly integrated into the bean definition, which makes the whole framework convincing and consistent. In addition, most of the development and configuration processes are already familiar to programmers who have used Spring beans. Second, it gives a good balance between configuration and Java programming. Even though most AOP basic features are usable through property configuration, it is always possible to customize the AOP model programmatically, or even to provide new configurable AOP concepts. The clean interface-based design of Spring is actually of a great help here.

From an abstract model perspective, Spring AOP defines the same concepts as classical AOP (advice, pointcuts, introductions, cflows), except that it materializes the link between an advice and a pointcut with the concept of an *advisor*. Introductions are handled as a special type of advice; it is our feeling that some of the concepts provided need further enhancement and refinement, which is understandable since Spring AOP is a young framework. The open design of Spring, especially interface-based design and IoC, will make it easy to improve the model in the future.

From an implementation perspective, Spring AOP relies on a proxy framework implemented on top of the JDK and the CGLIB proxies, which allows for a more dynamic AOP. Compared to other AOP implementations, it makes some of the Spring AOP support less efficient and less flexible. In particular, the distinction between "call" and "execution" advice is not clear, and the cflow mechanism is not as flexible as in AspectJ or JBoss-AOP. Having to create a lot of proxies is also less efficient than more intrusive implementations such as AspectJ. On the other hand, the Spring proxying mechanism, and especially the Spring auto-proxying mechanism, gives a way to better integrate AOP in a J2EE environment that includes complex legacy code.

CHAPTER 7

■ ■ ■

AOP Tools Comparison

The previous chapters presented four of the most widely used tools for AOP: AspectJ, JAC, JBoss AOP, and Spring AOP. This chapter compares these four tools with regard to programming aspect-oriented applications.

AspectJ, JAC, JBoss AOP, and Spring AOP each has its own techniques for implementing the concepts of AOP presented in Chapter 2. The three main concepts of AOP—*aspect*, *pointcut*, and *advice*—can be implemented with each of the four tools, but their forms as well as the means for programming them, such as syntax and API, vary. The terms used to describe these concepts may also vary among the tools; for example, the term *advice* is used by AspectJ, whereas JAC uses the term *wrapper* and JBoss AOP uses *interceptor*.

Besides some minor conceptual and terminology differences, these tools can be classified into two types of approaches: the language approach (AspectJ) and the framework approach (JAC, JBoss, and Spring). These two types of approaches imply some important differences, which we'll cover in this chapter.

Table 7-1 sums up and compares the features of AspectJ, JAC, JBoss AOP, and Spring AOP, which we'll cover in more detail throughout this chapter.

Table 7-1. *Comparison of Features of AspectJ, JAC, JBoss AOP, and Spring AOP*

Feature	AspectJ	JAC	JBoss AOP	Spring AOP
Approach	Language	Framework	Framework	Framework
Weaver implementation	Compile time or load time	Run time	Run time	Run time
Aspect	Keyword `aspect`	Class extending `AspectComponent`	Regular Java class	Set of advisors
Pointcut	Dedicated syntax	Method `pointcut` with GNU regular expression	XML tags with `java.util.regexp` expressions	XML with Perl 5 regular expressions
After/before code	Advice code	Wrapper	Interceptor	Interceptor
Intercepted object execution	`proceed`	`proceed`	`invokeNext`	`proceed`

Table 7-1. *Continued*

Feature	AspectJ	JAC	JBoss AOP	Spring AOP
Introduction mechanism	Intertype declaration	Role method	Mix-in	Introduction advice (mix-in)
Default aspect instantiation model	Singleton	Singleton	One aspect instance per aspectized class	Singleton
Aspect ordering	Keyword `declare precedence`	Property `jac.comp. wrappingOrder`	Declaration order in the `jboss-aop.xml` file	`org.springframework. core.Ordered` interface implementation

Weaver Implementation

The heart of an aspect-oriented system is the *aspect weaver*. It is a tool used for integrating aspects with classes. Several ways of performing the weaving exist. AspectJ employs a compile-time weaver, which is typical of the language approach, whereas JAC, JBoss AOP, and Spring AOP use run-time weavers, which are typical of the framework approach.

The AspectJ weaver can take either source code or bytecode as input. In addition to the compile-time weaving mode is a load-time mode, where aspects can be woven while the byte-code of the application is loaded into the JVM. The advantage of compile-time (or load-time) weaving is that it delivers woven applications with better execution times than are possible for run-time weaving. The disadvantage is that there is no distinction in the executed code between the aspect code and the application code. If the programmer needs to modify, add, or remove an aspect, then the entire application must be woven again.

With JAC, JBoss AOP, and Spring AOP, classes and aspects are compiled separately, and the weaving is performed while the application is loaded and executed. Aspect and class instances are separate run-time entities, and the weaver orchestrates the execution according to the weaving directives. In such a mode, the weaving is an operation very similar to binding: an aspect instance is bound to the objects where the aspect applies. The advantage of this mode is that the binding can be dynamically modified, thus enabling the removal of aspects and the weaving of new aspects without recompiling the application. This feature can be useful for applications such as web servers, which have to be readily available, since new features can be deployed without stopping the application. One of the disadvantages of run-time weaving is that the applications are generally slower than statically woven ones.

Note that although AspectJ could also implement run-time weaving, it is less natural as AspectJ follows the language approach. Most of the type checking performed by the compiler would then be disabled, which would erase most of the advantages of the language approach. On the other hand, the framework approach can hardly implement compile-time weaving, since it would imply some preprocessing tool, which is implemented much more efficiently by the language approach.

Aspect

We already mentioned that AspectJ is a language with its own syntax (with the AspectJ version 5, this dedicated syntax can be replaced by annotations), whereas JAC, JBoss AOP, and Spring AOP are frameworks.

With AspectJ, aspects are software entities that define pointcuts and advice code, and they may also define fields and methods. Aspect inheritance has been implemented, but with some restrictions compared to class inheritance. A concrete aspect can extend an abstract aspect, but not another concrete one.

With JAC, aspects are regular Java classes that extend the `AspectComponent` class provided by the JAC library. An aspect defines pointcuts, and advice code is written in separate *wrapper classes*. One of the key features of JAC is the mechanism known as *aspect configuration*. This tool allows the programmer to define the way an aspect can be reused with different applications while also tailoring to each application's needs. For this, a set of configuration elements is externalized from the aspects into some configuration files that can be modified without recompiling the whole application.

The concept of an aspect in JBoss AOP is split in two kinds of files: intercepting methods or interceptors implement advice code and are defined in Java classes, and pointcuts associate these interceptors with joinpoints and are defined in XML files. With newer versions of JBoss AOP, this distinction disappears; like in AspectJ, pointcuts can be defined with Java 5 annotations.

With Spring AOP, advice and pointcuts are implemented in regular Java classes, which are configured as beans. The dependency injection principle allows for the configuration of the links between advice and pointcuts. There is no explicit aspect entity; however, an aspect can be seen as a set of *advisors*.

The study of these four tools shows that the concept of an aspect is not mandatory for AOP. The actual primary concepts are pointcuts and advice, as well as a way to link them together. An aspect is no more than a set of pointcuts and advice that are logically related to a given concern. However, making this logical link explicit is not mandatory, and it is also useful to be able to define advice and pointcuts independently from a given aspect. In this case, we can say that these are anonymous pointcuts or advice.

Besides gathering pointcuts and advice, an important role of an aspect is to be used as a configuration unit for a given concern. As just explained with the aspect configuration mechanism of JAC, the configuration capability is of primary importance for aspect reuse. We will detail this feature later in this chapter. However, when a system already natively supports a configuration level (such as the Spring bean configuration level), the aspect concept is not needed. It emerges from some configuration holding pointcuts and advice.

Pointcut

Recall that a *pointcut* is a set of code locations, called *joinpoints*, where an aspect can be woven. This idea is central in AOP. Pointcuts define the crosscutting nature of an aspect. A pointcut "talks about" the application and designates strategic locations where an aspect applies.

In this section, we'll summarize how to write pointcuts and the types of joinpoints supported by the various aspect-oriented languages and frameworks featured in this book.

Pointcut Definition

All existing aspect-oriented tools provide a pointcut language for defining the set of joinpoints that are included in a pointcut. Basically, this pointcut language can be seen as a query language. Instead of being a classic database, the structure to which the query is applied is a program. The goal here is to define a language that allows developers to write relevant queries in the simplest and most practical way possible. Consequently, a pointcut language typically defines a few keywords, the classical Boolean operators (AND, OR, NOT), and wildcards such as the character * for selecting joinpoint sets in a concise way.

With AspectJ, pointcuts are defined with a dedicated syntax (the keyword `pointcut`) or with a Java 5 annotation. JAC pointcuts are defined by invoking an API with GNU regular expressions that define the set of joinpoints based on class names, object names, and method signatures. JBoss AOP pointcuts are defined either as XML tags or as Java 5 annotations. Spring AOP pointcuts can be defined either in XML or programmatically in Java.

Most of the time, pointcuts are dependant on the structure of the application. If the application code changes, the locations where an aspect applies will most likely change too. The situation is similar when programmers want to reuse their aspects with distinct applications: pointcuts have to be adapted to the new application. This is why the aspect configuration process mentioned in the previous section is so important. Note that with the language approach (AspectJ), which implements the weaving at compile time, the joinpoints belonging to a given pointcut can be determined at compile time, which is hardly the case for frameworks. With the right tools (e.g., the AJDT Eclipse plug-in), aspect programmers can have better control over their programs with the language approach.

As we said, pointcuts can be seen as queries on the program. These queries return a set of joinpoints where the aspects apply. An aspect tool is characterized by the supported types of joinpoints. For a given program, a type of joinpoint is materialized as a set of joinpoint shadows—that is, all the program locations that correspond to a given joinpoint type. For instance, the *method call* joinpoint type corresponds to all the places where a method is called.

In the next section, we'll look at a comparison of the tools' supported joinpoint types.

Joinpoint Types

AspectJ is the AOP tool that supports the largest set of joinpoint types. We'll examine in this section the types of joinpoints supported by AspectJ, JAC, JBoss AOP, and Spring AOP.

- *Method execution*: All AOP tools support this except Spring, which supports transparent proxying.

- *Method call*: This type is supported by AspectJ and JBoss AOP. JAC does not support it. When programming applications with remote communications, however, the method calls can be intercepted by wrapping the client-side proxy, which is rather similar to a method call joinpoint. Spring supports transparent proxying, which can be seen as a method call pointcut.

- *Constructor execution*: All AOP tools except Spring support this type of joinpoint.

- *Inherited constructor execution*: When a constructor calls a superconstructor, AspectJ can distinguish the execution of the current constructor from that of the inherited one.

- *Field read*: AspectJ and JBoss AOP can weave aspects around this joinpoint type. JAC and Spring do not support it directly. However, JAC performs a bytecode analysis to detect methods that read fields.

- *Field write*: This joinpoint type is similar to the field read type.

- *Exception*: AspectJ can intercept the start of an exception catch block. Neither JBoss AOP, JAC, nor Spring supports this joinpoint type. However, they support some "after throwing" advice (exception handlers in JAC), which modularize the handling of an exception for all the joinpoints included in a pointcut. Note that the "after throwing" advice (which is also supported by AspectJ) is less powerful than the catch block notification, because it does not allow the aspect to modify the way a base program deals with existing exceptions.

- *Static block execution*: This joinpoint type is supported by AspectJ, but not by the other tools.

- *Advice code execution*: This is an AspectJ joinpoint type. With the other tools, advice code is defined in a regular Java method. Programmers can thus aspectize the executions and the calls of these methods.

- *Control flow*: AspectJ supports joinpoint types that correspond to entry into and the exit from a control flow. This feature is not available with JBoss AOP or JAC; however, programmers can emulate it. Spring AOP supports some kinds of cflow.

It is interesting to note that tools that follow the framework approach (JAC, JBoss, and Spring) support fewer joinpoint types than AspectJ. There are several reasons for this, both technology and integration related.

On the technology side, since frameworks are written in pure Java and use reflection, bytecode manipulation, and proxying techniques for their implementations, it is more complicated for them to implement fine-grained joinpoint types such as, for instance, exception catches.

Regarding integration, since the framework approaches are placed in the context of component frameworks (EJB for JBoss and simple beans for JAC and Spring), they often deliberately decide to not support very fine-grained joinpoints in order to maintain the encapsulation principle for the aspectized components. For instance, Spring and JAC deliberately do not support field read/write joinpoint types so that the advice can be applied only to the component interface (i.e., the fixed part of the components). As another example, Spring AOP does not support constructor execution joinpoints because it may interfere with the construction process implemented in the Spring factory. Of course, these restrictions make the AOP frameworks less flexible than AspectJ. On the other hand, they prevent the programmers from misusing the framework, and they make the AOP programs more reusable. For example, refactoring a class by changing its implementation and fields, but not its interface, may impact an AspectJ pointcut, but it will never impact a JAC or Spring pointcut, since they do not support field interception.

Another important point is that some advanced joinpoint types of AOP provided by AspectJ can be implemented by using less advanced features. For instance, the cflow feature can be simply implemented by using execution advice and standard thread-local variables (java.lang.ThreadLocal). This justifies the fact that these types of joinpoints, although useful for simplification and clarity, are not always provided.

Advice

Pointcuts allow programmers to define where an aspect applies. The concept of advice code defines the behavior of an aspect—in other words, advice code states what an aspect is doing.

The terms used for the code structure that defines the behavior of an aspect varies from *advice code* (AspectJ), to *wrapper* (JAC), to *interceptor* (JBoss AOP and Spring AOP). However, the idea behind these terms is the same: to define the instructions that will be executed before and after the joinpoints.

Advice Code Types

The three main types of advice code are "before," "after," and "around."

- "Before" advice code is executed before the joinpoints.

- "After" advice code is executed after the joinpoints. There are two main types of "after" advice code:

  - "After returning" advice code is executed after a normal execution/invocation.

  - "After throwing" advice code is executed after an abnormal execution/invocation, which leads to an exception being thrown.

- "Around" advice code is executed both before and after the joinpoints.

AspectJ and Spring provide all of these advice code types, while JAC and JBoss AOP chose to provide only the "around" advice code type. Indeed, "around" advice code entails all the other kinds of advice. For instance, "before" advice code can be seen as "around" code that calls proceed and where the "after" part is missing. As another example, "after throwing" advice code is "around" advice code that encapsulates the call to proceed in a try/catch block.

Providing the "before" and "after" constructs has several advantages. First, it makes the aspect code clearer, as programmers can easily see what kind of function is implemented, without having to look at the advice code. Second, it helps programmers avoid programming mistakes such as forgetting to proceed to the joinpoint. Third, "before" and "after" advice code can be implemented more efficiently by the AOP frameworks, since the reification of the joinpoint is not needed in these cases (see the "before" and "after" advice code in Chapter 6). However, these advantages are not crucial when programming complicated aspects that need, for instance, to proceed or catch exceptions depending on particular execution contexts. In these cases, the "around" advice code general form is preferred, and this explains why some approaches stick with "around" advice code only.

Note that in all AOP tools, a special construction is provided for delimiting the "after" and the "before" parts of "around" advice code. This construction takes the form of a keyword (proceed) with AspectJ or a method call (proceed with JAC and Spring AOP, and invokeNext with JBoss AOP). This is, however, a minor difference, and the underlying semantics remain the same.

Finally, the major difference between AspectJ (language approach) and the other tools (framework approach) is that AspectJ provides typed advice. Indeed, in AspectJ, advice code can take well-typed parameters that are bound to some joinpoint contextual elements (e.g., parameters, targets, and callers). Well-typed advice code improves the program quality, readability, and performance (static binding). However, the advantages of typed advice code need to be balanced against the fact that it is not always possible to implement advice code in a typed way, especially when it has to perform generic functions on the base program (e.g., a persistence aspect should be applied generically on all the objects of the program and thus cannot be typed).

Joinpoint Introspection

When advice code is executed before, after, or around a joinpoint, programmers sometimes need to retrieve information about the current joinpoint. For example, a programmer may need to know what the method associated with the joinpoint is or what the arguments of the call are. The gathering of such information is called *joinpoint introspection*. All four AOP tools presented in this book support this feature.

AspectJ provides the keyword `thisJoinPoint` for introspecting joinpoints in advice code. This keyword returns a reference to an object created by AspectJ for each encountered joinpoint. This object implements the `org.aspectj.lang.JoinPoint` interface and, depending on the joinpoint type, several distinct methods exist for retrieving information about the current joinpoint.

With JAC, Spring AOP, and JBoss AOP, advice code consists of regular Java methods. These methods are called each time a joinpoint matches a defined pointcut. These methods take as a parameter an object that, similar to the AspectJ keyword `thisJoinPoint`, provides information about the current joinpoint. With JAC and Spring AOP, the interface implemented by this object is `org.aopalliance.intercept.Joinpoint`, which belongs to the AOP Alliance standard API. JBoss AOP uses a similar but JBoss-specific interface: `org.jboss.aop.joinpoint.Invocation`.

Introduction Mechanism

The *introduction mechanism* allows for extending an application with code elements (fields, methods, etc.) defined in aspects.

With AspectJ, this mechanism is known as *intertype declaration*. The idea is that a type (an aspect) performs declarations for a target type. AspectJ can introduce fields, methods, and constructors. The target of the introduction is a class or an interface. If an interface is used, all the classes that implement the interface are the target of the introduction. Interfaces can also be introduced by AspectJ.

With JAC, two types of code elements can be introduced: methods and exception handlers. The introduced methods (called *role methods*) and the exception handlers are defined in wrapper classes. The role methods can be invoked with an API that relies on the Java runtime reflection capabilities. The advantage of using reflection here is that the introduction mechanism is very flexible: it is easy to add or remove an introduction at run time. The disadvantages are that no type check of any kind is performed by JAC before the actual invocation, and the invocation process is relatively slow due to reflection overhead.

JBoss AOP and Spring AOP provide a mechanism known as *mix-in* for introducing code elements into an application. With this mechanism, the fields and methods defined in the mix-in class are appended to the classes that are the target of the mix-in. Well-formed mix-ins should implement an interface that declares the introduced methods. Under the hood, the AOP framework will use bytecode manipulation to make the target class implement the mix-in interfaces. Then, when invoking a mix-in method, programmers must cast the target object to the interface declaring the method. This mechanism is not type-safe either, since Java does not implement any strong type checks on the interfaces (dynamic binding). However, it has the advantage of being far more efficient than reflection. Besides, once the cast is done on the target object, the IDE will be able to provide some support, such as contextual help and code completion.

To summarize the introduction mechanism, only the AspectJ language approach is type-safe regarding this feature, since some type-checking mechanism is implemented by the compiler. Tools that follow the framework approach cannot be type-safe, since they remain pure Java, which does not support such a feature. However, the mix-in approach implemented by JBoss and Spring seems to be a good trade-off. Indeed, most programmers would argue that it is more natural to cast an object to a given interface to be allowed to call an introduced method. With AspectJ, the code can sometimes be difficult to read and understand since it can refer to methods that do not exist in any classes or interfaces supported by the target objects.

Advanced Features

This section compares the various advanced features implemented by AspectJ, JAC, JBoss AOP, and Spring AOP. Specifically, we cover aspect instantiation, ordering, and reuse.

Aspect Instantiation

Similar to classes, aspects are code elements that can be instantiated, and the term *aspect* refers to either a type or an instance. However, unlike with classes, aspects are not directly instantiated by programmers; in other words, programmers never call new for instantiating an aspect. Aspect instances are automatically created by the AOP language or framework.

With AspectJ, the default policy is to create only one instance of each existing aspect, such as aspects for singletons. As a consequence, the data defined in an aspect are shared by all the joinpoints where the aspect applies. Programmers can redefine this default policy by specifying that one instance of the aspect must be created for every object that is the executing object of a pointcut (clause perthis) or for every object that is the target object of a pointcut (clause pertarget). Similarly, an aspect instance can be created each time the program enters a control flow (clauses percflow and percflowbelow). AspectJ 5 provides a new instantiation policy (clause pertypewithin).

With JAC, the instantiation policy deals with aspects and wrappers, both of which are by default singletons. A distinct instantiation policy can be chosen for wrappers by specifying that an instance of a wrapper must be created for every joinpoint included in a pointcut. When programming distributed applications with JAC, aspect and wrapper instances are replicated on each host.

The default policy implemented by JBoss AOP is to associate one instance of a wrapper class per aspectized application class—in other words, one instance per class where one of the pointcuts defined in the aspect matches. This default policy can be redefined by specifying a factory that will be responsible for creating aspect instances according to the programmers' needs.

Finally, Spring AOP default policy is also to instantiate aspects as singleton.

Although the framework approach provides default policies, it is always possible to instantiate an aspect dynamically by using a lower-level Java API. In each framework (JAC, JBoss, and Spring), it is thus possible to dynamically add new pieces of advice and introductions to a target object. These features make the framework approach much more flexible than the language approach.

Aspect Ordering

When several aspects apply around the same joinpoint, the execution order of these aspects must be specified. Most of the time, this ordering depends on the semantics of aspects, and no automatic rules can be defined. When considering a trace and a security aspect, for example, the trace may be executed before the security if programmers want to trace every request. Alternatively, the security may be executed first if programmers need only tracing requests from unauthorized users. In such a case, the programmers must explicitly specify the ordering.

With AspectJ, aspect ordering is defined with the instruction `declare precedence`. The order is global and applies to the whole application. Some ordering may be left unspecified, and in this case, there is no guarantee of the execution order.

With JAC, aspect ordering is defined with the system property `jac.comp.wrappingOrder`. JBoss AOP uses the tag `<precedence>` in the XML file `jboss-aop.xml`. Spring AOP provides an interface (`org.springframework.core.Ordered`) that must be implemented to specify the order. In all cases, the order is global, and there is no guarantee that some orderings will not be left unspecified.

At first glance, it may appear that the precedence feature adopted by AspectJ and JBoss is the most powerful, since it allows the ordering of aspects declaration. The precedence relationship is transitive, and the aspect system will determine the final order by looking at all the declared orders of all the aspects. However, we think that the precedence construct can lead to maintainability issues when refactoring the program (i.e., when adding, removing, renaming, or changing aspects). It indeed may happen that all the precedence declarations would need to be changed across the program. Consequently, a centralized ordering declaration like JAC's seems to be reasonable for more complex programs. Hence, we advise programmers to use the precedence feature of AspectJ and JBoss in a centralized way by creating a specific aspect for managing all other aspect ordering. Unfortunately, the Spring ordering feature would not allow any centralized ordering declaration.

Aspect Reuse

Just as programmers can reuse a library of classes with different applications, they can also write libraries of aspects. Remember that, when writing an aspect, advice code defines the behavior of the aspect, whereas pointcuts define where the aspect must be integrated in the application. Pointcuts are therefore highly application-dependant and can seldom be reused, so the issue of reusing aspects is essentially a matter of reusing aspect codes.

With AspectJ, inheritance and abstract pointcuts allow for the reuse of aspects. As with abstract methods, an abstract pointcut is a pointcut declared with a name and a signature, but without an expression. Abstract pointcuts can be used like any other pointcut to define advice code. As with classes, the inheritance mechanism allows for extending an aspect, reusing the existing definitions of the superaspect, defining new advice code in the subaspects, and making abstract pointcuts concrete. With AspectJ, an aspect can extend an abstract aspect, but not a concrete aspect. Reusing aspects is then a matter of writing abstract aspects with advice code and abstract pointcuts and extending them to adapt the aspects to a given application by making the pointcuts concrete.

With JAC, the writing of aspects is separated in two regular Java classes: one for the wrapper and one for the aspect component. In addition, a configuration mechanism allows for the definition of application-dependant parameters such as pointcut expressions and system properties in so-called configuration files. Most of the time, reusing aspects with JAC is simply a matter of writing a new configuration file for adapting the aspect component and the wrapper classes to the new application.

JBoss AOP separates the writing of interceptors and of pointcuts. The former are regular Java classes, whereas the latter are XML files. Interceptors are then easily reused, whereas pointcuts must be adapted to each new application.

Finally, Spring AOP relies on its bean configuration mechanism to configure the aspects for different contexts.

When we look at aspect reuse for these tools, we can see that the language approach uses a language-level concept such as inheritance, while the framework approach uses configuration. Both have their advantages and disadvantages. For instance, the inheritance approach is less flexible than configuration, but it ensures better compatibility between the aspects and the inherited aspects. In our opinion, a combination of the two approaches represents a complete solution for aspect reuse.

Summary

In this chapter, we compared the four AOP tools presented in this book: AspectJ, JAC, JBoss AOP, and Spring AOP. We outlined some of the minor differences among the tools, and we explained that the major differences are the result of implementation dissimilarities between the language approach (AspectJ) and the framework approach (JAC, JBoss AOP, and Spring AOP).

As we have seen in this chapter, the language approach allows for static typing and more compile-time checks, which improve the quality of the programs (see, for example, the "The Joinpoint Types" section). The language approach is also more efficient, since compilers can optimize the woven code for static binding and avoid run-time reflection or dynamic proxying when they are not needed.

On the other hand, the framework approach uses run-time reflection and joinpoint introspection. These techniques make the frameworks less efficient, but also more flexible than the languages. Using the framework approach, it is possible to dynamically adapt an application while it is running. In addition, the framework approach uses existing languages or tools such as Java, XML, or Ant, which make it easier to integrate these tools within standard development environments. This last point is key, since it explains the success of the framework approach, while only one representative of the language approach is actually widely used: AspectJ.

The success of AspectJ is the result of the major work by AspectJ's creators to integrate the tool into IDEs such as Eclipse. Once AspectJ is well integrated, the use of AOP becomes simpler than a dedicated language, since the IDE can provide support such as contextual help, code completion, and design error detection, which can sometimes be tedious to support with the framework approach since these tools perform less type checking.

Although the language and framework approaches sometimes compete, our feeling is that they should be seen as complementary, since they have very different properties. The work done with AspectJ 5, which aims to integrate the AspectJ language and the AspectWerkz framework, is a step in the right direction. However, a lot of work is still needed to create an ideal tool that cleanly integrates the fexibility of frameworks and the type-checking capabilities of languages.

CHAPTER 8

■■■

Design Patterns and AOP

Design patterns offer generic solutions for recurring design problems. Most developers who use object-oriented programming are familiar with their use. Patterns are not specific to a particular language; in fact, most of the problems they tackle are not even specific to a particular programming paradigm. Consequently, many design problems usually resolved through object-oriented programming can be solved using AOP.

The core design patterns became popular in 1995 with Addison-Wesley's publishing of *Elements of Reusable Object-Oriented Software* by Erich Gamma, Richard Helm, Ralph Johnson, and John Vlissides (commonly known as the Gang of Four, or GoF). Although several other design patterns have been defined since then, most are based on this work.

This chapter aims to redefine selected design patterns with the aspect-oriented approach. We compare these redefined patterns with their object-oriented definitions so that the advantages of AOP will be highlighted.

The first section of this chapter gives a quick introduction to these reusable models. We then present and discuss the design patterns that show the most significant modularity improvements with an AOP implementation.

Design Patterns, or Elements of Reusable Software

Design patterns are one approach for reusability, which is one of the key concepts of object-oriented programming.

The idea of a pattern is not unique to programming; in fact, the idea stems from a similar concept that is used in architecture and town planning, an idea formalized by architect Christopher Alexander. The ideas were adapted to object-oriented programming by Ward Cunningham and Ken Beck in their article "Using Pattern Languages for Object-Oriented Programs," which was presented in 1987 at a conference in Orlando, Florida.

As stated previously, design patterns offer generic solutions to recurrent problems in specific contexts. The context in which a design pattern is used is important because a problem may be solved differently depending on the context. A good quality design pattern must be the abstraction of a concrete and well-tested solution.

A design pattern must be well documented if it is to be used efficiently. Several catalogues of design patterns are available, the GoF book being the most well known. Each catalogue is split into sections that contain descriptions of the design patterns.

With this documentation, almost anyone can use these design patterns and allow best practices to be applied easily in application development; however, it is still necessary to understand the possible applications of a design pattern in order to use it correctly.

Implementation of Design Patterns with AOP

Currently, a great deal of research is being carried out on the implementation of design patterns using AOP. This is because many design patterns crosscut, and therefore it is difficult to ensure sufficient modularity of these patterns within the object-oriented paradigm.

In 2002, an OOPSLA conference article by Jan Hannemann and Gregor Kiczales[1] discussed precursory research in this area. This work highlighted that implementing certain design patterns in AOP can lead to the following advantages:

- *Locality*: The code of the functionality is contained within the aspect rather than within the classes and, as a result, modularization is improved.

- *Reusability*: Refactoring code into aspects allows a greater degree of abstraction and better reusability.

- *Composition transparency*: An object can have several patterns applied to it without the global implementation becoming confusing.

- *(Un)pluggability*: The overall structure of the application depends less on the design patterns implemented. With AOP, a simple parameter change allows you to activate or deactivate a design pattern, for example, when making a class a singleton.

However, these four advantages were not apparent for all design patterns. Some show all four benefits, others none. Of the 23 GoF design patterns, 17 show improvements with an implementation using AOP; 12 benefit in all four ways.

The next sections apply AOP techniques to a sample of the GoF design patterns.

The Singleton Design Pattern

The first design pattern that we study with regards to aspect-oriented programming techniques is the Singleton. We begin by providing a quick description of this pattern, and proceed by giving two implementations of the pattern, one with JBoss AOP and one with AspectJ. We then conclude this section with an evaluation of the implementations.

Description

The Singleton design pattern can be described as follows:

- *The problem and its context*: Certain classes should only have a single instance during the execution of a program. This can be necessary for two reasons: either the class models a unique object, such as a set of global variables for the application, and having

---

1. Jan Hannemann and Gregor Kiczales. "Design Pattern Implementation in Java and AspectJ." Proceedings of the 17th Conference on Object-Oriented Programming: Systems, Languages and Applications (OOPSLA'02), ACM SIGPLAN Notices, 37(11): 161–173, November 2002.

two instances, may lead to run-time errors; or alternatively, because one instance is sufficient to offer all the services required, and by ensuring that not more than one instance is created, you economize memory and resources.

- *The solution to the problem*: The class must have a static attribute, usually called instance, to store a reference to the unique instance, as well as a method, generally called getInstance, that returns the value of instance. If the instance is null, getInstance creates a new instance of the class and stores its reference in the instance attribute, and then returns it to the caller.

Listing 8-1 shows one way in which the singleton can be implemented using Java.

Listing 8-1. *Implementation of the Singleton Design Pattern Using Java*

```
public class MySingleton {

  private static MySingleton instance = null;

    public static MySingleton getInstance() {
      if (instance==null) {
        instance = new MySingleton();
      }
     return instance;
    }
}
```

Because of the method getInstance, any class using MySingleton is ensured to be using the same instance of this class. The inconvenience of this is that the new operator cannot be used directly by the other classes to instantiate MySingleton. Using the Singleton design pattern is therefore not transparent for the classes that use MySingleton because these classes have to call getInstance instead of the usual constructor.

The issue of "transparency" in a design pattern, with respect to the other classes of an application, is not limited to the Singleton design pattern. In general, the use of a design pattern in an application has important implications for the classes with which it interacts. Design patterns can therefore have a huge impact on the structure of an application and may compromise the original object model.

While it is easy to recognize a singleton simply by reading the code, other design patterns such as the Command design pattern are more difficult to identify. Although design patterns are reusable in the sense that they structure the code, their implementation usually contains elements that are specific to a particular context, and the code itself is therefore less reusable.

A First Implementation of the Singleton Aspect with JBoss AOP

This section presents two implementations of the Singleton design pattern, one with JBoss AOP, and one with AspectJ.

As we saw in the previous example, the main issue preventing better modularization was the fact that classes had to call the method getInstance rather than the usual constructor.

JBoss AOP and AspectJ allow you to solve the problem simply and effectively by defining an aspect to modify the behavior of the constructor, which is invoked by the new operator to create a new instance of the class. When the constructor is invoked, the aspect intercepts and substitutes the new method with the code needed to manage the singleton.

With JBoss AOP, we can define the interceptor presented in Listing 8-2.

Listing 8-2. *Implementation of the Singleton Design Pattern Using JBoss AOP*

```java
package aop.patterns.singleton;

import org.jboss.aop.advice.Interceptor;
import org.jboss.aop.joinpoint.Invocation;

public class SingletonInterceptor implements Interceptor {

  private Object singleton;

  public String getName() {
    return "SingletonInterceptor";
  }

  public Object invoke(Invocation invocation) throws Throwable {
    if (singleton==null) {
      singleton = invocation.invokeNext();
    }
    return singleton;
  }
}
```

The code of this interceptor is similar to the object-oriented implementation of the singleton: it includes an attribute, which is used to store the unique instance of the singleton, and the method invoke, which uses the same kind of test to check the existence of the instance when a constructor is called. If the instance does not exist, invoke calls the constructor and stores the instance generated in the singleton attribute.

Note that the interceptor contains the code to handle the singleton and that it can be applied to a class in a way that is completely transparent for the rest of the application.

For the purpose of our example, we use a class called Stats, which contains various statistics for an e-commerce site (see Listing 8-3).

Listing 8-3. *Sample Class to Test theSingleton Design Pattern*

```java
package aop.patterns.singleton;
public class Stats {
  private int orders = 0;
  private float totalAmount = 0;
  private String status = "OK";

  public int getOrders() {
    return orders;
  }
```

```
public void incOrders() {
  orders++;
}

public float getTotalAmount() {
  return totalAmount;
}

public void addAmount(float p) {
  totalAmount+=p;
}

public String getStatus() {
  return status;
}

public void setStatus(String p) {
  status = p;
}

public void reset() {
  orders = 0;
  totalAmount = 0;
  status = "OK";
}
}
```

We will apply the Singleton design pattern to this class by parameterizing the file jboss-aop. xml in the way shown in Listing 8-4.

Listing 8-4. *Binding the Singleton Design Pattern to the Stats Class*

```
<bind pointcut="execution(aop.patterns.singleton.Stats->new())">
  <interceptor class="aop.patterns.singleton.SingletonInterceptor">
</bind>
```

It is easy to check if the design pattern has been applied correctly by using the class in Listing 8-5.

Listing 8-5. *Main Class for Testing the Singleton Design Pattern with JBoss AOP*

```
package aop.patterns.singleton;
public class SingletonExample {

  public static void main(String[] args) {
    Stats stats1 = new Stats();
    Stats stats2 = new Stats();
    if (stats1==stats2) {
```

```
      System.out.println("These instances are the same!");
    } else {
      System.out.println("These instances are not the same!");
    }
  }
}
```

We no longer need the method getInstance since the Singleton is accessed through a standard call to the constructor. The Singleton design pattern is now entirely transparent with respect to the application.

The result obtained by running this program is the following:

```
These instances are the same!
```

We have successfully applied the Singleton design pattern to the class Stats without needing to modify the code of Stats, or any class that uses it.

A Second Implementation of the Singleton Aspect with AspectJ

The same result can be obtained with AspectJ. We start by defining an abstract aspect independent of the pointcut that determines the classes to be transformed into singletons (see Listing 8-6).

Listing 8-6. *Implementation of the Singleton Design Pattern Using AspectJ*

```
package aop.patterns.singleton;

public abstract aspect AbstractSingletonAspect {

  private Object singleton = null;

  abstract pointcut singletonPointcut();

  Object around(): singletonPointcut() {
    if (singleton == null) {
      singleton = proceed();
    }
    return singleton;
  }
}
```

The abstract aspect defines two elements: an abstract pointcut, which must be defined by the concrete aspects and with subclass AbstractSingletonAspect; and an "around" advice, which is similar to the invoke method in the JBoss AOP interceptor.

This implementation presents a flow. In AspectJ, an aspect is a singleton by default, which means that one instance of the aspect is shared by all the classes designated by the `singletonPointcut` pointcut. Therefore, the aspect contains a reference to one unique instance of the singleton class. Each time the advice is executed, the existing singleton is obliterated by one of the newly created classes.

The AspectJ keywords `perthis` and `pertarget` cannot be used here since they would generate one instance of the aspect for every instance of the class, which is the opposite of the desired effect.

This problem can be solved in the following way:

- Define an abstract aspect as a superaspect for several concrete aspects: one for each class to be turned into a singleton. This way, the individual classes will not interfere with the other singletons. This is the solution we have chosen to implement in the preceding example.

- Use a hash table (`java.util.Hashtable`) to store the singleton for each of the transformed classes. We give an example of this solution in the next section.

We can now define a concrete aspect for each of the classes to be made into a singleton. If we want to transform the `Stats` class into a singleton, as we did previously with JBoss AOP, we must program the aspect shown in Listing 8-7.

Listing 8-7. *Concrete AspectJ Aspect to Bind the Singleton Design Pattern to the Stats Class*

```
package aop.patterns.singleton;

public aspect SingletonAspect extends AbstractSingletonAspect {
  pointcut singletonPointcut() : call(Stats.new(..));
}
```

Once the application is compiled, we execute the test class shown previously, obtaining the following result:

```
These instances are the same!
```

We obtain the same result as with the JBoss AOP implementation: the `Stats` class has been transformed into a singleton.

Evaluation of the Implementation

Unfortunately, this implementation of the Singleton design pattern has limited capability and can cause execution errors.

The first problem is the multiple constructor issue. In the example, only one instance reference is stored so that we always return the same instance of the class, regardless of the constructor.

Another problem is that this implementation is intrusive and can have damaging side effects on the way the application behaves, as will be described later.

Managing Multiple Constructors

In another context, we could use the singleton aspect with a class that contains several constructors. Although multiconstructor classes are not as adaptable to the singleton design pattern since it is designed to work with only one constructor, multiconstructor classes are frequently used in real applications, and therefore we can extend the pattern to deal with this case.

With different constructors, we can expect the creation of different instances (which is not the case with our current implementation). This difficulty is, however, by no means insurmountable. It is possible to store one instance for each constructor. Besides, we can store an instance not only depending on the header, but also on the values of the parameters.

With AspectJ, we obtain the result shown in Listing 8-8 for the abstract aspect.

Listing 8-8. *Second Implementation of the Singleton Design Pattern Using AspectJ*

```
package aop.patterns.singleton;

import java.util.Hashtable;

public abstract aspect AbstractMultipleSingletonAspect {

  private Hashtable singletons = new Hashtable();
  abstract pointcut singletonPointcut();

  private String getValue(Object o) {
    if (!o.getClass().isArray()) {
      return Integer.toString(o.hashCode());
    } else {
      StringBuffer value = new StringBuffer();
      Object[] temp = (Object[]) o;
      for (int i=0;i<temp.length;i++) {
        value.append(getValue(temp[i]));
        value.append('|');
      }
      return value.toString();
    }
  }

  Object around(): singletonPointcut() {

    String arguments;
    String signature = thisJoinPoint.getSignature().toString();
    if(thisJoinPoint.getArgs().length>0) {
      arguments = getValue(thisJoinPoint.getArgs());
    } else {
      arguments = "";
    }
```

```
      Object singleton = singletons.get(signature+arguments);
      if (singleton == null) {
        singleton = proceed();
        singletons.put(signature+arguments,singleton);
      }
      return singleton;
    }
}
```

This new implementation of the abstract aspect is more complex than the previous example because we have used a hash table to store the singleton instances. The key used in the hash table is determined according to the signature of the constructor and the value of the arguments. The value is obtained using the method getValue (this method is explained in Chapter 9 in the section "Nonregression Tests.")

Now, to support multiple constructors, we have to create the aspect SingletonAspect by subclassing the abstract aspect AbstractMultipleSingletonAspect. Using a hash table could also solve the problem stated previously, whereas a concrete aspect cannot be shared by several aspectized classes.

The Invasive Nature of the Aspect

The fact that we can transform any class into a singleton simply by applying an aspect to it seems initially both simple and useful. However, this invasive modification of the Java new operator is far from benign.

First, transforming a class into a singleton has consequences for the rest of the development. The advantage of using the method getInstance in the object-oriented approach is that we know immediately that this class is a singleton. With the AOP implementation of the singleton, any class is potentially a singleton, since all we must do to achieve this transformation is change the pointcut definition. For the final programmer, not knowing whether a class is a singleton could lead to programming mistakes.

Second, it is important to take precautions when we make an existing class into a singleton. If the singleton is called by more than one object, we have to ensure that multiple calls to this shared instance of the class do not lead to errors. A classic mistake when implementing a singleton is that the singleton attributes are obliterated each time a new object calls it, leading to incoherencies. These attributes must be considered as global shared variables.

Finally, this aspect makes it difficult to use aspect composition, which is an important functionality of AOP. For example, we cannot compose the singleton aspect with another aspect that also replaces the instance returned by the constructor. This could be a real problem, for example, when using a factory pattern aspect to replace a local instance of an object by an instance provided by a remote proxy.

The Observer Design Pattern

The second design pattern that we study with regards to aspect-oriented programming techniques is the Observer. We begin by providing a quick description of this pattern, and proceed by giving an implementation of the pattern using AspectJ. We then conclude this section with an evaluation of the implementation.

Description

In many situations, programmers need to be aware of objects' state changes or pay attention to the events produced by objects. For example, a text editor must activate the saving functionality when a file is modified. Other examples can be found in frameworks for building graphical user interfaces. For instance, Swing heavily relies on the mechanism known as *listeners*; listeners are objects that consume events emitted by other objects and react to these events.

The Observer design pattern consists of notifying observer objects when the states of other objects, called subjects, change.

Hence, a pure object-oriented, aspect-free implementation of the observer design pattern generally relies on two interfaces: Observer and Subject. The Subject interface is implemented by all observed classes and provides methods for registering and removing observers. The Observer interface is implemented by observers and provides methods for notifying state changes.

Aspect-oriented Implementation

In this section, we propose an aspect-oriented implementation of the Observer design pattern. With our solution, the management of observers and the detection of state changes are handled by an aspect. First, an AspectJ abstract aspect is defined to implement the generic part of the code. This aspect can be reused for all observers. Second, this aspect is extended to take into account the needs of real observers.

Generic Part of the Implementation

The code of the abstract aspect is presented in Listing 8-9.

Listing 8-9. *Implementation of the Observer Design Pattern Using AspectJ*

```
1 package aop.patterns.observer;
2
3 import java.util.Enumeration;
4 import java.util.Vector;
5
6 public abstract aspect AbstractObserverAspect pertarget (subject()) {
7
8   private Vector observers = new Vector();
9
10    public void addObserver(Object o) {
11      observers.add(o);
12    }
13
14    public void removeObserver(Object o) {
15      observers.remove(o);
16    }
17
18    protected abstract pointcut subject();
19
```

```
20   protected abstract pointcut event();
21
22   protected abstract void notifyEvent(Object subject,Object observer);
23
24   after(Object s) : event() && target(s) {
25     Enumeration elements = observers.elements();
26     while (elements.hasMoreElements()) {
27       Object o = elements.nextElement();
28       notifyEvent(s,o);
29     }
30   }
31 }
```

The AbstractObserverAspect aspect provides two methods, addObserver and removeObserver, to register and remove observers.

In the method notifyEvent (line 22), the pointcuts subject (line 18) and event (line 20) are code elements that are specific to the subject being observed. They are left abstract and will be defined in subaspects. The notifyEvent method will implement the reaction to a state change. The event pointcut will define the state changes of the event being observed. The subject pointcut will define the subject to be observed.

An important point to notice is that the aspect AbstractObserverAspect is not a singleton (clause pertarget on line 6). One instance of this aspect exists per subject to be observed.

The advice code defined on line 24 notifies all registered observers when a state change occurs.

Implementation of Observers

With the class Stats defined previously, this section illustrates the definition of an observer to monitor the addition and the removal of an order.

The code of this observer is shown in Listing 8-10.

Listing 8-10. *Concrete AspectJ Aspect to Bind the Observer Design Pattern to the Stats Class*

```
1 package aop.patterns.observer;
2
3 public aspect OrdersObserverAspect extends AbstractObserverAspect {
4
5   protected pointcut subject() : initialization(Stats.new(..));
6
7   protected pointcut event() : set(int Stats.orders);
8
9   protected void notifyEvent(Object s,Object o) {
10     Stats statistics = (Stats)s;
11     OrdersObserver observer = (OrdersObserver)o;
12     observer.eventHandler(statistics.getOrders());
13   }
14 }
15
```

```
16 public class OrdersObserver {
17   public void eventHandler(int value) {
18     System.out.println("Orders observer called with value: "+value);
19   }
20 }
```

The OrdersObserver class implements the observer, and the OrdersObserverAspect aspect defines the events and the observed subjects.

The pointcut event (line 7) defines the events that are observed: in this example, the pointcut matches all the write operations performed on the field Stats.order. Thus, the observed events are the addition or the removal of an order.

When such events occur, the advice code defined in the abstract AbstractObserverAspect aspect calls the notifyEvent method. Here, this method (line 9) retrieves the number of orders and forwards this number to the observer.

The observer (line 16) displays the total number of orders.

To test this observer, use the class shown in Listing 8-11.

Listing 8-11. *Main Class for Testing the Singleton Design Pattern*

```
package aop.patterns.observer;

public class ObserverExample {
  public static void main(String[] args) {
    Stats stats = new Stats();
    OrdersObserver observer1 = new OrdersObserver();

    OrdersObserverAspect.aspectOf(stats).addObserver(observer1);

    stats.incOrders();
    stats.addAmount(10);
    stats.incOrders();
    stats.addAmount(10);

    OrdersObserverAspect.aspectOf(stats).removeObserver(observer1);

    stats.incOrders();
    stats.addAmount(10);
  }
}
```

This program displays the following result:

```
Orders observer called with value: 1
Orders observer called with value: 2
```

Evaluation of the Implementation

With the four criteria defined by Hannemann and Kiczales, we can evaluate our implementation as follows:

- *Locality*: The subject is free from any code managing observers. This code is located in the `AbstractObserverAspect` abstract aspect. The code elements specific to subjects are handled by concrete aspects, which extend `AbstractObserverAspect`.

- *Reusability*: The management of observers is reused systematically.

- *Composition transparency*: The aspect is not invasive. The behavior of the observed subjects is extended, but not modified.

- *(Un)pluggability*: The link between the observed subject and its observers is weak. The pointcuts for events and subjects define precisely where the design pattern must be integrated.

The Command Design Pattern

The third design pattern that we study with regards to aspect-oriented programming techniques is the Command. We begin by providing a quick description of this pattern, and proceed by giving an implementation of the pattern using AspectJ. We then conclude this section with an evaluation of the implementation.

Description

Through classes, the object-oriented approach offers a good way for modularizing treatments that can be applied on data. These treatments are defined in methods. All the instances of a class share the same treatments. Moreover, these treatments are immutable: they never change as long as the instance exists. Because of this immutability, the notion of a method is a safe, but rigid, way for defining treatments.

The Command design pattern provides a way of defining treatments independently from the class where they will be applied. Several different commands can be defined and assigned to as many classes as needed.

Aspect-oriented Implementation

This section defines our aspect-oriented implementation of the Command design pattern. As with the Observer design pattern, we define an abstract aspect that provides the generic part of the implementation. This aspect is then extended to be specialized for a real command.

Generic Part of the Implementation

The code that is shared by all commands is defined in the `AbstractCommandAspect` aspect. Listing 8-12 presents the code of this aspect.

Listing 8-12. *Implementation of the Command Design Pattern Using AspectJ*

```
1 package aop.patterns.command;
2
3 public abstract aspect AbstractCommandAspect pertarget(receiver()){
4
5   private Command command = null;
6   public void setCommand(Command c) {
7     command = c;
8   }
9
10  protected abstract pointcut receiver();
11
12  protected abstract pointcut execute();
13
14  before(Object receiver) : execute() && target(receiver) {
15    command.execute(receiver);
16  }
17 }
```

The preceding aspect implements the setCommand method, which sets the command to be executed. Commands implement the Command interface, which defines a single execute method. This method takes as a parameter the object (a Receiver's instance) that receives the command. The code of these two types appears in Listing 8-13.

Listing 8-13. *Interfaces to Be Used with the Command Design Pattern*

```
public interface Command {
  public void execute(Receiver receiver);
}

public interface Receiver {
  public void setCommand(Command command);
}
```

Two abstract pointcuts, receiver and execute, are defined in the AbstractCommandAspect aspect. The receiver pointcut designates the classes where the command is run. The execute pointcut designates the event that triggers the execution of the command. Notice that only one instance of the AbstractCommandAspect aspect exists per receiver: commands are not shared by receivers, and each different receiver handles its own commands.

Finally, a "before" advice (line 14) is defined to launch the execution of the command. This advice code is executed before the joinpoints included in the execute pointcut; in other words, before the events that will be designated as triggers. Notice that this pointcut is parameterized with the target object of the joinpoint, that is to say, the object where the command is to be performed.

Implementation of Commands

A concrete aspect can now be defined to integrate the Command pattern into the Stats class (see Listing 8-14).

Listing 8-14. *Concrete AspectJ Aspect to Bind the Command Design Pattern to the Stats Class*

```
1 package aop.patterns.command;
2 public aspect CommandAspect extends AbstractCommandAspect {
3   public void Stats.save() {}
4   protected pointcut receiver() : initialization(Stats.new(..));
5   protected pointcut execute() : call(void Stats.save());
6 }
```

This aspect designates the instances of the Stats class as the receivers of the pattern (line 4). An empty method, named save, is introduced in the Stats class. Call operations on this method are included in the execute pointcut (line 5). Given the definition of the "before" advice in AbstractCommandAspect, the command will be executed before the calls to the save method.

Several new commands can now be defined and associated to the Stats class. The FileSaver class, shown in Listing 8-15, provides an example of such a command.

Listing 8-15. *FileSaver Command*

```
package aop.patterns.command;

import java.io.FileOutputStream;
import java.io.PrintWriter;

public class FileSaver implements Command {

  private String fileName;

  public FileSaver(String fileName) {
    this.fileName = fileName;
  }

  public void execute(Receiver receiver) {
    Stats stats = (Stats)receiver;
    try {
      FileOutputStream output = new FileOutputStream(fileName);
      PrintWriter writer = new PrintWriter(output);
      writer.println("STATISTICS");
      writer.println("Number of orders: "+stats.getOrders());
      writer.println("Total amount: " +stats.getTotalAmount());
      writer.println("Status: "+stats.getStatus());
      writer.flush();
      writer.close();
    }
```

```
      catch (Exception e) {
        System.err.println(e);
      }
    }
  }
}
```

The `CommandExample` class in Listing 8-16 provides a way of testing the aspect-oriented implementation of the Command design pattern with the command `FileSaver`.

Listing 8-16. *Main Class for Testing the Command Design Pattern*

```
package aop.patterns.command;

public class CommandExample {
  public static void main(String[] args) {
    Stats stats = new Stats();
    CommandAspect.aspectOf(stats)
      .setCommand(new FileSaver("c://temp/statistics.txt"));

    stats.incOrders();
    stats.addAmount(10);
    stats.incOrders();
    stats.addAmount(10);
    stats.incOrders();
    stats.addAmount(10);

    stats.save();
  }
}
```

When run, this program generates a text file that contains the following data:

```
STATISTICS
Number of orders: 3
Total amount: 30.0
Status: OK
```

Evaluation of the Implementation

With the four criteria defined by Hannemann and Kiczales, we can evaluate our implementation as follows.

- *Locality*: The class that receives commands is free from any code managing these commands. This code is located in the `AbstractCommandAspect` abstract aspect. The calls to commands are handled by concrete aspects that extend `AbstractCommandAspect`.

- *Reusability*: The management of commands is reused systematically.

- *Composition transparency*: The aspect is not invasive. The behavior of the classes that receives commands is extended, but not modified.

- *(Un)pluggability*: The link between the commands and the receivers of a command is weak. The pointcuts for receivers and executions define precisely where the design pattern must be integrated.

The Chain of Responsibility Design Pattern

The fourth design pattern that we study with regards to aspect-oriented programming techniques is the Chain of Responsibility. We begin by providing a quick description of this pattern, and proceed by giving an implementation of the pattern using AspectJ. We then conclude this section with an evaluation of the implementation.

Description

The Command design pattern presented in the previous section allows the definition of commands that are executed by objects. The Chain of Responsibility design pattern is more or less an extension of this principle and allows you to group several commands in a chain. When the chain is executed, each element of the chain is visited. When visited, an element either performs a command or does nothing.

A pure object-oriented, aspect-free implementation of the Chain of Responsibility design pattern generally relies on a `Handler` interface. Each command of a chain must implement this interface, which generally provides two methods: `setSuccessor` for setting the successor of the current command in the chain, and `handle` for performing the command. Depending on the conditions chosen by the programmer, the `handle` method can perform the command and delegate the call to the next element in the chain; it can also just perform the command or just delegate the call.

Aspect-oriented Implementation

The implementation that we propose for the Chain of Responsibility design pattern uses the notion of aspect precedence. In the previously presented design patterns, an abstract aspect was defined to implement the code that was shared by all the commands in a chain. This abstract aspect was then extended for each concrete command. Aspect precedence is the notion used for ordering the execution of these commands in the chain.

Generic Part of the Implementation

The generic part of our implementation of the Chain of Responsibility design pattern is defined in the `AbstractChainAspect` abstract aspect shown in Listing 8-17.

Listing 8-17. *Implementation of the Chain of Responsibility Design Pattern Using AspectJ*

```
1 package aop.patterns.chainOfResponsibility;
2
3 public abstract aspect AbstractChainAspect pertarget(receiver()){
4     protected abstract pointcut receiver();
```

```
 5      protected abstract pointcut execute();
 6      protected abstract void handle();
 7      after() : execute() {
 8          handle();
 9      }
10 }
```

With our implementation of the Observer and Command design pattern, the abstract `receiver` pointcut will designate the objects where the Chain of Responsibility pattern needs to be integrated.

The abstract `execute` pointcut defines the "condition," which triggers the execution of the chain.

The "after" advice (line 7) calls the abstract method `handle`. This method will be concretized into subaspects to define the behavior implemented by each command in the chain.

Implementation of a Chain of Commands

We now define two simple commands, `Step1ChainAspect` and `Step2ChainAspect`, which will be put in a chain (see Listing 8-18).

Listing 8-18. *Concrete Aspect to Bind the Chain of Responsibility Design Pattern to the Stats Class*

```
 1 package aop.patterns.chainOfResponsibility;
 2
 3 public aspect Step1ChainAspect extends AbstractChainAspect {
 4   protected pointcut receiver() : initialization(Stats.new(..));
 5   protected pointcut execute() : call(void Stats.incOrders());
 6
 7   protected void handle() {
 8     System.out.println("OrderHandler 1");
 9   }
10 }
11
12 public aspect Step2ChainAspect extends AbstractChainAspect {
13
14   declare precedence : Step1ChainAspect;
15
16   protected pointcut receiver() : initialization(Stats.new(..));
17   protected pointcut execute() : call(void Stats.incOrders());
18
19   protected void handle() {
20     System.out.println("OrderHandler 2");
21   }
22 }
```

Both aspects apply on the instances of the `Stats` class (see the pointcut receiver on lines 4 and 16). Both are also triggered when the `Stat.incOrders` method is called (see the pointcut execute on lines 5 and 17).

The important point in this example is the use of the `declare precedence` clause at line 14, which allows the definition of the aspect order in the chain. Here, the aspect `Step2ChainAspect` will be executed after `Step1ChainAspect`.

The `ChainExample` class in Listing 8-19 illustrates the usage of our implementation of the Chain of Responsibility design pattern.

Listing 8-19. *Main Class for Testing the Chain of Responsibility Design Pattern*

```
package aop.patterns.chainOfResponsibility;

public class ChainExample {
  public static void main(String[] args) {
    Stats stats = new Stats();
    stats.incOrders();
    stats.addAmount(10);
    stats.incOrders();
    stats.addAmount(10);
    stats.incOrders();
    stats.addAmount(10);
  }
}
```

When run, this program displays the following output:

```
OrderHandler n°1
OrderHandler n°2
OrderHandler n°1
OrderHandler n°2
OrderHandler n°1
OrderHandler n°2
```

Evaluation of the Implementation

With the four criteria defined by Hannemann and Kiczales, we can evaluate our implementation as follows:

- *Locality*: The class where the chain of responsibility applies is free from any code related to the management of this pattern. The aspect composition mechanism handles the ordering of commands within a chain.

- *Reusability*: The management of the chain is reused systematically. The implementation of any new chain only requires the definition of the new chain elements by extending the abstract aspect.

- *Composition transparency*: The aspect is not invasive. The behavior of the classes that receives commands is extended, but not modified.

- *(Un)pluggability*: The link between the chain of commands and the receivers is weak. The pointcuts for receivers and executions define precisely where the design pattern must be integrated.

The Proxy Design Pattern

The last design pattern that we study with regards to aspect-oriented programming techniques is the Proxy. We begin by providing a quick description of this pattern, and proceed by giving an implementation of the pattern using AspectJ.

Description

In many situations, the objects involved in a program cannot communicate directly through local method calls. For example, objects in a distributed program are separated by a network. In such situations, a proxy is used to transfer the communications from client to server over the network. Distribution is not the only situation where proxies are useful. For example, if the access to an object needs to be restricted to authorized users, a proxy can be inserted to perform access checks.

A proxy is an object that acts as a representative for another object. A proxy can be generic; in this case, it acts as a representative for any kind of object. Conversely, a proxy can be specific and implement the same interface as the object it is representing.

The treatments performed by the proxy are out of the scope of design patterns. The simplest existing proxy delegates the call to the main object without performing any additional treatments.

In the remainder of this section, we take the example of a proxy that performs access control checks.

Aspect-oriented Implementation

Our implementation of the Proxy design pattern for access control checks relies on an abstract aspect. Concrete aspects will be defined later when we set the authorization rights and denote the actual methods where the checks are to be applied.

Generic Part of the Implementation

The code of the abstract aspect is shown in Listing 8-20.

Listing 8-20. *Implementation of the Proxy Design Pattern Using AspectJ*

```
1 package aop.patterns.accessproxy;
2
3 public abstract aspect AbstractAccessProxyAspect {
4     protected String user;
5     protected String password;
6
```

```
 7   public void setAuthentication(String user,String password) {
 8      this.user = user;
 9      this.password = password;
10   }
11
12   protected abstract boolean isAuthorized();
13   protected abstract pointcut accessControl();
14
15   before() : accessControl() {
16     if (!isAuthorized()) {
17       throw new RuntimeException("Unauthorized access to: "+
18          thisJoinPoint.getSignature().getName());
19     }
20   }
21 }
```

The setAuthentication method sets the current user's login and password. The
isAuthorized method is concretized into subaspects to define the access policy.

The accessControl abstract pointcut is associated to methods that should be protected
against unauthorized accesses. The "before" advice (line 15) performs the check and throws an
exception if the access is denied.

Implementation of Proxies

In Listing 8-21, we define a simple concrete aspect where the access is only granted to the user
with the login "admin" and the password "admin" for the methods of the Stats class.

Listing 8-21. *Concrete Aspect to Bind the Proxy Design Pattern to the Stats Class*

```
package aop.patterns.accessproxy;

public aspect AccessProxyAspect extends AbstractAccessProxyAspect {

  protected boolean isAuthorized() {
    if ("admin".equals(user)&&"admin".equals(password)) {
      return true;
    }
    return false;
  }

  protected pointcut accessControl() : call(* Stats.*(..));
}
```

The program in Listing 8-22 uses this aspect. The login and password must be provided as
command-line arguments.

Listing 8-22. *Main Class for Testing the Proxy Design Pattern*

```
package aop.patterns.accessproxy;

public class ProxyExample {
  public static void main(String[] args) {
    Stats stats = new Stats();
    if (args.length==2) {
      AccessProxyAspect.aspectOf().setAuthentication(args[0],args[1]);

      stats.incOrders();
      stats.addAmount(10);
      stats.incOrders();
      stats.addAmount(10);
      stats.incOrders();
      stats.addAmount(10);
    }
  }
}
```

Summary

In this chapter, we presented the aspect-oriented implementation of five well-known design patterns: Singleton, Observer, Command, Chain of Responsibility, and Proxy.

For these five cases, the implementation follows this principle: an abstract aspect is defined to hold the code that is generic in the implementation of the pattern. This abstract aspect defines abstract pointcuts that designate the locations in the program where the pattern is to be integrated and the conditions under which the pattern must be triggered. This abstract aspect is then extended to define the code, which is specific to, for example, a command or a proxy.

The aspect-oriented implementations of these five design patterns lead to solutions that are more interesting than pure object-oriented, aspect-free implementations. It is, however, not the case for all existing design patterns. Patterns such as the Factory pattern or the Interpreter pattern do not benefit as much from aspects.

Deciding whether a design pattern will benefit from an aspect-oriented implementation is a matter of evaluating whether

- The pattern defines a crosscutting structure.

- The four criteria of locality, reusability, composition transparency, and (un)pluggability defined by Hannemann and Kiczales are met.

- The pattern leaves the structure of the base program unchanged.

CHAPTER 9

Quality of Service and AOP

Since computing capacity follows the famous Moore's law, software limits are constantly being pushed back, and applications are becoming increasingly more complex. This complexity has to be managed and controlled because it can induce shortcomings and failures that can impact the application's *Quality of Service*. Quality of Service is a broad topic that covers several complex issues. In this chapter, we will not enter into the details of the topic, but we will focus on techniques that help to ensure that the functions implemented by the application are correctly defined and executed. These techniques can be seen as a first step toward more complex Quality of Service issues.

Several techniques can be used to manage the complexity of an application. This chapter introduces three complementary techniques, all of which can be improved by using AOP:

- *Design by Contract*: This design methodology aims to formalize the constraints that are linked to the use of classes. The principles of Design by Contract are far from being integrated into languages; they can, however, be implemented by using AOP.

- *Coverage Analysis*: This technique checks for completeness through the implementation of sound test cases and nonregression tests, which check whether the functions that are related to an implementation change are still behaving according to the initial specification. These tests can use the AOP code-instrumentation capabilities to better watch over the application's executions.

- *Administration and Supervision*: This technique keeps track of the running application in order to prevent incidents or repair failures. With AOP, the Administration and Supervision functions can be easily separated from the rest of the application.

Design by Contract

Design by Contract is a design methodology that consists of formalizing the use of application components. To do this, a number of logical constraints must be specified and checked by the components to guarantee that their behavior is consistent with their specifications.

Design by Contract concepts were popularized by Bertrand Meyer in his book, *Object-Oriented Software Construction, Second Edition* (Prentice Hall, 1997). Contracts were used in a number of languages, such as Eiffel, as early as 1985. AOP provides the basic techniques to efficiently implement Design by Contract.

Before detailing the AOP implementation of Design by Contract, we will first explain the main principles of this methodology in the Java context.

Foundations of Design by Contract

Most languages' basic consistency-control mechanisms, such as type checking, are not sufficient to ensure that a given class is properly used by a client program. The consistency of an instance state with a method call or result necessitates the use of a more evolved concept—*contracts*.

By implementing contracts, an application benefits in the following ways:

- Testing and debugging is improved. Contracts allow the strict definition of execution conditions.

- Documentation and reusability are improved. Contracts are clearly materialized in the component code or interface. The contracts can be taken into account to help avoid mistakes when a component is reused.

- Error handling is improved. When a contract is not fulfilled, the initial error can be more easily identified, and strategies can be implemented to overcome the problem.

Languages supporting Design by Contract can usually activate or deactivate the contracts at compile time or at run time to improve performance. Note that contracts may be of different natures, but they are not meant to replace any kinds of tests, such as security-related tests. This is so even though some of these tests might then become redundant and possibly be removed from the test suite.

Taxonomy of a Contract

A software-level contract can be compared to a legal contract. In a contract, there are typically two contracting parties (the contractors). In software, the two contractors are a user component and a provider component. A contract also defines an object, which defines what kind of relationship is materialized between the two contractors. In addition to the contractors and the object, a contract must also define mutual obligations, which regulate how the two contractors realize the object of the contract. In software, these obligations are defined through *assertions*.

■**Definition** Assertion—A logical Boolean expression that must be `true` at a given point in the program's execution.

In theory, an assertion can be used anywhere in the program's code. For instance, an assertion can be applied to a division operation to check that the divisor is different from zero. An assertion condition must be literal and should avoid method calls, which have some side effects.

Assertions have a generic form. However, object-oriented languages such as Java can use four well-known forms: *precondition*, *postcondition*, *class invariant*, and *internal invariant*.

■**Definition** Precondition—An assertion that must be verified before the execution of a method. If the precondition is `false`, the method must not be executed. For instance, a square-root method (`sqrt`) would have the precondition `parameter>=0`.

■**Definition** Postcondition—An assertion that must be verified at the end of a method execution. The postcondition allows you to verify that the method has been correctly executed. (From the user's perspective, the postcondition allows some assumptions about the values of that user's variables, so redundant tests can be avoided.) For instance, a square-root method (`sqrt`) would have the postcondition `result>=0`.

■**Definition** Class invariant—An assertion that must be verified by the state of the class (in other words, by all the states of all the class instances). The class invariant guarantees that the objects remain in consistent states. For instance, a `Triangle` class would have the class invariant `vertexes=3`, where `vertexes` is either an attribute of the class or the result of a calculation on several attributes of the class.

■**Definition** Internal invariant—An assertion that must be verified within the body of a method. The internal invariant helps to guarantee that the method is correctly implemented. For instance, in a method that simulates a loan calculation would have the internal invariant `total interest ratio >=0`.

Conflict Handling

A contract conflict occurs when one or several assertions are not verified. This conflict can arise for any reason, such as a hardware failure, the failure of a called routine, or a software bug that makes it impossible to satisfy the contract.

In such cases, three strategies can be applied:

- *Retrying*: An alternative strategy is available. The contractors should restore the invariants and make another attempt using a different strategy.

- *Organized panic*: No alternative is available. The contractors must restore the invariants, terminate, and report failure to the user by triggering an exception.

- *False alarm*: It is possible to continue, maybe after some corrective measures are taken.

Contract Inheritance

One of the key mechanisms of OOP is inheritance. When inheritance is used, obligations are also inherited, and the subclasses can modify the inherited contracts. To ensure that the subclasses offer at least the same level of service as the superclasses, these modifications must follow certain rules:

- For preconditions, subclasses keep the same conditions or make them less restrictive.

- For postconditions, subclasses keep the same conditions or make them more restrictive.

- For class invariants, the invariants of a superclass are automatically part of the invariants of the subclasses.

- For internal invariants, the invariants of a superclass are kept identical only if the subclass does not redefine the method that the invariant is defined about.

Contracts in Java

As requested by *Java Specification Request (JSR) 41: A Simple Assertion Facility*, Java 1.4 introduced some limited contract support, which is similar to that offered by the C language through the `assert` macro. The `assert` keyword that was added to Java can be in two forms:

- `assert <condition>`
- `assert <condition> : <value>`

In the first form, `assert` behaves as follows:

- If the Boolean `condition` returns `true`, the program execution continues.

- If the Boolean `condition` returns `false`, a `java.lang.AssertionError` is thrown.

In the second form, `assert` behaves as follows:

- If the Boolean `condition` returns `true`, the program execution continues.

- If the Boolean `condition` returns `false`, a `java.lang.AssertionError` is built by passing value to the error's constructor. The passed `value` must be either a constant string or a function returning an object (which is then converted into a string by the `toString` method).

Implementing Contracts with AOP

As shown in the previous section, Java provides very limited support for Design by Contract. In particular, Java 1.4 does not implement any of the notions of preconditions, postconditions, or class invariants. As we will show here, AOP provides useful techniques for implementing these notions in Java.

To illustrate this point, we will use the JBoss AOP framework, which allows you to activate and deactivate assertions without having to recompile the code. This process is not as straightforward with AspectJ. The provided examples can be easily transported into the JAC framework.

Implementing Preconditions

The program in Listing 9-1 defines and uses the `sqrt` method.

Listing 9-1. *An Example of the Use of the sqrt Method*

```
package aop.contracts.preconditions;

public class PreConditionExample {

    public double sqrt (double p) {
        return Math.sqrt(p);
    }

    public static void main(String[] args) {
        PreConditionExample t = new PreConditionExample();
        System.out.println("sqrt of 4 : "+t.sqrt(4));
        System.out.println("sqrt of 0 : "+t.sqrt(0));
        System.out.println("sqrt of -4 : "+t.sqrt(-4));
        System.out.println("sqrt of 9 : "+t.sqrt (9));
    }
}
```

If you run the program without any preconditions, you obtain the results that are shown in Listing 9-2.

Listing 9-2. *An Execution Trace Without Preconditions*

```
sqrt of 4 : 2.0
sqrt of 0 : 0.0
sqrt of -4 : NaN
sqrt of 9 : 3.0
```

As you can see, no exceptions are thrown when sqrt is called with a negative parameter (−4). In this case, the value returned by java.lang.Math.sqrt(double) is java.lang.Double.NaN to indicate that the result is "not a number."

By using JBoss AOP, you can implement a sqrt precondition within an interceptor (which corresponds to the notion of advice code), as shown in Listing 9-3.

Listing 9-3. *A Precondition Interceptor for the sqrt Method*

```
01   package aop.contracts.preconditions;
02
03   import java.lang.reflect.Method;
04
05   import org.jboss.aop.Interceptor;
06   import org.jboss.aop.Invocation;
07   import org.jboss.aop.InvocationResponse;
08   import org.jboss.aop.InvocationType;
09   import org.jboss.aop.MethodInvocation;
10
```

```
11  public class PreConditionInterceptor implements Interceptor {
12
13    public String getName() {
14      return "PreConditionInterceptor";
15    }
16
17    public InvocationResponse invoke(Invocation invocation) throws Throwable {
18      if (invocation.getType() == InvocationType.METHOD) {
19        MethodInvocation methodInvocation = (MethodInvocation)invocation;
20        Method method = methodInvocation.method;
21        if ("sqrt".equals(method.getName())) {
22          Double parameter = (Double) methodInvocation.arguments[0];
23          if (parameter.doubleValue() < 0) {
24            throw new Error("Unfulfilled precondition");
25          }
26        }
27      }
28      InvocationResponse rsp = invocation.invokeNext();
29      return rsp;
30    }
31  }
```

The interceptor in Listing 9-3 implements the org.jboss.aop.Interceptor interface and its two methods, getName and invoke. The invoke method behaves as follows:

1. The invocation type—InvocationType.CONSTRUCTOR, InvocationType.METHOD, InvocationType.FIELD_READ, or InvocationType.FIELD_WRITE—is tested (see line 18). This program is interested only in method invocations.

2. If the name of the invoked method is sqrt, the precondition is checked (see line 21).

3. The value of the sqrt argument is obtained from the arguments attribute of the methodInvocation object (see line 22).

4. If the parameter has a negative value, an error is thrown (see line 24).

To actually apply the precondition to the program, the jboss-aop.xml file must be modified to declare that a new pointcut is associated with the interceptor. For this example, the jboss-aop.xml file must contain the code that is shown in Listing 9-4.

Listing 9-4. *The Deployment of the Precondition Interceptor*

```
01  <interceptor-pointcut
02      methodFilter="ALL" fieldFilter="NONE" constructorFilter="NONE"
03      class="aop.contracts.preconditions.PreConditionExample">
04
05        <interceptors>
06          <interceptor class=
07                  "aop.contracts.preconditions.PreConditionInterceptor"/>
```

```
08        </interceptors>
09
10  </interceptor-pointcut>
```

The XML tags in Listing 9-4 define the class (see line 3) that the interceptor is applied to (see line 6). The `methodFilter`, `fieldFilter`, and `constructorFilter` parameters define the pointcut; in this case, only the methods are advised. Note that because of these parameters, the first `if` of the `invoke` method is not needed. Since no consistency checks are performed on the interceptor type by JBoss AOP, the `if` test can be kept to make sure that the interceptor works only on methods—even if a pointcut tries to apply the interceptor to something else.

Finally, after the program is compiled and correctly parameterized, the execution gives the results that are shown in Listing 9-5.

Listing 9-5. *The Execution Trace with the Precondition Interceptor*

```
sqrt of 4 : 2.0
sqrt of 0 : 0.0
java.lang.Error: Unfulfilled precondition
    ...
Exception in thread "main"
```

When the precondition is not fulfilled, the program cannot continue its execution—unless some conflict-resolution strategy is explicitly implemented. This behavior is better than the default. Note that you can activate and deactivate the precondition—without any recompilation—by modifying the `jboss-aop.xml` file.

Implementing Postconditions

Postconditions often access more data than preconditions. This data includes:

- The result of the invoked method
- The values of the parameters object attributes before and/or after the execution of the invoked method

The implementation of postconditions is illustrated by the example—which purposely contains a bug—that is shown in Listing 9-6.

Listing 9-6. *An Example of an Incorrect Increment Function*

```
package aop.contracts.postconditions;

public class PostConditionExample2 {

    public int increment(int p) {
        return p++;
    }
```

```
    public static void main(String[] args) {
        PostConditionExample2 t = new PostConditionExample2();
        System.out.println("incrémente 1 : "+t.increment(1));
    }
}
```

The body of the increment method should be return ++p;. For this method, the postcondition is implemented by the interceptor that is shown in Listing 9-7.

Listing 9-7. *A Postcondition Interceptor for the Increment Function*

```
package aop.contracts.postconditions;

import java.lang.reflect.Method;

import org.jboss.aop.Interceptor;
import org.jboss.aop.Invocation;
import org.jboss.aop.InvocationResponse;
import org.jboss.aop.InvocationType;
import org.jboss.aop.MethodInvocation;

public class PostConditionInterceptor implements Interceptor {

  public String getName() {
    return "PostConditionInterceptor";
  }

  public InvocationResponse invoke(Invocation invocation)  throws Throwable {
    boolean incrementInvocation = false;
    int incrementParameterValue = 0;

    if (invocation.getType() == InvocationType.METHOD) {
      MethodInvocation methodInvocation = (MethodInvocation)invocation;
      Method method = methodInvocation.method;
      if ("increment".equals(method.getName())) {
        incrementInvocation = true;
        incrementParameterValue = ((Integer) methodInvocation.arguments[0])
                                  .intValue();
      }
    }
    InvocationResponse rsp = invocation.invokeNext();
    if (incrementInvocation) {
      int result = ((Integer)
      rsp.getResponse()).intValue();
      if (result != (incrementParameterValue + 1)) {
        ...
        throw new Error(errorMsg.toString());
      }
```

```
    }
    return rsp;
  }
}
```

The interceptor is activated by adding the pointcut in Listing 9-8 to the jboss-aop.xml file.

Listing 9-8. *The Deployment of the Postcondition Interceptor*

```
<interceptor-pointcut
    methodFilter="ALL" fieldFilter="NONE" constructorFilter="NONE"
    class="aop.contracts.postconditions.PostConditionExample">

    <interceptors>
        <interceptor class="aop.contracts.postconditions.PostConditionInterceptor"/>
    </interceptors>
</interceptor-pointcut>
```

Now, if the program is executed, the trace messages in Listing 9-9 are obtained.

Listing 9-9. *The Trace of the Increment Function when the Postcondition is Applied*

```
java.lang.Error: Unfulfilled post-condition for increment.
The result (1) is not equal to an incrementation of the passed parameter (1).
    ...
Exception in thread "main"
```

This example shows that a clean Design by Contract approach, implemented with AOP, will help you detect bugs concerning program values.

Implementing Invariants

There are two types of invariants—class and internal—that we have spoken about. A class invariant usually needs to be checked after the execution of a method that can potentially modify the state of the object. Not all methods should be checked. Indeed, an intermediate method, which is part of a higher-level method defined for the same class, may leave the object in an inconsistent state. It is only when the higher-level method ends that the object should be left in a consistent state. Selecting the methods that the invariant is checked for can be achieved either by advising only certain methods or by using cflow. The latter solution disables the checking of the invariant when the advised method is in the control flow of a higher-level method (usually belonging to the same class). This solution is more generic but slightly less efficient than the former one because the aspect system adds some run-time tests to determine whether the current method execution belongs to a given control flow. These run-time tests are called *residues*.

The advice code in Listing 9-10 shows the implementation of an invariant that ensures that a state field always equals 1.

Listing 9-10. *Advice Code for a* state *Invariant*

```
...
public InvocationResponse invoke(Invocation invocation)
  throws Throwable {
    InvocationResponse rsp = invocation.invokeNext();

    if (invocation.getType() == InvocationType.METHOD) {
        MethodInvocation methodInvocation = (MethodInvocation)invocation;
        Method method = methodInvocation.method;
        Object target = methodInvocation.targetObject;
        int state = target.getClass().getDeclaredField("state").getInt(target);
        if (state != 1) {
            throw new Error("Broken class invariant.");
        }
    }
    return rsp;
}
...
```

As you can see, testing an invariant is similar to testing a postcondition, except that the target object's state has to be accessed through the java.lang.reflect API.

Testing Applications

To guarantee Quality of Service for the end user, applications need to be tested. Since AOP allows code instrumentation for controlling and logging an application's execution, AOP is a useful tool for implementing tests in a simple way.

Two main categories of tests exist:

- Structural

- Functional

A *structural test*, or *white-box test*, verifies the application by checking its static structure (its code or any equivalent representation). Such a test aims to identify static problems—such as bad programming practice, unused variables, and unused methods—in the implementation of the application. A typical structural test is *coverage analysis*, which consists of executing the application in order to detect unused parts. Note that the Java compiler already implements some of these verifications—locally, within method bodies.

A *functional test*, or *black-box test*, verifies that the behavior of the application is consistent with its specification. Functional tests are widely used in the development process. In particular, these tests can be automatically generated from scenarios, which are identified during the analysis and design stages. Among the functional tests, the *nonregression tests* consist of executing two different versions of the application with the same scenarios. The purpose of such tests is to detect potential differences in the behavior of the different versions.

The following sections show how AOP can be used to implement some of these tests.

Coverage Analysis

Coverage analysis can be implemented at several granularity levels. With most of the AOP technologies, the granularity is limited to the accessing of fields and the invocation of methods and constructors. This type of coverage analysis is called *function coverage analysis.*

A coverage-analysis tool is composed of two elements: the *recorder* and the *comparator.* The recorder is in charge of executing the application and recording all the invoked methods and accessed attributes. The comparator compares the record with the program's structure to detect unused fields or methods.

We now present an example that implements only the recorder, which is the part that specifically uses AOP. The recorder generates a comma-separated value (CSV) file so that the file will be readable using standard tools such as Microsoft Excel. The following columns are defined:

- The type of call or access

- The name of the class that the called or accessed element belongs to

- The name of the element

- The type (for fields) or the return type (for methods)

- The parameter types (for methods and constructors)

- The declared exceptions (for methods and constructors)

The JBoss AOP interceptor is defined in Listing 9-11.

Listing 9-11. *A Simple Code-Coverage Analyzer Implemented with AOP*

```
001   package aop.tests.cover;
002
003   import java.io.FileNotFoundException;
004   import java.io.FileOutputStream;
005   import java.io.PrintWriter;
006   import java.lang.reflect.Constructor;
007   import java.lang.reflect.Field;
008   import java.lang.reflect.Method;
009
010   import org.jboss.aop.ConstructorInvocation;
011   import org.jboss.aop.FieldInvocation;
012   import org.jboss.aop.Interceptor;
013   import org.jboss.aop.Invocation;
014   import org.jboss.aop.InvocationResponse;
015   import org.jboss.aop.InvocationType;
016   import org.jboss.aop.MethodInvocation;
017   import org.jboss.util.xml.XmlLoadable;
018   import org.w3c.dom.Element;
019
020   public class CoverRecorderInterceptor implements Interceptor, XmlLoadable {
021       private PrintWriter out;
```

```
022
023     public String getName() {
024        return "CoverRecorderInterceptor";
025     }
026
027     public void importXml(Element parameter) {
028       Element t=(Element)parameter.getElementsByTagName("record-file").item(0);
029        String fileName = "";
030        if (t != null) {
031          fileName = t.getAttribute("value");
032          if ("".equals(fileName)){
033            throw new RuntimeException("...");
034          }
035        } else {
036          throw new RuntimeException("...");
037        }
038        try {
039          FileOutputStream stream=new FileOutputStream(fileName);
040          out = new PrintWriter(stream);
041        } catch (FileNotFoundException e) {
042          throw new RuntimeException("...");
043        }
044        out.println("Call type,Class,Name,ReturnType,parameters,exceptions");
045     }
046
047     public void recordMethodCall(String className,
048           String methodName,Class returnType,Class[] parameters,
049           Class[] exceptions) {
050        ...
051     }
052
053     public InvocationResponse invoke(Invocation invocation)
054            throws Throwable {
055       String filter = (String) invocation.getMetaData("cover", "filter");
056       if (filter != null && filter.equals("true")) {
057          return invocation.invokeNext();
058       }
059       InvocationResponse rsp = invocation.invokeNext();
060       InvocationType invocationType = invocation.getType();
061       if (invocationType == InvocationType.METHOD) {
062          MethodInvocation methodInvocation = (MethodInvocation)invocation;
063          Method method = methodInvocation.method;
064          String className = method.getDeclaringClass().getName();
065          String methodName = method.getName();
066          Class returnType = method.getReturnType();
067          Class[] parameters = method.getParameterTypes();
068          Class[] exceptions = method.getExceptionTypes();
```

```
069            out.print("Method call,");
070            recordMethodCall(className,methodName,returnType, parameters,
071                                        exceptions);
072        } else if (invocationType==InvocationType.CONSTRUCTOR) {
073            ConstructorInvocation constructorInvocation =
074                    (ConstructorInvocation)invocation;
075            Constructor constructor = constructorInvocation.constructor;
076            String className = constructor.getDeclaringClass().getName();
077            String methodName = "N/A";
078            Class returnType = null;
079            Class[] parameters = constructor.getParameterTypes();
080            Class[] exceptions = constructor.getExceptionTypes();
081            out.print("Constructor call,");
082            recordMethodCall(className,methodName,returnType, parameters,
083                                    exceptions);
084        } else if (invocationType == InvocationType.FIELD_WRITE ||
085                invocationType == InvocationType.FIELD_READ) {
086            if (invocationType == InvocationType.FIELD_READ) {
087                out.print("Field read access,");
088            } else {
089                out.print("Field write access,");
090            }
091            FieldInvocation fieldInvocation = (FieldInvocation)invocation;
092            Field field = fieldInvocation.field;
093            out.print(field.getDeclaringClass().getName());
094            out.print(',');
095            out.print(field.getName());
096            out.print(',');
097            out.print(field.getType());
098        }
099        out.println();
100        out.flush();
101        return rsp;
102    }
103    ...
104 }
```

The importXml method (see line 27) initializes the interceptor from the information contained in the jboss-aop.xml file—in particular, from the value parameter of the record-file tag, which defines the output file name.

The recordMethodCall method (see line 50) uses the out attribute to write the passed parameters in a readable way. This method is used to record method and constructor calls.

The invoke method is the heart of the recorder. It verifies that the invoked element needs to be recorded (see line 55), performs an introspection on the invocation, and writes the expected data to the file (which is accessible through the out field).

The recorder will be tested on the program that is shown in Listing 9-12.

Listing 9-12. *A Simple Example to be Recorded*

```java
package aop.tests.cover;

public class CoverExample {

    private static int myField = 0;

    public int increment(int value) {
        return ++value;
    }

    public int decrement(int value) {
        return --value;
    }

    public static int[] test(Object[] t,Object j)
            throws Exception,ArrayIndexOutOfBoundsException {
        System.out.println("Reading myField : "+myField);
        return null;
    }

    public static void main(String[] args) {
        CoverExample t = new CoverExample();
        System.out.println("Increment 1 : "+t.increment(1));
        System.out.println("Decrement 1 : "+t.decrement(1));
        try {
            test(null,null);
        } catch (Exception e) {}
    }
}
```

The running of the recorder on the program in Listing 9-12 is parameterized by the jboss-aop.xml file that is shown in Listing 9-13.

Listing 9-13. *The Deployment of the Recorder Interceptor*

```xml
<interceptor-pointcut methodFilter="ALL" constructorFilter="ALL"
                                    fieldFilter="ALL" group="cover">
    <interceptors>
        <interceptor class="aop.tests.cover.CoverRecorderInterceptor"
                            singleton="true">
            <record-file value="d:\\temp\\recordcover.csv" />
        </interceptor>
    </interceptors>
</interceptor-pointcut>

<class-metadata group="cover" class="aop.tests.cover.CoverExample">
```

```
<default>
    <filter>false</filter>
</default>
<method name="main">
  <filter>true</filter>
</method>
</class-metadata>
```

The pointcut is defined for all the potentially recorded elements (constructors, methods, and fields) in the cover group, which is defined through the class-metadata tag. (Here, only one tag is used for the sole class of the program.) When associating the interceptor with the pointcut, a recorder-specific tag (record-file) is added. This tag defines the output file name and is handled by the importXml method.

Metadata is then associated with the CoverExample class, which is defined as part of the cover group. The filter variable, which is used by the interceptor to determine whether a method should be analyzed, is initialized.

Running CoverExample produces the trace file that is shown in Listing 9-14.

Listing 9-14. *The Recording Output File*

```
Call type,Class,Name,Return / Type,parameters,exceptions
Field write access,aop.tests.cover.CoverExample,myField,int
Constructor call,aop.tests.cover.CoverExample,N/A,N/A,,
Method call,aop.tests.cover.CoverExample,increment,int,int,
Method call,aop.tests.cover.CoverExample,decrement,int,int,
Field read access,aop.tests.cover.CoverExample,myField,int
Method call,aop.tests.cover.CoverExample,test,int[],\
java.lang.Object[];java.lang.Object,\
java.lang.Exception;java.lang.ArrayIndexOutOfBoundsException
```

Figure 9-1 shows what the trace file looks like when it is opened with Microsoft Excel.

Call Type	Class	Name	Return/Type	Parameters	Exceptions
Field write access	aop.tests.cover.CoverExample	myField	int		
Constructor call	aop.tests.cover.CoverExample	N/A	N/A		
Method call	aop.tests.cover.CoverExample	increment	int	int	
Method call	aop.tests.cover.CoverExample	decrement	int	int	
Field read access	aop.tests.cover.CoverExample	myField	int		
Method call	aop.tests.cover.CoverExample	test	int[]	java.lang.Object[];java.lang.Object	java.lang.Exception;java.

Figure 9-1. *A coverage-analysis trace file in Microsoft Excel*

Nonregression Tests

Detecting regressions consists of recording a reference behavior in one version of an application and, then, while a newer version of the application is running, comparing the obtained record to the newer version (the version to be tested). If a difference is detected, that difference must be analyzed to determine whether it is a regression.

This technique relies on two assumptions:

- The reference record corresponds to the correct behavior of the application and is bug free.

- The reference record is deterministic. In other words, recording the same version of the application with the same input always gives the same result.

To implement regression detection, both a recorder and a comparator must be implemented. The granularity is at the level of method invocations. The regression-recorder interceptor shown in Listing 9-15 is quite similar to the interceptor that was previously developed for coverage analysis.

Listing 9-15. *A Simple Regression Analyzer Implemented with AOP*

```
package aop.tests.regression;

import java.io.FileNotFoundException;
import java.io.FileOutputStream;
import java.io.PrintWriter;
import java.lang.reflect.Method;

import org.jboss.aop.Interceptor;
import org.jboss.aop.Invocation;
import org.jboss.aop.InvocationResponse;
import org.jboss.aop.InvocationType;
import org.jboss.aop.MethodInvocation;
import org.jboss.util.xml.XmlLoadable;
import org.w3c.dom.Element;

public class RegressionRecorderInterceptor implements Interceptor, XmlLoadable {
    private PrintWriter out;
    private String version;

    public String getName() {
        return "RegressionRecorderInterceptor";
    }

    public void importXml(Element parameter) {
        ...
    }

    public InvocationResponse invoke(Invocation invocation)  throws Throwable {
        String filter = (String) invocation.getMetaData("regression", "filter");
        if ((invocation.getType() != InvocationType.METHOD)
                || (filter != null && filter.equals("true"))) {
            return invocation.invokeNext();
        }
        InvocationResponse rsp = null;
```

```java
Object response = null;
Throwable exception = null;

try {
    rsp = invocation.invokeNext();
    response = rsp.getResponse();
} catch (Throwable e){
    exception = e;
}
MethodInvocation methodInvocation = (MethodInvocation)invocation;
Method method = methodInvocation.method;

String className = method.getDeclaringClass().getName();
String methodName = method.getName();
Object[] parameters = methodInvocation.arguments;

out.print(version);
out.print(',');
out.print(className);
out.print(',');
out.print(methodName);
out.print(',');
if (response!=null) {
    out.print(getValue(response));
} else if (method.getReturnType().isAssignableFrom(java.lang.Void.TYPE)) {
    out.print("void");
} else {
    out.print("null");
}
out.print(',');
StringBuffer temp = new StringBuffer();
for (int i = 0; i < parameters.length; i++) {
    if (parameters[i]!=null) {
        temp.append(getValue(parameters[i]));
    } else {
        temp.append("null");
    }
    temp.append(';');
}
if (temp.length()>0) {
    temp.deleteCharAt(temp.length()-1);
    out.print(temp);
}
if (exception!=null){
    out.print(',');
    out.print("throws ");
    out.print(exception.getClass().getName());
```

```
        }
        out.println();
        out.flush();

        return rsp;
    }

    private String getValue(Object o) {
        if (!o.getClass().isArray()) {
            return Integer.toString(o.hashCode());
        } else {
            StringBuffer value = new StringBuffer();
            Object[] temp = (Object[]) o;
            for (int i=0;i<temp.length;i++) {
                value.append(getValue(temp[i]));
                value.append('|');
            }
            return value.toString();
        }
    }
}

    ...
}
```

The major difficulty of the implementation shown in Listing 9-15 involves dealing with object values that are not easily represented as simple strings (for instance, arrays and user-defined class instances). For the sake of the example, we have defined the getValue method, which uses the java.lang.Object.hashCode method to get a unique representation of an object and that also deals with arrays. Note that the call to invocation.invokeNext() is performed within a try/catch block in order to record potential exceptions.

The recorder is tested on the program shown in Listing 9-16, which corresponds to the earlier version of the application.

Listing 9-16. *A Simple Example to Test for Regressions: Version 1*

```
package aop.tests.regression;

import java.util.Vector;

public class RegressionExample {

    public int increment(int value) {
        return ++value;
    }

    public int decrement(int value) {
        return --value;
    }
```

```
    public static void test(Object[] t,Object j)
                    throws Exception,ArrayIndexOutOfBoundsException {
        System.out.println("calling test ");
        throw new Exception("error in test");
    }

    public static void main(String[] args) {
        RegressionExample t = new RegressionExample();
        System.out.println("Increment 1 : "+t.increment(1));
        System.out.println("Decrement 1 : "+t.decrement(1));
        try {
            String[] array = {"str1","str2"};
            Object[] arrayOfArray = {array,"str3"};
            Vector v = new Vector();
            v.add("str4");
            v.add("str5");
            test(arrayOfArray,v);
        } catch (Exception e) {}
    }
}
```

To record the program's execution, we must now define the jboss-aop.xml file, which is shown in Listing 9-17.

Listing 9-17. *The Deployment of the Regression Interceptor*

```xml
<interceptor-pointcut methodFilter="ALL" constructorFilter="NONE"
                                fieldFilter="NONE" group="regression">
    <interceptors>
        <interceptor class="aop.tests.regression.RegressionRecorderInterceptor"
                    singleton="true">
            <record-file value="d:\\temp\\recordreg.csv" />
            <version value="1" />
        </interceptor>
    </interceptors>
</interceptor-pointcut>

<class-metadata group="regression"
                class="aop.tests.regression.RegressionExample">
    <default>
        <filter>false</filter>
    </default>
</class-metadata>
```

When the application is run, the record is generated, and the file opened with Excel gives the result shown in Figure 9-2.

Version	Class Name	Method Name	Response	Parameters	Exception
1	aop.tests.regression.RegressionExample	increment	2	1	
1	aop.tests.regression.RegressionExample	decrement	0	1	
1	aop.tests.regression.RegressionExample	test	void	3541024|3541025||3541026|;113313826	throws java.lang.Exception
1	aop.tests.regression.RegressionExample	main	void		

Figure 9-2. *The nonregression trace file generated for version 1 of the example*

The next step is to perform the same recording on a different version of the application. (Note that the version number in the `jboss-aop.xml` file must be changed before running the application.) The code for version 2 is shown in Listing 9-18.

Listing 9-18. *A Simple Example to Test for Regressions: Version 2*

```
package aop.tests.regression;

import java.util.Vector;

public class RegressionExample {
    public int increment(int value) {
        return value++;
    }

    public int decrement(int value) {
        return value--;
    }

    public static void test(Object[] t,Object j)
            throws Exception,ArrayIndexOutOfBoundsException {
        System.out.println("calling test");
        throw new ArrayIndexOutOfBoundsException("error in test");
    }

    public static void main(String[] args) {
        RegressionExample t = new RegressionExample();
        System.out.println("Increment 1 : "+t.increment(1));
        System.out.println("Decrement 1 : "+t.decrement(1));
        try {
            String[] array = {"str1","str2"};
            Object[] arrayOfArray = {array,"str3"};
            Vector v = new Vector();
            v.add("str4");
            v.add("str5");
            test(arrayOfArray,v);
        } catch (Exception e) {}
    }
}
```

After its execution is recorded, the application gives the trace file that is shown in Figure 9-3.

Version	Class Name	Method Name	Response	Parameters
1	aop.tests.regression.RegressionExample	increment	2	1
1	aop.tests.regression.RegressionExample	decrement	0	1
1	aop.tests.regression.RegressionExample	test	void	3541024|3541025||3541026|;113313826
1	aop.tests.regression.RegressionExample	main	void	
2	aop.tests.regression.RegressionExample	increment	1	1
2	aop.tests.regression.RegressionExample	decrement	1	1
2	aop.tests.regression.RegressionExample	test	void	3541024|3541025||3541026|;113313826
2	aop.tests.regression.RegressionExample	main	void	

Figure 9-3. *The nonregression trace file generated for version 2 of the example*

Finally, by using the filtering features of Excel, you can compare the two trace files and detect regressions. Figure 9-4 shows this comparison for the `increment` method. The comparison highlights the fact that the `increment` method does not return the same result in version 1 as it does in version 2.

Version	Class Name	Method Name	Response	Parameters	Exception
1	aop.tests.regression.RegressionExample	increment	2	1	
2	aop.tests.regression.RegressionExample	increment	1	1	

Figure 9-4. *A comparison of the* increment *method in version 1 and in version 2*

AOP for Application Administration and Supervision

Even though administration and supervision are of primary importance for n-tier applications, these tasks are barely taken into account by developers, who naturally tend to focus on the applications' main functions. Since they are not tackled up front, administration and supervision can benefit from the greater degree of separation among concerns that is provided by AOP. Indeed, it is interesting to independently develop some administration and supervision features so as to be able to plug and unplug these features when needed.

Certain standards—Simple Mail Transfer Protocol (SMTP) and Java Management Extensions (JMX)—are available for administration and supervision, and it is preferable to use them rather than code from scratch. In fact interoperability is often a requirement for administration and supervision because these tasks can crosscut several subsystems of an enterprise application.

JMX

With JMX, Java provides a standard specification and a library for administration and supervision. JMX relies on two main functionalities:

- The opening of Java components through a specific API so that the components become fully accessible to the administration and supervision tools

- A notification mechanism for implementing automatic checks when needed

Note that JMX is widely used by the administration consoles of the existing application servers.

The JMX architecture is composed of the three following layers:

- *Instrumentation*: The role of this layer consists of opening the components to the other layers. The components are then called *manageable resources.*

- *Agent*: This layer exploits the manageable resources of the previous layer and makes them accessible, through adapters, to the outer application (in other words, to the distributed services layer). This layer also offers several services—such as dynamic class loading, manageable-resources monitoring, and timers—that can be used by the distributed services layer.

- *Distributed services*: This layer gathers the application's external components. These components communicate with the agent layer through adapters and are mainly composed of the administration and supervision tools.

The JMX architecture is designed to be open and easy to use. The adapters of the agent layer make it easy for a JMX application to interoperate with standards and with existing administration and supervision tools (such as IBM Tivoli and Hewlett-Packard OpenView). The following sections present the different layers of JMX.

Instrumentation Layer

The instrumentation layer relies on the notion of the manageable resource. Resources are implemented as regular Java objects (beans) that must follow a set of conventions to be administered and supervised by JMX. These resources are called *MBeans*, which stands for *Manageable Beans.*

There are four types of MBeans: standard, dynamic, open, and model. Since this book is not dedicated to JMX, we will deal only with standard MBeans, which are general enough to demonstrate our point.

An MBean is a Java class if it implements an interface that is named from the class and the *MBean* suffix. For instance, a Stats class is an MBean if it implements a StatsMBean interface, as shown here:

```
package aop.management.jmx.simple;

public class Stats implements StatsMBean {
    ...
}
```

The role of the MBean interface is to define the fields and methods that are accessible from the agent layer. For each attribute, you must define a getter method and, if the attribute is modifiable, a setter method. The example in Listing 9-18 defines three read-only attributes and a reset method.

Listing 9-19. *A Simple MBean for Statistics Managment*

```
package aop.management.jmx.simple;

public interface StatsMBean {
    public int getOrders();
    public float getTotalOrdersAmount();
    public String getStatus();
    public void reset();
}
```

Agent Layer

The agent layer is implemented by a specific JMX component, named MBeanServer, that is defined in the MBeans specification. This component controls the communications between the manageable resources and the outer world.

The MBeanServer component defines useful services, such as the monitoring service that generates a notification when a field value is modified—thus allowing for the monitoring of the manageable resources. There are three types of monitors:

- CounterMonitor: This type monitors the numeric attributes and sends a notification event when a threshold value is reached. A new threshold value can then be calculated.

- GaugeMonitor: This type monitors the attributes and sends a notification event when a value goes under or over a limit value.

- StringMonitor: This type monitors the string values and can send a notification event when a string equals or differs from a reference string.

To be notified of monitoring events, Java classes must implement the javax.management. NotificationListener interface.

Distributed Services Layer

The distributed services layer consists of a set of tools that can be connected to the JMX agent through an adapter. The remainder of this chapter uses the HTTP adapter provided by MX4J (an open-source implementation of JMX 1.1). As shown in Figure 9-5, the HTTP adapter contains a GUI for administering the MBeans, creating new monitors, and more.

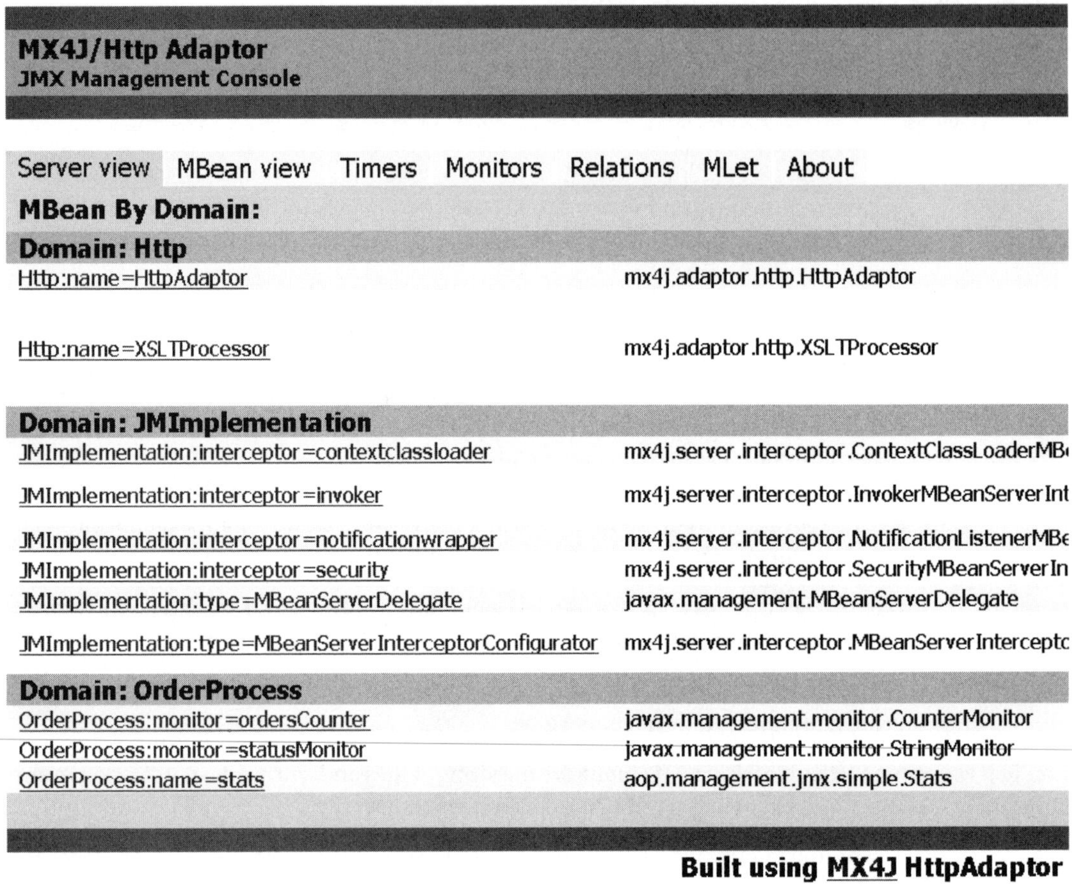

Figure 9-5. *The GUI for the HTTP adapter provided by MX4J*

Using JMX with AOP

As stated previously, to transform a regular Java object into a manageable resource, you need
to implement an MBean interface. When using JMX with an existing application, it can be
useful to leave the existing objects untouched and transparently integrate the MBean interface
with aspects.

As a reference example, we will use a simplified order-management application. The
application is composed of two parts:

- The order-management part, which updates certain statistics about the orders

- The order-creation part, which generates certain arbitrary orders to test the order-
  management part

Statistics are implemented in the Stats class, which is shown in Listing 9-20.

Listing 9-20. *An Implementation of the Statistics Manageable Bean*

```
public class Stats {
    private int orders = 0;
    private float totalAmount = 0;
    private String status = "OK";

    public int getOrders() {
        return orders;
    }

    public void incOrders() {
        orders++;
    }

    public float getTotalAmount() {
        return totalAmount;
    }

    public void addAmount(float p) {
        totalAmount+=p;
    }

    public String getStatus() {
        return status;
    }

    public void setStatus(String p) {
        status = p;
    }

    public void reset() {
        orders = 0;
        totalAmount = 0;
        status = "OK";
    }
}
```

The fields of the class are:

- orders: This field contains an order counter.

- totalAmount: This field accumulates the amounts of all the orders.

- status: This field represents the status ("OK" or "KO") of the ordering process.

As its name implies, the reset method resets the fields to their initial values. The Stats class is used by the main JMXExample class, which is shown in Listing 9-21.

Listing 9-21. *A Simple Client Program for the Stats MBean*

```
package aop.management.jmx.simple;

public class JMXExample {

    private static Stats statistics = new Stats();

    public static void sendOrder(float amount) {
        if (amount>0) {
            statistics.incOrders();
            statistics.addAmount(amount);
        } else {
            statistics.setStatus("KO");
            try {
                Thread.sleep(200);
            }
            catch (InterruptedException e) {
            }
            statistics.setStatus("OK");
        }
    }
```

```
    public static void main(String[] str) throws Exception {
        Injector injection = new Injector();
        injection.start();
    }
}
```

The sendOrder method is used by the Injector instance to simulate orders. If the passed amount is positive, statistics are updated. Otherwise, an error is generated, and the status attribute is set to "KO" for 200 milliseconds before being reset to "OK".

The Injector class shown in Listing 9-22 is a Java thread that generates arbitrary orders. More precisely, it generates ten random orders. Every five orders, an invalid order (with an amount of –1000) is generated.

Listing 9-22. *A Thread for the Random Generation of Orders*

```
package aop.management.jmx.simple;

public class Injector extends Thread {

    public void run() {
        float amount = 0;

        for (int i=1;i<=10;i++) {
            try {
```

```
            System.err.println("Order #"+i);
            sleep(Math.round(Math.random() * 5000));
        } catch (InterruptedException e) {}
        if ((i%5)==0) {
            JMXExample.sendCommand(-1000);
        } else {
            amount = Math.round(Math.random() * 1500);
            JMXExample.sendCommand(amount);
        }
      }
    }
}
```

Creating a Manageable Resource with an Aspect

To become a manageable resource, the Stats class must implement a StatsMBean interface, as shown in Listing 9-23.

Listing 9-23. *The MBean Interface for Ordering Statistics*

```
package aop.management.jmx.simple;

public interface StatsMBean {
    public int getOrders();
    public float getTotalAmount();
    public String getStatus();
    public void reset();
}
```

With MX4J, you must also define a class named StatsMBeanDescription, which is used for documenting the attributes and methods of the MBean. This class is shown in Listing 9-24.

Listing 9-24. *The MX4J Stats Bean Description*

```
package aop.management.jmx.simple;

import java.lang.reflect.Method;
import mx4j.MBeanDescriptionAdapter;

public class StatsMBeanDescription extends MBeanDescriptionAdapter {

    public String getAttributeDescription(String attribute) {
        if (attribute.equals("Orders")) {
            return "Number of orders ";
        } else if (attribute.equals("Status")) {
            return "Status of the ordering process";
        } else if (attribute.equals("TotalAmount")) {
            return "Total amount of the orders";
```

```
    } else {
        return "Unknown attribute";
    }
}

    public String getOperationDescription(Method method) {
        if (method.getName().equals("reset")) {
            return "Resets the attributes to their initial values ";
        } else {
            return "Unkown operation";
        }
    }
}
}
```

Once we have defined our interface and description class, we can use the introduction mechanism of AOP to transform our Java class into a manageable resource. With JBoss AOP, an empty interceptor must be defined, as shown in Listing 9-25.

Listing 9-25. *An Empty Interceptor for Allowing Introductions*

```
package aop.management.jmx.simple;

import org.jboss.aop.Interceptor;
import org.jboss.aop.Invocation;
import org.jboss.aop.InvocationResponse;

public class StatsMBeanInterceptor implements Interceptor {
    public String getName() {
        return "StatsMBeanInterceptor";
    }

    public InvocationResponse invoke(Invocation invocation) throws Throwable {
        return invocation.invokeNext();
    }
}
```

Finally, `jboss-aop.xml` defines the introduction, as shown in Listing 9-26.

Listing 9-26. *The Deployment of the MBean-Interface Introduction*

```
<interceptor-pointcut methodFilter="NONE" constructorFilter="ALL"
                      fieldFilter="NONE"
                      class="aop.management.jmx.simple.Stats">
  <interceptors>
    <interceptor class="aop.management.jmx.simple.StatsMBeanInterceptor"/>
  </interceptors>
</interceptor-pointcut>

<introduction-pointcut class="aop.management.jmx.simple.Stats">
```

```
<interfaces>aop.management.jmx.simple.StatsMBean</interfaces>
</introduction-pointcut>
```

In addition, the main class must be modified as shown in Listing 9-27.

Listing 9-27. *The Modification of the Example to Make it a JMX Client*

```
01  package aop.management.jmx.simple;
02
03  import javax.management.MBeanServer;
04  import javax.management.MBeanServerFactory;
05  import javax.management.ObjectName;
06  import javax.management.JMException;
07  import javax.management.Attribute;
08  import javax.management.monitor.GaugeMonitor;
09  import javax.management.monitor.StringMonitor;
10  import javax.management.monitor.CounterMonitor;
11  import javax.management.NotificationListener;
12  import javax.management.Notification;
13  import java.net.URL;
14  import java.net.MalformedURLException;
15  import java.util.Map;
16  import java.util.HashMap;
17  import java.util.List;
18  import java.util.ArrayList;
19
20  public class JMXExample {
21
22    private int port = 8080;
23    private String host = "localhost";
24    private static Stats statistics = new Stats();
25
26    public static void sendCommand(float amount) {
27        ...
28    }
29
30    public void start() throws JMException, MalformedURLException {
31      MBeanServer server = MbeanServerFactory.createMBeanServer("OrderProcess");
32      ObjectName serverName = new ObjectName("Http:name=HttpAdaptor");
33      server.createMBean("mx4j.adaptor.http.HttpAdaptor",serverName,null);
34      server.setAttribute(serverName,new Attribute("Port",new Integer(port)));
35      server.setAttribute(serverName,new Attribute("Host",host));
36      ObjectName processorName = new ObjectName("Http:name=XSLTProcessor");
37      server.createMBean("mx4j.adaptor.http.XSLTProcessor",processorName,null);
38      server.setAttribute(processorName, new Attribute("UseCache",new
                                        Boolean(false)));
39      server.setAttribute(serverName, new
                        Attribute("ProcessorName",processorName));
```

```
40
41     server.registerMBean(statistics, new ObjectName("OrderProcess:name=stats"));
42     ...
43     server.invoke(serverName, "start", null, null);
44   }
45
46   public static void main(String[] str) throws Exception {
47       JMXExample t = new JMXExample();
48       t.start();
49       Injector injection = new Injector();
50       injection.start();
51   }
52 }
```

The purpose of this modification is to handle the initialization of the MBeanServer component and the HTTP adapter and to register the manageable resource. In our example, the
adapter is accessible through the http://localhost:8080 address, which is defined by the
added fields on lines 22 and 23 in Listing 9-27. An instance of MBeanServer is created on line 31,
and the adapter is initialized on line 39. The manageable resource is then registered in the
MBeanServer component (see line 5). Finally, we define two monitors. (For clarity, the actual
code of line 42 is shown in Listing 9-28.)

Listing 9-28. *The Definitions of the Monitors for Listing 9-27*

```
01   CounterMonitor ordersCounter = new CounterMonitor();
02   ObjectName ordersCounterName =
03         new ObjectName("OrderProcess","monitor","ordersCounter");
04   server.registerMBean(ordersCounter, ordersCounterName);
05   ordersCounter.setThreshold(new Integer(5));
06   ordersCounter.setOffset(new Integer(5));
07   ordersCounter.setNotify(true);
08   ordersCounter.setDifferenceMode(false);
09   ordersCounter.setObservedObject(new ObjectName("OrderProcess:name=stats"));
10   ordersCounter.setObservedAttribute("Orders");
11   ordersCounter.setGranularityPeriod(100L);
12   ordersCounter.addNotificationListener(
13       new NotificationListener() {
14           public void handleNotification(Notification notification,
16                                           Object handback) {
17               System.out.println(
18               "JMX Notification - Orders : threshold overflow");
19           }
20       }, null, null);
21   ordersCounter.start();
22
23   StringMonitor statusMonitor = new StringMonitor();
24   ObjectName statusMonitorName = new ObjectName("OrderProcess","monitor",
25       "statusMonitor");
```

```
26  server.registerMBean(statusMonitor,statusMonitorName);
27  statusMonitor.setNotifyDiffer(true);
28  statusMonitor.setNotifyMatch(true);
29  statusMonitor.setStringToCompare("OK");
30  statusMonitor.setObservedObject(new ObjectName("OrderProcess:name=stats"));
31  statusMonitor.setObservedAttribute("Status");
32  statusMonitor.setGranularityPeriod(100L);
33  statusMonitor.addNotificationListener(
34      new NotificationListener() {
35          public void handleNotification(Notification notification,
36                                                  Object handback) {
37              if (notification.getType().equals("jmx.monitor.string.differs")) {
38                  System.out.println("JMX notification - Abnormal process ");
39              } else {
40                  System.out.println("JMX notification - Process OK");
41              }
42          }
43      }, null, null);
44  statusMonitor.start();
```

The monitor of line 1 in Listing 9-28 checks the number of incoming orders. Every five orders, the monitor emits a notification event, which is received by the listener of line 13. The monitor of line 20 checks the status attribute of the Stats bean and emits a notification when the attribute's state changes. These notifications are received by the listener of line 34.

When run, the application gives the output that is shown in Listing 9-29.

Listing 9-29. *The Output of the JMX Example*

```
JMX notification - Process OK
Order #1
Order #2
Order #3
Order #4
Order #5
JMX notification - Abnormal process
Order #6
JMX notification - Process OK
Order #7
JMX notification - Orders : threshold overflow
Order #8
Order #9
Order #10
JMX notification - Abnormal process
JMX notification - Process OK
```

As you can see, the application emitted notifications as expected. The delay comes from the monitors' granularity period, which must be set to 100 milliseconds with the setGanularityPeriod method of the javax.management.monitor.Monitor class.

We can now use the HTTP adapter's GUI to reset the Stats class, as shown in Figure 9-6.

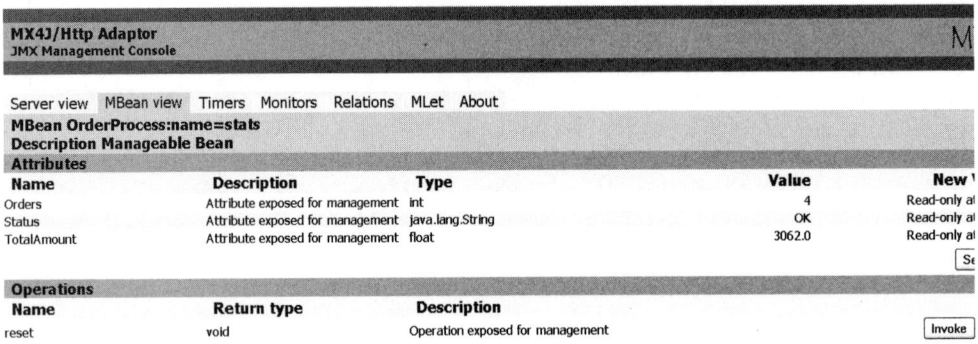

Figure 9-6. *Invoking the* reset *method through the HTTP adapter of MX4J*

Extending a Manageable Resource with an Aspect

Through the use of AOP, we have been able to extend a regular Java class into a manageable resource. In some cases, it is interesting to transparently introduce new functions or attributes. Here, we propose to add a property that contains the mean amount of orders. To do so, we will first modify StatsMBean and StatsMBeanDescription to take the new attribute into account, as shown in Listing 9-30.

Listing 9-30. *The Enhanced* Stats *MBean*

```
package aop.management.jmx.mixin;

public interface StatsMBean {
    public int getMOrders();
    public float getMTotalAmount();
    public float getMeanOrderAmount();
    public String getMStatus();
    public void mReset();
}
```

Next, we will create a mix-in class that implements the new attribute, as shown in Listing 9-31.

Listing 9-31. *A Mix-in Implementation that Defines the Introduction*

```
01   package aop.management.jmx.mixin;
02
03   public class StatsMBeanMixin implements StatsMBean {
04
05       private Stats advised;
06
```

```
07      public StatsMBeanMixin(Object p) {
08          advised = (Stats)p;
09      }
10
11      public float getMeanOrderAmount() {
12          if (advised.getOrders() > 0) {
13              return advised.getTotalAmount()/advised.getOrders();
14          } else {
15              return 0;
16          }
17      }
18
19  }
```

In JBoss AOP, a mix-in class constructor takes the advised object as a parameter (see line 7 in Listing 9-31). This parameter allows the mix-in class to access the advised object's public members, which here are those of the Stats class (see lines 12 and 13).

Finally, we can modify the introduction pointcut in the jboss-aop.xml file, as shown in Listing 9-32.

Listing 9-32. *The Deployment of the Introduced MeanOrderAmount Attribute*

```
<introduction-pointcut class="aop.management.jmx.mixin.Stats">
   <mixin>
      <interfaces>aop.management.jmx.mixin.StatsMBean</interfaces>
      <class>aop.management.jmx.mixin.StatsMBeanMixin</class>
      <construction>new aop.management.jmx.mixin.StatsMBeanMixin(this)
      </construction>
   </mixin>
</introduction-pointcut>
```

To check that the program is operational, this new, aspect-added attribute can be monitored with the JMX program that is shown in Listing 9-33.

Listing 9-33. *Monitoring the Introduced Attribute*

```
GaugeMonitor meanOrderAmountGauge = new GaugeMonitor();
ObjectName meanOrderAmountGaugeName =
    new ObjectName("OrderProcess","monitor","meanOrderAmountGauge");
server.registerMBean(meanOrderAmountGauge, meanOrderAmountGaugeName);
meanOrderAmountGauge.setThresholds(new Float(1000), new Float(500));
meanOrderAmountGauge.setNotifyHigh(true);
meanOrderAmountGauge.setNotifyLow(true);
meanOrderAmountGauge.setDifferenceMode(false);
meanOrderAmountGauge.setObservedObject(new ObjectName("OrderProcess:name=stats"));
meanOrderAmountGauge.setObservedAttribute("MeanOrderAmount");
meanOrderAmountGauge.setGranularityPeriod(100L);
meanOrderAmountGauge.addNotificationListener(
    new NotificationListener() {
```

```
    public void handleNotification(Notification notification,Object handback) {
        if (notification.getType().equals("jmx.monitor.gauge.low")) {
            System.out.println("JMX notification - Mean amount < 500 euros");
        } else {
            System.out.println("JMX notification - Mean amount > 1000 euros");
        }
    }
}, null, null);
meanOrderAmountGauge.start();
```

The JMX program gives the expected result, which is shown in Listing 9-34.

Listing 9-34. *The Output of the JMX Example with the Introduced Attribute*

```
JMX notification - Mean amount < 500 euros
JMX notification - Process OK
Order #1
Order #2
JMX notification - Mean amount > 1000 euros
Order #3
Order #4
Order #5
JMX notification - Abnormal process
Order #6
JMX notification - Process OK
Order #7
JMX notification - Orders : threshold overflow
Order #8
Order #9
Order #10
JMX notification - Abnormal process
JMX notification - Process OK
```

Summary

In this chapter, you saw how AOP—by verifying that an application's definition and execution correspond to its identified requirements—can be used to improve the application's Quality of Service. First, we showed how AOP can help to implement contracts in a straightforward way. Second, we showed the AOP implementation of two testing techniques: coverage analysis and nonregression tests. Finally, we showed how to use AOP for the seamless integration of JMX with a Java application.

Our AOP implementations did not provide more features than the existing tools do. However, our implementations showed how AOP can be used at a developmental level to improve code quality—without needing any specific support. Besides, an important advantage of AOP technologies is that it provides the ability to plug and unplug Quality of Service support when needed—even at run time if dynamic AOP tools are used.

CHAPTER 10

Presentation of the Sample Application

This chapter discusses the architecture and design details of a sample application that we'll use as a case study to demonstrate the strengths of AOP within the J2EE environment. This well-known, simple sample application serves to present the material in an understandable manner. The sample is developed from the Duke's Bank application of the Sun ONE J2EE application server. This application does not depend on Sun ONE specifically, and it can be used efficiently on any J2EE application server by adapting the deployment scripts.

Since this book focuses on AOP, this chapter does not go into the details of J2EE programming, but instead provides sufficient information on AOP and where it can be useful. A portion of this chapter, however, is a review of the J2EE design patterns used by the sample application. Please note that these patterns are different from the GOF patterns presented in Chapter 8. Additionally, we do not present the application's full code here; rather, we simply depict its design.

If you'd like more detailed information on the application, please visit the Downloads area of the Apress web site (http://www.apress.com) to access the case study code. If you aren't familiar with J2EE, we highly recommend doing some further reading on the subject before you examine the code in detail.

Sample Application Architecture

Duke's Bank is a classic J2EE application composed of tiers commonly found when developing enterprise applications. It is packaged so that the modules corresponding to each tier are clearly separated.

To simplify the code, we have slightly modified the Duke's Bank application, notably its packaging. For means of comparison, please refer to the original application, which is available on the Sun Microsystems web site.

The Application at a Glance

Before we cover the details of the tiers, we'll provide an overview of the whole application and its organization in the sections that follow.

The Participating Tiers

As J2EE advises, the application is composed of several tiers, as shown in Figure 10-1.

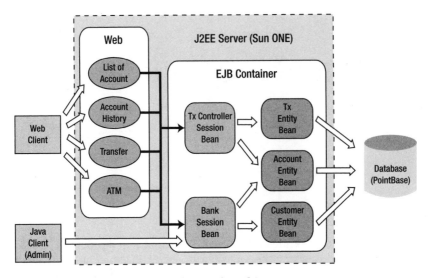

Figure 10-1. *The Duke's Bank application's architecture*

The tiers and their roles are as follows:

- The *data tier* allows for storage of the persistent data and is implemented within the PointBase relational database.

- The *business tier* contains EJBs that implement the application's logic. These EJBs are the session EJB, which provides a client's view of the application's business logic, and the entity EJB, which represents the persistent objects manipulated by the application. The business tier directly accesses the data tier, especially through the entity EJBs.

- The *presentation tier* allows the application to be accessed through a browser. It contains a web servlet/JSP container and accesses the business tier. Relative to the business tier, the presentation tier can be considered as a specific Java client tier.

- The *client tier* can be either a web (thin client) or a Java application. In this case, it is a web application, as it accesses the presentation tier through HTTP; in the case of Java, it directly accesses the business tier for locating the EJBs and goes through RMI for remote communication. In the latter case, the Java client self-manages its presentation on the client site (thick client).

Organizing and Packaging the Code

Although you can use any IDE, we recommend using the Eclipse open source IDE (we used Eclipse to develop the application presented in this chapter). Eclipse can be downloaded from http://www.eclipse.org. You can import the Eclipse project from the file system. The AJDT plug-in for AspectJ is required to compile it, and the installation of this plug-in is depicted in the appendixes.

In contrast with the original application, we structured this application by separating the code into several independent projects. This structure allows developers to work more efficiently, especially in the case of a large project, where different teams could more easily be assigned to the development of a given tier.

The Eclipse projects are as follows:

- The Commons project contains all the classes common to several tiers. For example, it contains the transfer objects and the service locators, described later in more detail, which are used by the client, business, and presentation tiers.

- The BusinessUtils project contains all the classes used by the business tier.

- The BusinessComponents project contains all the business Plain Old Java Objects (POJOs).

- The EJBComponents project contains all the business EJBs.

- The ClientUtils project contains all the classes used by the client tier.

- The BusinessDelegates project contains all the delegates, described later in further detail, that allow the clients to access the business objects transparently with regard to the communication layer.

- The ApplicationClient project contains the client application and its logic.

Figure 10-2 illustrates the project dependencies.

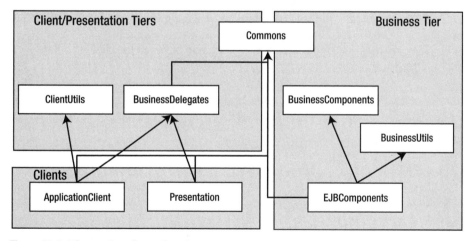

Figure 10-2. *The project dependencies*

For further clarification on the Eclipse project's packaging, please refer to the screen shots later in this chapter, which show the internal organization of the tiers.

Packages contain regular and aspectized application classes. This organization allows programmers to compare aspectized and regular code more efficiently, especially when using the AJDT plug-in and its aspect visualizer.

Deploying the Application

The application is packaged and deployed on the Sun ONE J2EE application server. Our web site publishes the packaging and compilation scripts, which allow the project to remain independent from the chosen IDE. Although they are developed under Eclipse, the projects do not use any specific plug-in or Eclipse technology, therefore it is easy to use a different IDE.

The relevant files are as follows:

- The deploySunONE.bat file, located at the root of the EJBComponent project, deploys the application on the Sun ONE server and uses the Ant script SunONE.xml in the same location. To execute this script, Ant must be installed and the Sun ONE server must be launched.

- The SunONE.properties file is used to configure and connect the server during the deployment phase.

- The property file of the client application, j2eeclient.properties, configures remote access to the Sun ONE server. This file, which must be installed on the client side, declares that the facade EJBs are accessible from the client. This file is independently published.

The next sections cover the AOP-specific details of the different tiers.

The Data Tier

The data tier is implemented by a set of tables within a relational database. Since this tier is based on the RDBMS technology, it does not benefit from AOP improvements. Only its access by another tier can be improved using AOP.

For our simple application, the direct object-relational mapping can be applied (one table equals one business class). The table-creation script is shown in Listing 10-1. The table customer_account_xref (line 34) implements the association between the clients and the accounts (multiple cardinality).

Listing 10-1. *Table Creation Script for the Sample Application*

```
1    // table creation
2    CREATE TABLE account
3       (account_id VARCHAR(8)
4           CONSTRAINT pk_account PRIMARY KEY,
5        type VARCHAR(24),
6        description VARCHAR(30),
7        balance DECIMAL(10,2),
8        credit_line DECIMAL(10,2),
9        begin_balance DECIMAL(10,2),
10       begin_balance_time_stamp TIMESTAMP);
11
12   CREATE TABLE customer
13      (customer_id VARCHAR(8)
14          CONSTRAINT pk_customer PRIMARY KEY,
15       last_name VARCHAR(30),
16       first_name VARCHAR(30),
17       middle_initial VARCHAR(1),
18       street VARCHAR(40),
```

```
19      city VARCHAR(40),
20      state VARCHAR(2),
21      zip VARCHAR(5),
22      phone VARCHAR(16),
23      email VARCHAR(30));
24
25  CREATE TABLE tx
26    (tx_id VARCHAR(8)
27        CONSTRAINT pk_tx PRIMARY KEY,
28      account_id VARCHAR(8),
29      time_stamp TIMESTAMP,
30      amount DECIMAL(10,2),
31      balance DECIMAL(10,2),
32      description VARCHAR(30));
33
34  CREATE TABLE customer_account_xref
35    (customer_id VARCHAR(8),
36      account_id VARCHAR(8));
37
38  CREATE TABLE next_account_id (id INTEGER);
39  CREATE TABLE next_customer_id (id INTEGER);
40  CREATE TABLE next_tx_id (id INTEGER);
```

The Business Tier

The application is composed of two distinct parts: a bank administration interface (accounts and users) and an interface that allows the users to perform transactions on their accounts. These two interfaces use a model that is implemented with EJBs and that directly accesses the data tier.

Session Facades

Session facades are session EJB components that implement the application logic or, more specifically, the business functions. A facade defines a high-level interface that enables the subsystems accessed through it to be used more easily. Among other roles, it implements an isolation layer that permits the subsystems to evolve with minimal impact for the facades' users.

Facades are generally stateless and delegate to the entity EJBs. Usually, the client tier accesses the entity EJBs through these facades. For this simple application, we define only two facades: the Bank facade and the TXController facade.

The Bank facade manages accounts and users, and is therefore used mainly for administrative purposes; users cannot, for example, create or delete accounts. Since the code is self-explanatory we do not describe all the services in detail.

The code in Listing 10-2 shows the interface that corresponds to the public services of the Bank facade—that is to say, the services that are accessible through an administration client.

Listing 10-2. *The Bank Interface*

```
package aop.j2ee.business.session.bank;
// imports
[...]
public interface Bank extends EJBObject {
  public String createAccount(String customerId, String type,
      String description, BigDecimal balance, BigDecimal creditLine,
      BigDecimal beginBalance, Date beginBalanceTimeStamp)
      throws RemoteException, IllegalAccountTypeException,
      CustomerNotFoundException, InvalidParameterException;

  public void removeAccount(String accountId)
  throws RemoteException, AccountNotFoundException,
         InvalidParameterException;

  public void addCustomerToAccount(String customerId,
    String accountId)
    throws RemoteException,
           AccountNotFoundException, CustomerNotFoundException,
           CustomerInAccountException, InvalidParameterException;

  public void removeCustomerFromAccount(String customerId,
    String accountId)
    throws RemoteException,
           AccountNotFoundException, CustomerRequiredException,
           CustomerNotInAccountException,
           InvalidParameterException;

  public ArrayList getAccountsOfCustomer(String customerId)
    throws RemoteException, AccountNotFoundException,
           InvalidParameterException;

  public AccountDetails getAccountDetails(String accountId)
    throws RemoteException, AccountNotFoundException,
           InvalidParameterException;

  public void setAccountType(String type, String accountId)
    throws RemoteException, AccountNotFoundException,
           IllegalAccountTypeException, InvalidParameterException;

  public void setAccountDescription(String description,
    String accountId)
    throws RemoteException, AccountNotFoundException,
           InvalidParameterException;

  public void setAccountBalance(BigDecimal balance,
                                String accountId)
```

```
      throws RemoteException, AccountNotFoundException,
            InvalidParameterException;

  public void setAccountCreditLine(BigDecimal creditLine,
                                   String accountId)
    throws RemoteException, AccountNotFoundException,
          InvalidParameterException;

  public void setAccountBeginBalance(BigDecimal beginBalance,
                                     String accountId)
    throws RemoteException, AccountNotFoundException,
          InvalidParameterException;

  public void setAccountBeginBalanceTimeStamp(
    Date beginBalanceTimeStamp, String accountId)
    throws RemoteException, AccountNotFoundException,
          InvalidParameterException;

  public String createCustomer (String lastName,
    String firstName, String middleInitial, String street,
    String city, String state, String zip, String phone,
    String email)
    throws InvalidParameterException, RemoteException;

  public void removeCustomer(String customerId)
    throws RemoteException, CustomerNotFoundException,
          InvalidParameterException;

  public ArrayList getCustomersOfAccount(String accountId)
    throws RemoteException, CustomerNotFoundException,
          InvalidParameterException;;

  public CustomerDetails getCustomerDetails(String customerId)
    throws RemoteException, CustomerNotFoundException,
          InvalidParameterException;

  public ArrayList getCustomersOfLastName(String lastName)
    throws InvalidParameterException, RemoteException;

  public void setCustomerName(String lastName, String firstName,
    String middleInitial, String customerId)
    throws RemoteException, CustomerNotFoundException,
          InvalidParameterException;

  public void setCustomerAddress(String street, String city,
    String state, String zip, String phone, String email,
    String customerId)
```

```
        throws RemoteException, CustomerNotFoundException,
            InvalidParameterException;
}
```

The TXController facade manages all the possible bank account transactions through a web application (i.e., an online banking application) or an ATM. Listing 10-3 shows the interface that corresponds to the TXController facade.

Listing 10-3. *The Transaction Controller (TxController) Interface*

```
package aop.j2ee.business.session.txcontroller;
// imports
[...]

public interface TxController extends EJBObject {

  public ArrayList getTxsOfAccount(Date startDate, Date endDate, String accountId)
    throws RemoteException, InvalidParameterException;

  public TxDetails getDetails(String txId)
    throws RemoteException, TxNotFoundException, InvalidParameterException;

  public void withdraw(BigDecimal amount, String description, String accountId)
    throws RemoteException, InvalidParameterException,
        AccountNotFoundException, IllegalAccountTypeException,
        InsufficientFundsException;

  public void deposit(BigDecimal amount, String description, String accountId)
      throws RemoteException, InvalidParameterException,
      AccountNotFoundException, IllegalAccountTypeException;

  public void transferFunds(BigDecimal amount, String description,
                                       String fromAccountId,
                                       String toAccountId)
      throws RemoteException, InvalidParameterException,
      AccountNotFoundException, InsufficientFundsException,
      InsufficientCreditException;

  public void makeCharge(BigDecimal amount, String description, String accountId)
     throws InvalidParameterException,
      AccountNotFoundException, IllegalAccountTypeException,
      InsufficientCreditException, RemoteException ;

  public void makePayment(BigDecimal amount, String description,
                      String accountId)
      throws InvalidParameterException, AccountNotFoundException,
      IllegalAccountTypeException, RemoteException;
}
```

Entity EJBs

The entity EJBs define the model on which the application's functions are applied, and they are usually implemented within the session facade EJBs. A client may directly access an EJB without going through a facade, but this is not advised for the following reasons. First, it can result in application services that are not well defined. Second, it couples the client's implementations to the business model, which reduces the application evolution possibilities.

The entity EJBs of our model are the accounts, the users, and the transactions. As explained earlier in reference to the data tier, each EJB corresponds to a table. The accounts implement the Account interface, as shown in Listing 10-4.

Listing 10-4. *The Accounts Interface*

```
package aop.j2ee.business.entity.account;
import aop.j2ee.commons.to.AccountDetails;
[...] // other imports

public interface Account extends EJBObject {
  public AccountDetails getDetails() throws RemoteException;
  public BigDecimal getBalance() throws RemoteException;
  public String getType() throws RemoteException;
  public BigDecimal getCreditLine() throws RemoteException;
  public void setType(String type) throws RemoteException;
  public void setDescription(String description) throws RemoteException;
  public void setBalance(BigDecimal balance) throws RemoteException;
  public void setCreditLine(BigDecimal creditLine) throws RemoteException;
  public void setBeginBalance(BigDecimal beginBalance) throws RemoteException;
  public void setBeginBalanceTimeStamp(Date beginBalanceTimeStamp)
    throws RemoteException;
}
```

The users are implemented using the Customer interface shown in Listing 10-5.

Listing 10-5. *The Customer Interface*

```
package aop.j2ee.business.entity.customer;
import aop.j2ee.commons.to.CustomerDetails;
[...] // other imports

public interface Customer extends EJBObject {
  public CustomerDetails getDetails() throws RemoteException;
  public void setLastName(String lastName) throws RemoteException;
  public void setFirstName(String firstName) throws RemoteException;
  public void setMiddleInitial(String middleInitial) throws RemoteException;
  public void setStreet(String street) throws RemoteException;
  public void setCity(String city) throws RemoteException;
  public void setState(String state) throws RemoteException;
  public void setZip(String zip) throws RemoteException;
  public void setPhone(String phone) throws RemoteException;
  public void setEmail(String email) throws RemoteException;
}
```

Transactions are EJBs implementing the Tx interface, as shown in Listing 10-6.

Listing 10-6. *The Tx Interface*

```
package aop.j2ee.business.entity.tx;
import aop.j2ee.commons.to.TxDetails;
[...] // other imports

public interface Tx extends EJBObject {
    public TxDetails getDetails() throws RemoteException;
}
```

Organizing the Business Tier Code

Figure 10-3 shows the organization of the EJBComponents Eclipse project, which corresponds to
the business tier and contains the EJBs.

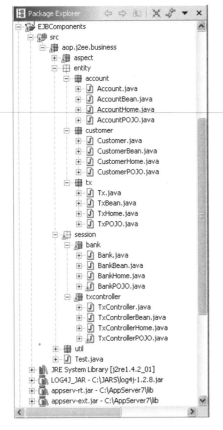

Figure 10-3. *Organization of the EJBComponents project (business tier)*

The root package is aop.j2ee.business. The entity and session EJBs are placed in two subpackages: aop.j2ee.business.entity and aop.j2ee.business.session. Within these packages, the EJB is defined within a specific package, which contains at least three implementation files:

- The file that defines the Remote interface (by convention, the business name)

- The file that defines the Home interface (by convention, the business name followed by Home)

- The file that defines the Bean implementation (by convention, the business name followed by Bean)

For example, for the EJB that implements the banking facade, the files are Bank.java, BankHome.java, and BankBean.java, respectively.

A fourth file, which ends with POJO, corresponds to the POJO implementation of the bean defined in the package; for instance, BankPOJO corresponds to BankBean in the bank package. This non-EJB implementation is made possible through the use of aspects, as we'll explain further in Chapter 12. Since this file contains the aspectized implementation of the EJB, it is easy for the developer to compare these two implementations and to visualize the impact of the aspects.

Choosing one of these functionally equivalent implementations is done within the deployment descriptor file, ejb-jar.xml, which is located in the META-INF directory of the Eclipse project. Listing 10-7 shows an example.

Listing 10-7. *Sample of a Deployment Descriptor File for the Sample Application (Bank)*

```
1    <ejb-jar>
2     <enterprise-beans>
3      [...]
4      <session>
5       <display-name>Bank</display-name>
6       <ejb-name>Bank</ejb-name>
7       <home>aop.j2ee.business.session.bank.BankHome</home>
8       <remote>aop.j2ee.business.session.bank.Bank</remote>
9       <ejb-class>aop.j2ee.business.session.bank.BankBean</ejb-class>
10      <session-type>Stateless</session-type>
11      <transaction-type>Bean</transaction-type>
12     </session>
13     [...]
14    </enterprise-beans>
15   </ejb-jar>
```

To use the aspectized implementation rather than the regular one, you must replace the line that declares the EJB class (line 9) with the following line:

```
<ejb-class>aop.j2ee.business.session.bank.BankPOJO</ejb-class>
```

All the aspects applied to the POJOs are defined in the aop.j2ee.business.entity.aspect package, which we discuss later in this chapter. Note that since this is an AspectJ project, it contains aspectj.jar in its CLASSPATH and uses ajc for compiling.

The Client Tier

The application defines two distinct clients: a Java client that uses Swing and allows for bank administration and a web client that accesses the presentation tier through HTTP, programmed using the Servlets/JSP technologies.

The Swing Client

The Swing client is an administration application developed using Java Swing API. It allows for the creation, modification, and deletion of users and accounts.

Figure 10-4 shows the Swing administration GUI, which consists of a simple two-part interface. The left side is used to print out messages, such as requested information or errors, and the right side is an input panel that allows for the creation or modification of user- and account-related information. The possible operations are accessible through the menu bar. The administration client's implementation depends solely on the Bank business facade.

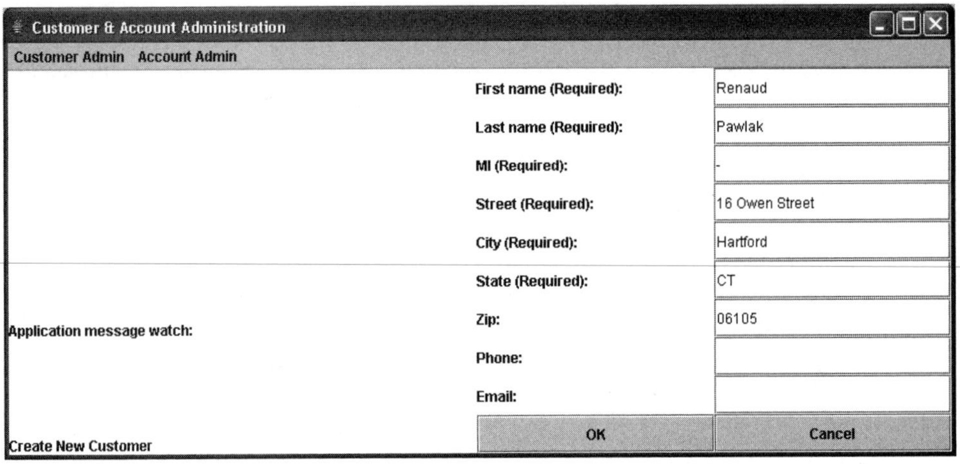

Figure 10-4. *The Swing GUI for the bank administration*

The Web Client

The web client is the interface that allows bank users to access and manage their accounts through a browser. Its logic is defined in the presentation tier, which is developed with the Servlets/JSP technologies. Figure 10-5 shows the web GUI.

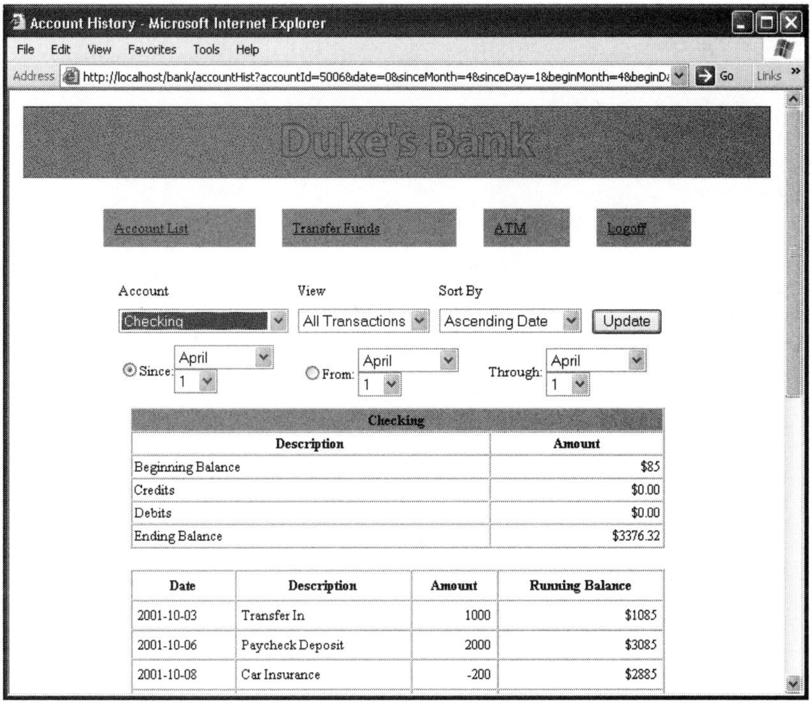

Figure 10-5. *The bank's web GUI*

Organizing the Java Swing Client Code

This section describes the Java Swing client code used for the bank administration. Figure 10-6 shows the Java client project's organization.

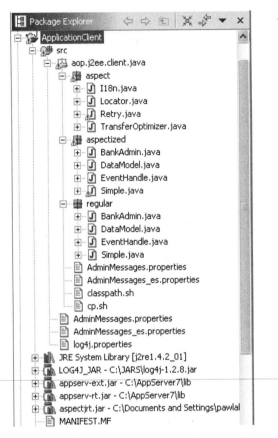

Figure 10-6. *Organization of the ApplicationClient project (Java Swing client tier)*

The root package is aop.j2ee.client.java. Within this package, you can find two versions of the application: the regular application developed without aspects (the regular package), and the aspectized version (the aspectized package). The aspect package contains all the AspectJ aspects of this latter version; this is an AspectJ project.

As shown in Figure 10-6, the Java administration client of the original version is simple. It is composed of four Java classes: BankAdmin, DataModel, EventHandle, and Simple. The BankAdmin class builds the actual GUI. It throws events that correspond to the possible actions of the users. These events are handled by the event managers as defined and installed in EventHandle. The DataModel class implements the effects of the actions in terms of calls to the business tier, specifically to the aop.j2ee.business.session.bank facade. Note that the Simple class is not part of the original application, but it will be used in the next chapter to test simple client-side logic without having to deal with the whole client.

The client layer is by no means a design to be followed; we use it simply as a means to describe the concerns that may arise when programming the Java client.

The Web Presentation Tier

The web presentation tier, which is programmed using Struts, is not aspectized because, in this context, the benefits are limited. In Chapter 13 we discuss the possible aspectization of the presentation tier design patterns in an application context not using Struts.

Sample Application Design

The design of the sample application was inspired by J2EE applications in general, and more specifically by J2EE good practices and design patterns.

We'll begin this section by presenting a selection of design patterns and solutions that are specific to J2EE and that have been used previously in this context. We'll then explain the ways in which using AOP improves the design of the sample application.

The original Duke's Bank application is included in the free distribution of the Sun ONE application server, which is available on the Sun Microsystems site. Please refer to the original application if you wish to make comparisons with the design presented here.

Using J2EE Design Solutions

The design of the original Duke's Bank application is simple. Not all the available J2EE design solutions are used, causing deficiencies in code modularity. For this case study, we have changed the application slightly, notably by following J2EE design patterns to improve the modularity of the application and also by modifying the organization of the code.

The use of J2EE design patterns offers two main advantages:

- These design patterns are well-tested, reusable design elements that allow us to follow J2EE best practices.

- J2EE design patterns are well documented and developers are familiar with their use (see http://java.sun.com/blueprints/corej2eepatterns/Patterns/index.html). Using J2EE design patterns allows developers to understand the design of the application better and makes it easier to identify the problems that we are looking to resolve using aspects.

Using EJBs in addition to J2EE design patterns allows us to integrate services automatically. For example, persistence can be managed in this way by the component container or container-managed persistence (CMP) by applying it to the entity EJB. The same applies to transactions, or container-managed transactions (CMTs), which can be integrated declaratively using the EJB deployment descriptors.

The next few sections briefly describe the different J2EE design solutions that we will develop further later in the chapter. For more details, please refer to the J2EE documentation (http://java.sun.com/j2ee/docs.html) and to the catalog of J2EE design patterns (see the references section at the end of this book).

J2EE Business Tier Design Patterns

In applications built using J2EE, the business tier is the middle tier, and it forms the interface between the client and the enterprise resources (data sources). It is therefore extremely important that this tier is implemented in a way that ensures good performance, as well as provides for ease of maintenance, evolution, scalability, and so on.

Use of a business tier is not compulsory, but it is, however, highly recommended. In applications with a business tier, clients can access the company's different data sources in a logical and consistent way, which is not the case if the application allows direct access to the database. Making data access consistent enables easier optimization of the application architecture. For example, global performance can be improved by using load balancing or caching on application servers. These improvements are linked to the use of a business layer and are only possible if certain basic rules are respected. J2EE design patterns state these rules explicitly.

The two most important design patterns for the business layer are the session facade pattern and the business object pattern, both of which are described in the sections that follow.

The Session Facade Pattern

The *session facade pattern* is simply a session EJB. Its principal functions are as follows:

- To ensure that the client is independent from the business model (the latter being subject to modifications over time).

- To allow access to the data via objects without shared states that can be managed and optimized automatically by the application server. Since the problem of state synchronization is avoided, the server itself constructs pools of session objects according to the different sessions opened by the clients.

- To create a functional interface to adding extra nonfunctional properties declaratively using deployment descriptors, as we will explain later.

- To provide remote access to identified services via the J2EE lookup and communication layers (*Java Naming and Directory Interface*, or *JNDI*, and *Remote Method Invocation*, or *RMI*). This access is also configured in the deployment descriptors.

The Business Object Pattern

The *business object pattern* allows the session facade objects to access data via entity EJBs, without resorting to direct use of the connectors for the different resources. As with the session facade, use of business objects is not compulsory but is recommended.

The principal functions of the business object pattern are as follows:

- The encapsulation of data access within the object-oriented model, which simplifies data access and avoids, for example, the need for SQL queries. The EJB model advocates, among other things, use of Home interfaces for resolving business objects.

- Use of deployment descriptors for the declarative and automatic introduction of nonfunctional properties such as persistence.

The Transfer Object Pattern

The use of other design patterns can also improve the design of a J2EE application, particularly in terms of performance. The *transfer object pattern* allows us to group together services used by a facade. This is useful when the services have fine-grained parameters that can cause multiple sequences of calls between the client and the server, as these calls tend to induce a great deal of network traffic, especially costly connections.

A transfer object implements the java.io.Serializable interface. The state of the transfer object corresponds to a set of parameters and return values for a group of services. A transfer object can be grouped inside another transfer object recursively; this is called a *composite transfer object*.

Transfer objects are shared by the client and business layers. They must be accessible to both layers and are therefore defined in the application's Commons project.

J2EE Client Tier Design Patterns

The client tier must use the remote resolving and communication APIs to access the services of the business tier. However, this can make the client-side code complicated. When this complication occurs, J2EE design pattern guidelines recommend the use of two design patterns: the service locator and business delegate. We describe these patterns in the sections that follow.

The Service Locator Pattern

The *service locator pattern* allows generic access to a service by hiding from the client the access mechanisms involved. Examples of this are the use of Home interfaces and using cache management to improve service resolution performance.

The service locator is generally implemented in the form of a singleton with a resolve method that the client uses directly. Service resolution is not limited to the session facades; we can, for example, access data sources in the same way.

The service locator pattern can also be used in the business layer when EJBs such as facades need to access services. Because different layers use the service locator, its code is contained within the application's Commons project.

Figure 10-7 shows the organization of the Commons project, which contains the classes and interfaces used by the client and business layers. As you would expect, it contains a package for managing exceptions (aop.j2ee.commons.exception), but also the transfer objects (aop.j2ee.commons.to) and the service locators (aop.j2ee.commons.util.locator) explained in this section.

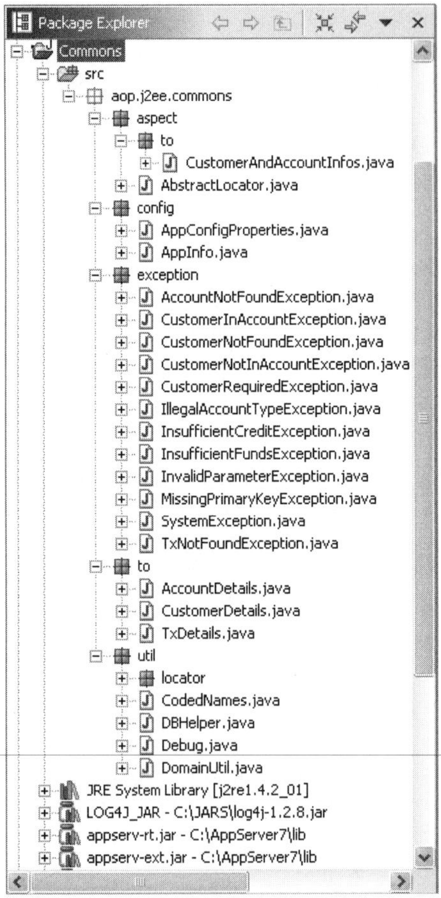

Figure 10-7. *Organization of the Commons project*

The Business Delegate Pattern

The *business delegate pattern* creates a client-side object, allowing the client to access the facades of the business layer. In general, a delegate has the same interface as the facade to which it is delegating, but this is not a requirement.

The main functions of the business delegate are as follows:

- To make the client independent of the facades, guaranteeing better application structure and independence of the projects. For example, with an application programmed in this way, recompiling the business layer has no effect on the clients.

- To simplify the client-side code by regrouping common or generic functions within the delegates. For example, a delegate can be used to group together replay policies or the processing of certain exceptions.

- To make the client more independent of the way services are resolved. The business delegate usually uses the service locator.

In our application, the client-side administration application uses a delegate to access the Bank facade. For organizational reasons, delegates can be put in a separate project, as shown in Figure 10-8.

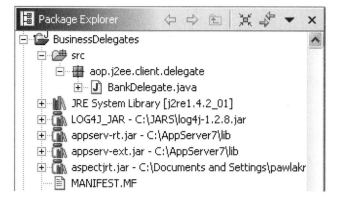

Figure 10-8. *Organization of the BusinessDelegates project*

J2EE Presentation Tier Design Patterns

A number of design patterns are recommended for use when developing the business tier of an application:

- The *front controller pattern* is used to centralize the management of requests.

- The *application controller pattern* is used to transparently manage application-level requests.

- The *context object pattern* is used to allow object encapsulation of the request parameters simplifying the code of the presentation layer.

- The *view helper pattern* is used to migrate complex processing in JSP pages to Java objects.

- The *intercepting filter pattern* is used to allow specific objects to systematically intercept requests and process them with additional functions in a modular and parameterizable way.

Although these design patterns are documented, using several together is not an easy task for designers or developers. It is often preferable to use frameworks that integrate the full range of presentation tier design patterns in a consistent and transparent manner. This is the chosen solution for the original version of the sample application, Duke's Bank, which is implemented using the Struts open source framework.

Automatic Integration Solutions

In the context of J2EE, we use deployment descriptors (see the XML code in this section) to configure nonfunctional services that are managed by the container. This technique allows us, for example, to integrate transactions into the facade services or declaratively add persistence to business objects. It is also possible to configure the components to include remote access features such as naming or declaring a remote interface, as well as features for managing rights. These solutions for automatic integration are referred to as *declarative management* or *container-managed* solutions.

Listing 10-8 shows a section of the XML file ejb-jar.xml.

Listing 10-8. *The ejb-jar.xml File for Automatic Integration of Technical Services*

```
<enterprise-beans>
 <session>
  <description>no description</description>
  <display-name>BankEJB</display-name>
  <ejb-name>BankEJB</ejb-name>
  <home>aop.j2ee.business.session.bank.BankHome</home>
  <remote>aop.j2ee.business.session.bank.Bank</remote>
  <ejb-class>aop.j2ee.business.session.bank.BankBean</ejb-class>
  <session-type>Stateless</session-type>
  <transaction-type>Container</transaction-type>
 </session>
</enterprise-beans>

<assembly-descriptor>
 <security-role>
  <role-name>BankCustomer</role-name>
 </security-role>
 <security-role>
  <role-name>BankAdmin</role-name>
 </security-role>

<container-transaction>
 <method>
  <ejb-name>BankEJB</ejb-name>
  <method-intf>Remote</method-intf>
  <method-name>getCustomersOfAccount</method-name>
  <method-params>
   <method-param>java.lang.String</method-param>
  </method-params>
 </method>
  <trans-attribute>Required</trans-attribute>
</container-transaction>
[...]
```

Listing 10-9 shows a section of the XML file sun-ejb-jar.xml.

Listing 10-9. *The sun-ejb-jar.xml File for Naming and Access*

```
<sun-ejb-jar>
<security-role-mapping>
  <role-name>BankCustomer</role-name>
```

```
    <group-name>Customer</group-name>
</security-role-mapping>
<security-role-mapping>
  <role-name>BankAdmin</role-name>
  <group-name>Admin</group-name>
</security-role-mapping>
  <enterprise-beans>
    <name>bank-ejb.jar</name>
    <unique-id>2059221019</unique-id>
    <ejb>
      <ejb-name>BankEJB</ejb-name>
      <jndi-name>ejb/bank</jndi-name>
      [...]
    </ejb>
  </enterprise-beans>
  [...]
</sun-ejb-jar>
```

These solutions simplify the programming task enormously, because rather than using APIs explicitly in our code, we configure the container declaratively. In this way, J2EE allows us to factor out a certain number of nonfunctional crosscutting concerns, a point that it has in common with AOP. The next section describes how AOP can be used to complement—or even replace—these solutions.

Using AOP

As you learned in Chapter 8, many design patterns can benefit from an aspect-oriented implementation. This also applies to a certain number of J2EE design patterns, where there are demonstrable advantages to using AOP. This is the case for the service locator and the business delegate, both evidently crosscutting. Other design patterns can also be improved by using AOP. For example, the facade and the business object can be made independent of the EJB technology used.

The automatic integration solutions discussed earlier can also be improved by using AOP, as they demonstrate the following associated problems:

- Because the container manages the integration automatically, there are very few ways to adjust this integration in cases where it is unsatisfactory or cannot be configured in the required way.

- Declarative configuration only works well for simple cases and often necessitates programming a complementary code fragment in Java, which limits its usefulness. It is sometimes preferable not to parameterize at all and rely on explicit design solutions such as design patterns and frameworks.

- Apart from in the case of normalized solutions, solutions for automatic integration often depend on the application server, which limits portability.

AOP avoids most of these limitations by integrating services in a modular way, using deployment descriptors when appropriate, but also AspectJ code, resulting in a technique that is both flexible and powerful.

Summary

This chapter presented a J2EE banking program that was constructed from the Duke's Bank sample application and showed its organization into projects and packages. This allowed us to explore its architecture and design comprehensively. After reading this chapter, you should now have a basic understanding of the design problems of this application and the ways in which AOP can resolve them.

The next two chapters present a detailed account of the use of AOP with this sample application, tier by tier. Although design elements may affect several tiers, it is best to concentrate on one at a time when implementing a design pattern. This allows the projects corresponding to each of the layers to remain independent of each another.

For each of the tiers, we will evaluate the improvements offered by AOP according to three criteria:

- Improvements in the implementation of the design patterns used, concentrating on J2EE design patterns

- Improvements to a design element that is recognized as being crosscutting, but that is not an identified design pattern or does not fit within the documented context of a design pattern

- Improvements whereby the design depends less on the J2EE technologies, especially EJBs

As far as the business layer is concerned, we will also evaluate the possibility of replacing automatic integration with a solution using AOP.

CHAPTER 11

■■■

Using AOP within the Sample Application's Business Tier

When implementing the business tier, programmers use J2EE design patterns. Most business tier J2EE design patterns rely on EJBs. The session facade pattern, for example, advises the use of a session EJB. Using EJBs allows for the automatic integration of additional concerns. J2EE design patterns are also simpler than GoF design patterns.

In this chapter, we will explore the use of AOP within the business tier of our reference application. You will see that, within this context, AOP has three main advantages:

- Making the application independent from EJB technology. In changing Enterprise environments, which rely on new technologies, independence is a desirable property.

- Bringing an alternative, more flexible solution to the existing automatic integration solutions.

- Simplifying the J2EE design pattern implementations and making them more transparent to the user.

AOP OR COMPONENT CONTAINERS?

AOP and component-based programming share the same goal: to separate the business logic from the technical concerns such as persistence and transactions, and to integrate them in a clear and automatic way. The major difficulty of integration comes from the interdependencies between the technical concerns, which are then interleaved at the code level, thus going against the fundamental principles of software engineering: encapsulation and separation of concerns.

Component containers integrate technical concerns at deployment time. For this, they rely on a component model, like EJB, and on deployment descriptors, which are defined as XML files for EJBs. The latter files parameterize the integration in a declarative manner. However, there is no simple solution to extend or modify the integration mechanics when needed. In these cases, the use of design patterns, external frameworks, or AOP can help the programmer to tune the integration.

Among all these solutions, AOP is the only one that specifies the integration in an imperative manner, that is to say, through a program, which keeps the base program unchanged and technologically independent. Indeed, in the case of design patterns, the program's structure must be modified. In the case of frameworks, dependencies need to be added towards the required APIs or classes need to be specialized. These are technological dependences that can be avoided with AOP.

Improving Business Tier Design Patterns

In this section, we present some design patterns that can be used in the business tier and discuss their weaknesses. We show that the use of AOP greatly increases the independence of the server tier objects when it comes to technological and design choices.

In particular, we stress the fact that all the server-side EJBs can be implemented as Plain Old Java Objects (POJOs) with the help of specific aspects. The use of EJBs then becomes transparent.

The Session Facade

In a J2EE application that uses EJBs, the session facade is a session EJB that manages a set of business objects and defines a middle-grained application interface. The advantages of using a facade have been outlined in the literature on standard GoF design patterns.

In J2EE design patterns, the session facade must implement the `javax.ejb.SessionBean` interface. This is how the application server automatically instantiates the class and handles session object pools for the clients. In addition, within the context of EJB, an EJB allows the facade to be directly accessible by remote clients through JNDI and RMI.

Regular Implementation

Without any aspects, the application facade for the `TxController` interface, from the package `aop.j2ee.business.session.txcontroller`, is implemented as shown in Listing 11-1. (Note that this interface has been introduced in Chapter 10 in the section "Session Facades.")

Listing 11-1. *The TxControllerBean Session Facade Implementation*

```
001    package aop.j2ee.business.session.txcontroller;
002
003    import java.sql.*;
004    import javax.sql.*;
005    import java.util.*;
006    import java.math.*;
007    import javax.ejb.*;
008    import javax.naming.*;
009    import java.rmi.RemoteException;
010    import aop.j2ee.business.entity.tx.Tx;
011    import aop.j2ee.business.entity.tx.TxHome;
012
013    import aop.j2ee.business.entity.account.AccountHome;
014    import aop.j2ee.business.entity.account.Account;
015    import aop.j2ee.commons.exception.*;
016    import aop.j2ee.commons.util.*;
017    import aop.j2ee.commons.to.*;
018    import aop.j2ee.business.util.EJBGetter;
019
020    public class TxControllerBean implements SessionBean {
021
```

```
022  // fields
023
024  private TxHome txHome;
025  private AccountHome accountHome;
026  private Connection con;
027  private SessionContext context;
028  private BigDecimal bigZero = new BigDecimal("0.00");
029
030  // implementation of the business interface
031
032    public void withdraw(BigDecimal amount,String descr,String accountId)
033      throws InvalidParameterException,
034                AccountNotFoundException,IllegalAccountTypeException,
035        InsufficientFundsException {
036      Account account = checkAccountArgsAndResolve(amount, descr, accountId);
037      try {
038        String type = account.getType();
039        if (DomainUtil.isCreditAccount(type))
040          throw new IllegalAccountTypeException(type);
041        BigDecimal newBalance = account.getBalance().subtract(amount);
042        if (newBalance.compareTo(bigZero) == -1)
043          throw new InsufficientFundsException();
044       executeTx(amount.negate(),descr,accountId,newBalance,account);
045      } catch (RemoteException ex) {
046        throw new EJBException("withdraw: " + ex.getMessage());
047      }
048  } // withdraw
049
050    public void transferFunds(BigDecimal amount,String descr,
051                              String fromAccountId,String toAccountId)
052    throws
053      InvalidParameterException,AccountNotFoundException,
054      InsufficientFundsException,InsufficientCreditException {
055      try {
056        Account fromAccount = checkAccountArgsAndResolve(
057          amount, descr, fromAccountId);
058        Account toAccount = checkAccountArgsAndResolve(
059          amount, descr, toAccountId);
060
061        String fromType = fromAccount.getType();
062        BigDecimal fromBalance = fromAccount.getBalance();
063
064        if (DomainUtil.isCreditAccount(fromType)) {
065          BigDecimal fromNewBalance = fromBalance.add(amount);
066          if (fromNewBalance.compareTo(
067              fromAccount.getCreditLine()) == 1)
068            throw new InsufficientCreditException();
```

```
069          executeTx(amount,descr,fromAccountId,fromNewBalance,fromAccount);
070        } else {
071          BigDecimal fromNewBalance = fromBalance.subtract(amount);
072          if (fromNewBalance.compareTo(bigZero) == -1)
073            throw new InsufficientFundsException();
074          executeTx(amount.negate(),descr,fromAccountId,
075                          fromNewBalance,fromAccount); } //transferFunds
076
077        String toType = toAccount.getType();
078        BigDecimal toBalance = toAccount.getBalance();
079
080        if (DomainUtil.isCreditAccount(toType)) {
081          BigDecimal toNewBalance = toBalance.subtract(amount);
082          executeTx(amount.negate(),descr,toAccountId,toNewBalance,toAccount);
083        } else {
084          BigDecimal toNewBalance = toBalance.add(amount);
085          executeTx(amount,descr,toAccountId,toNewBalance,toAccount);
086        }
087      } catch (RemoteException ex) {
088        throw new EJBException("transferFunds: " + ex.getMessage());
089      }
090    } // transferFunds
091
092    // same principles for other methods
093    [...]
094
095    // private methods
096
097    private void executeTx(BigDecimal amount,String descr,String accountId,
098      BigDecimal newBalance,Account account) {
099      try {
100        makeConnection();
101        String txId = DBHelper.getNextTxId(con);
102        account.setBalance(newBalance);
103        Tx tx=txHome.create(txId,accountId,new Date(),amount,newBalance,descr);
104      } catch (Exception ex) {
105        throw new EJBException("executeTx: " + ex.getMessage());
106      } finally {
107        releaseConnection();
108      }
109    } // executeTx
110
111    private Account checkAccountArgsAndResolve(
112      BigDecimal amount,String description,String accountId)
113    throws InvalidParameterException, AccountNotFoundException {
114
115      Account account = null;
```

```
116      if (description == null)
117        throw new InvalidParameterException("null description");
118      if (accountId == null)
119        throw new InvalidParameterException("null accountId");
120      if (amount.compareTo(bigZero) != 1)
121        throw new InvalidParameterException("amount <= 0");
122      try {
123        account = accountHome.findByPrimaryKey(accountId);
124      } catch (Exception ex) {
125        throw new AccountNotFoundException(accountId);
126      }
127      return account;
128    } // checkAccountArgsAndResolve
129
130    // ejb methods
131
132    public void ejbCreate() {
133      try {
134        txHome = EJBGetter.getTxHome();
135        accountHome = EJBGetter.getAccountHome();
136      } catch (Exception ex) {
137        throw new EJBException("ejbCreate: " + ex.getMessage());
138      }
139    } // ejbCreate
140
141    public void setSessionContext(SessionContext context) {
142      this.context = context;
143    }
144
145    public TxControllerBean() {}
146    public void ejbRemove() {}
147    public void ejbActivate() {}
148    public void ejbPassivate() {}
149
150    // Database functions
151
152    private void makeConnection() {
153      try {
154        InitialContext ic = new InitialContext();
155        DataSource ds =
156          (DataSource) ic.lookup(CodedNames.BANK_DATABASE);
157          con = ds.getConnection();
158      } catch (Exception ex) {
159        throw new EJBException("Unable to connect to database. ");
160      }
161    } // makeConnection
162
```

```
163    private void releaseConnection() {
164      try { con.close(); } catch (SQLException ex) {
165        throw new EJBException("releaseConnection: " + ex.getMessage());
166      }
167    } // releaseConnection
168  } // TxControllerEJB
```

This sample, taken in its original form from the Duke's Bank implementation, contains a set of concerns that is interesting to modularize:

- It implements the SessionBean interface (lines 20 and 27).

- In the business method implementations (line 30), there is a recurrent call to the method checkArgsAndResolve (lines 36, 57, 59, 111). This call has two roles: it allows the use of a method to check certain preconditions on the arguments, and it resolves the reference of an account by using its Home interface.

- It defines and handles references to other EJBs (lines 123, 134, 135).

- It implements and uses some database functions (lines 100, 101, 107, 150). The original Duke's Bank implementation does not use any particular integration technique for persistence but directly uses the JDBC API.

These concerns make the facade's code complicated and force the implementer to define private methods (line 95). These methods clarify the code; however, since they are ad hoc, their maintenance can be complex and error prone.

We will come back to these points in the remainder of the chapter. As for now, we focus primarily on the problem of implementing the J2EE facade design pattern (as depicted by Sun Microsystems) independently from the EJB session (lines 20 and 27).

AOP-based Implementation

AOP has a straightforward approach to making the code independent from the EJB technology: create an aspect for transforming POJOs into EJBs, and use an empty marker interface—similar to Serializable—to implement the aspect with intertype declarations based on this interface.

If the marker is

```
package aop.j2ee.business;
public interface SessionBeanProtocol {}
```

the following aspect POJOSession can transform a POJO implementing this interface into an EJB session:

```
package aop.j2ee.business.aspect;

import javax.ejb.*;
import aop.j2ee.business.aspect.marker.SessionBeanProtocol;

public aspect POJOSession extends EJBResolver {
  // common session bean behavior
```

```
declare parents: SessionBeanProtocol
                 extends javax.ejb.SessionBean;

private SessionContext SessionBeanProtocol.context;
public void SessionBeanProtocol
  .setSessionContext(SessionContext context) {
  this.context = context;
}
public void SessionBeanProtocol.ejbRemove() {}
public void SessionBeanProtocol.ejbActivate() {}
public void SessionBeanProtocol.ejbPassivate() {}
public void SessionBeanProtocol.ejbCreate() { [...] }
}
```

The implementation of the method ejbCreate (in the last line) contains certain initializations that are dedicated to EJBs.

In terms of modularity, the advantages are

- *Locality*: The code that implements the functions of the facade is located in a POJO, while the code dealing with the EJB session is in an aspect.

- *Reuse*: We can extend the SessionBeanProtocol interface depending on our needs and add new intertype declarations in POJOSession. Since the inheritance hierarchy is independent from the business, the reuse and factoring of functions common to EJB sessions are significantly increased.

- *Composition*: As the facade implementation is not coupled to the session facade design pattern, it is easier to use other patterns at the same time with less-complicated code.

Note that the POJOSession aspect extends the abstract aspect EJBResolver and does not impact the SessionBean's implementation. (This will be described later in this chapter, in the section "Business Tier Improvement: Beyond Design Patterns.")

The Business Object

J2EE design patterns advise the use of entity EJBs for the definition of persistent business objects. In theory, the use of an entity EJB allows the simple adding of transactional and persistence properties. However, several patterns or frameworks exist to deal with the same issues in a simpler and more efficient way.

For example, using the Hibernate Open Source framework for persistence is an efficient replacement for entity EJBs. Most of the available frameworks do not require specific extensions, and business objects are defined as POJO or traditional JavaBeans. For further evolutions, it is interesting for the application to leave the business objects as independent as possible from EJBs.

Regular Implementation

Listing 11-2 shows the implementation of an account as an entity EJB without the use of aspects.

Listing 11-2. *The Account EJB*

```
001  package aop.j2ee.business.entity.account;
002
003  import java.sql.*;
004  import javax.sql.*;
005  import java.util.*;
006  import java.math.*;
007  import javax.ejb.*;
008  import javax.naming.*;
009  import aop.j2ee.commons.exception.*;
010  import aop.j2ee.commons.util.Debug;
011  import aop.j2ee.commons.util.CodedNames;
012  import aop.j2ee.commons.util.DBHelper;
013  import aop.j2ee.commons.to.AccountDetails;
014
015  public class AccountBean implements EntityBean {
016
017    private String accountId;
018    private String type;
019    private String description;
020    private BigDecimal balance;
021    private BigDecimal creditLine;
022    private BigDecimal beginBalance;
023    private java.util.Date beginBalanceTimeStamp;
024    private ArrayList customerIds;
025
026    private EntityContext context;
027    private Connection con;
028
029    // business method
030
031    public AccountDetails getDetails() {
032      try {
033        loadCustomerIds();
034      } catch (Exception ex) {
035        throw new EJBException("loadCustomerIds:  " +ex.getMessage());
036      }
037      return new AccountDetails(
038        accountId, type, description, balance, creditLine, beginBalance,
039        beginBalanceTimeStamp, customerIds);
040    }
041
042    public BigDecimal getBalance() { return balance; }
043    public String getType() { return type; }
044    public BigDecimal getCreditLine() { return creditLine; }
045    public void setType(String type) { this.type = type; }
046    public void setDescription(String d) { this.description = d; }
```

```
047   public void setBalance(BigDecimal balance) { this.balance = balance; }
048   public void setCreditLine(BigDecimal n) { this.creditLine = n; }
049   public void setBeginBalance(BigDecimal n) { this.beginBalance = n; }
050   public void setBeginBalanceTimeStamp(java.util.Date beginBalanceTimeStamp) {
051     this.beginBalanceTimeStamp = beginBalanceTimeStamp;
052   }
053
054   // methods ejb home
055
056   public String ejbCreate(String accountId, String type, String description,
057     BigDecimal balance, BigDecimal creditLine, BigDecimal beginBalance,
058     java.util.Date beginBalanceTimeStamp, ArrayList customerIds)
059   throws CreateException, MissingPrimaryKeyException {
060     if ((accountId == null) || (accountId.trim().length() == 0)) {
061       throw new MissingPrimaryKeyException("ejbCreate: accountId is empty");
062     }
063     this.accountId = accountId;
064     this.type = type;
065     this.description = description;
066     this.balance = balance;
067     this.creditLine = creditLine;
068     this.beginBalance = beginBalance;
069     this.beginBalanceTimeStamp = beginBalanceTimeStamp;
070     this.customerIds = customerIds;
071     try { insertRow(); } catch (Exception ex) {
072       throw new EJBException("ejbCreate: " + ex.getMessage());
073     }
074     return accountId;
075   }
076
077   public String ejbFindByPrimaryKey(String primaryKey)
078     throws FinderException {
079     boolean result;
080     try {
081       result = selectByPrimaryKey(primaryKey);
082     } catch (Exception ex) {
083       throw new EJBException("ejbFindByPrimaryKey: " + ex.getMessage());
084     }
085     if (result) {
086       return primaryKey;
087     } else {
088       throw new ObjectNotFoundException("Row "+primaryKey+" not found.");
089     }
090   }
091
092   public Collection ejbFindByCustomerId(String customerId)
093     throws FinderException {
```

```
094      Collection result;
095      try {
096        result = selectByCustomerId(customerId);
097      } catch (Exception ex) {
098        throw new EJBException("ejbFindByCustomerId " + ex.getMessage());
099      }
100      return result;
101    }
102
103    public void ejbRemove() {
104      try {
105        deleteRow(accountId);
106      } catch (Exception ex) {
107        throw new EJBException("ejbRemove: " + ex.getMessage());
108      }
109    }
110
111    // ejb methods
112
113    public void setEntityContext(EntityContext context) {
114      this.context = context;
115      customerIds = new ArrayList();
116    }
117
118    public void unsetEntityContext() {}
119
120    public void ejbLoad() {
121      try {
122          loadAccount();
123      } catch (Exception ex) {
124        throw new EJBException("ejbLoad: " + ex.getMessage());
125      }
126    }
127
128    public void ejbStore() {
129      try {
130        storeAccount();
131      } catch (Exception ex) {
132        throw new EJBException("ejbStore: " + ex.getMessage());
133      }
134    }
135
136    public void ejbActivate() {
137      accountId = (String)context.getPrimaryKey();
138    }
139
140    public void ejbPassivate() {
```

```
141      accountId = null;
142    }
143
144    public void ejbPostCreate(String accountId, String type, String description,
145      BigDecimal balance, BigDecimal creditLine, BigDecimal beginBalance,
146      java.util.Date beginBalanceTimeStamp, ArrayList customerIds) {}
147
148    // database methods
149
150    private void makeConnection() { [...] }  // see TxControllerBean above
151    private void releaseConnection() { [...] } // idem
152    private void insertRow () throws SQLException {
153      makeConnection();
154      String insertStatement = "insert into account values (?,?,?,?,?,?,?)";
155      PreparedStatement prepStmt = con.prepareStatement(insertStatement);
156      prepStmt.setString(1, accountId);
157      prepStmt.setString(2, type);
158      prepStmt.setString(3, description);
159      prepStmt.setBigDecimal(4, balance);
160      prepStmt.setBigDecimal(5, creditLine);
161      prepStmt.setBigDecimal(6, beginBalance);
162      prepStmt.setDate(7, DBHelper.toSQLDate(beginBalanceTimeStamp));
163      prepStmt.executeUpdate();
164      prepStmt.close();
165      releaseConnection();
166    }
167
168    private void deleteRow(String id) throws SQLException {
169      makeConnection();
170      String deleteStatement ="delete from account where account_id = ? ";
171      PreparedStatement prepStmt =con.prepareStatement(deleteStatement);
172      prepStmt.setString(1, id);
173      prepStmt.executeUpdate();
174      prepStmt.close();
175      releaseConnection();
176    }
177
178    private boolean selectByPrimaryKey(String primaryKey) throws SQLException {
179      makeConnection();
180      String s = "select account_id from account where account_id = ? ";
181      PreparedStatement prepStmt = con.prepareStatement(s);
182      prepStmt.setString(1, primaryKey);
183      ResultSet rs = prepStmt.executeQuery();
184      boolean result = rs.next();
185      prepStmt.close();
186      releaseConnection();
187      return result;
```

```
188      }
189
190      Collection selectByCustomerId(String customerId) throws SQLException {
191        makeConnection();
192        String selectStatement = "select account_id from customer_account_xref " +
193          "where customer_id = ? ";
194        PreparedStatement prepStmt = con.prepareStatement(selectStatement);
195        prepStmt.setString(1, customerId);
196        ResultSet rs = prepStmt.executeQuery();
197        ArrayList a = new ArrayList();
198        while (rs.next()) {
199          a.add(rs.getString(1));
200        }
201        prepStmt.close();
202        releaseConnection();
203        return a;
204      }
205
206      private void loadAccount() throws SQLException {
207        makeConnection();
208        String selectStatement =
209          "select type, description, balance, credit_line, " +
210          "begin_balance, begin_balance_time_stamp " +
211          "from account where account_id = ? ";
212        PreparedStatement prepStmt =
213          con.prepareStatement(selectStatement);
214        prepStmt.setString(1, accountId);
215        ResultSet rs = prepStmt.executeQuery();
216        if (rs.next()) {
217          type = rs.getString(1);
218          description = rs.getString(2);
219          balance = rs.getBigDecimal(3);
220          creditLine = rs.getBigDecimal(4);
221          beginBalance = rs.getBigDecimal(5);
222          beginBalanceTimeStamp = rs.getDate(6);
223          prepStmt.close();
224          releaseConnection();
225        } else {
226          prepStmt.close();
227          releaseConnection();
228          throw new NoSuchEntityException("Row for id " +
229            accountId + " not found in database.");
230        }
231      }
232
233      private void loadCustomerIds() throws SQLException {
234        makeConnection();
```

```
235      String selectStatement = "select customer_id " +
236        "from customer_account_xref where account_id = ? ";
237      PreparedStatement prepStmt = con.prepareStatement(selectStatement);
238      prepStmt.setString(1, accountId);
239      ResultSet rs = prepStmt.executeQuery();
240      customerIds.clear();
241      while (rs.next()) {
242        customerIds.add(rs.getString(1));
243      }
244      prepStmt.close();
245      releaseConnection();
246    }
247
248    private void storeAccount() throws SQLException {
249      makeConnection();
250      String updateStatement =
251        "update account set type =  ? , description = ? , " +
252        "balance = ? , credit_line = ? , " +
253        "begin_balance = ? , begin_balance_time_stamp = ? " +
254        "where account_id = ?";
255      PreparedStatement prepStmt =
256        con.prepareStatement(updateStatement);
257      prepStmt.setString(1, type);
258      prepStmt.setString(2, description);
259      prepStmt.setBigDecimal(3, balance);
260      prepStmt.setBigDecimal(4, creditLine);
261      prepStmt.setBigDecimal(5, beginBalance);
262      prepStmt.setDate(6, DBHelper.toSQLDate(beginBalanceTimeStamp));
263      prepStmt.setString(7, accountId);
264      int rowCount = prepStmt.executeUpdate();
265      prepStmt.close();
267      if (rowCount == 0) {266      releaseConnection();
268        throw new EJBException("Storing row for id " + accountId + " failed.");
269      }
270    }
271  } // AccountBean
```

Similar to the session facade, the business object implementation shows some nonmodularized concerns:

- EJB technology dependency through the implementation of the EntityBean interface (lines 15, 26, 111).

- Implementation and management of references (here a collection) towards other EJBs (lines 24, 33, 233).

- Database access, more generally persistence management (lines 27, 71, 81, 96, 105, 148), since it is a bean-managed persistence (BMP) EJB and not a container-managed persistence (CMP) EJB.

- Business implementation (line 29).

- EJB instances resolving through the Home interface implementation (line 5).

The following sections illustrate how to clearly modularize these concerns with AOP by implementing nonbusiness concerns in aspects.

AOP-based Implementation

AOP, similar to facade objects, must implement the `javax.ejb.SessionBean` interface; business objects, such as entity EJBs, must implement the `javax.ejb.EntityBean` interface. AOP can be used, like for the session facade, through a marker interface.

```
package aop.j2ee.business;
public interface EntityBeanProtocol {}
```

This empty interface must be implemented by the business objects or any entity EJB that will have minimal impact on the code. An aspect (such as the one in Listing 11-3) transforms POJOs into EJBs and implements the needed methods.

Listing 11-3. *An Aspect to Transform POJO into an Entity EJB*

```
package aop.j2ee.business.aspect;

import java.sql.*;
import javax.ejb.*;
import aop.j2ee.business.aspect.marker.EntityBeanProtocol;

public abstract aspect POJOEntity extends EJBResolver {

  declare parents: EntityBeanProtocol extends javax.ejb.EntityBean;
  private EntityContext EntityBeanProtocol.context;

  // generic EJB home methods ==================================

  public String EntityBeanProtocol
       .ejbFindByPrimaryKey(String primaryKey)
  throws FinderException {
    boolean result;
    try {
      result = selectByPrimaryKey(primaryKey);
    } catch (Exception ex) {
      throw new EJBException("ejbFindByPrimaryKey: " +
                          ex.getMessage());
    }
    if (result) {
      return primaryKey;
    } else {
      throw new ObjectNotFoundException
```

```
        ("Row for id " + primaryKey + " not found.");
  }
}

// generic EJB methods =====================================

public void EntityBeanProtocol.ejbRemove() {
  try {
    deleteRow(getEntityId());
  } catch (Exception ex) {
    throw new EJBException("ejbRemove: " +  ex.getMessage());
  }
}

public void EntityBeanProtocol
            .setEntityContext(EntityContext context) {
  this.context = context;
  setExtraContext();
}

public void EntityBeanProtocol.unsetEntityContext() {}

public void EntityBeanProtocol.ejbLoad() {
  try {
    loadEntity();
  } catch (Exception ex) {
    throw new EJBException("ejbLoad: " + ex.getMessage());
  }
}

public void EntityBeanProtocol.ejbStore() {
  try {
    storeEntity();
  } catch (Exception ex) {
      throw new EJBException("ejbStore: " + ex.getMessage());
  }
}

public void EntityBeanProtocol.ejbActivate() {
  setEntityId((String)context.getPrimaryKey());
}

public void EntityBeanProtocol.ejbPassivate() {
  setEntityId(null);
}

// persistence protocol
```

```
    private void EntityBeanProtocol.makeConnection() {}
    private void EntityBeanProtocol.releaseConnection() {}
    private void EntityBeanProtocol.insertRow () throws SQLException {}
    private void EntityBeanProtocol.deleteRow(String id) throws SQLException {}
    private boolean EntityBeanProtocol.selectByPrimaryKey(String k) { return false; }
    private void EntityBeanProtocol.loadEntity() throws SQLException {}
    private void EntityBeanProtocol.storeEntity() throws SQLException {}
    private String EntityBeanProtocol.getEntityId() throws SQLException{return null;}
    private void EntityBeanProtocol.setEntityId(String id) {}
    private void EntityBeanProtocol.setExtraContext() {}
}
```

In this case, unlike the reference implementation, the common behaviors of the entity EJBs can be more easily factorized. Similar to session EJBs, you can decouple the factorizations into two independent inheritance hierarchies: a functional hierarchy, for the POJOs that implement the business, and, if needed, a technical hierarchy that can be formed by the aspects and the markers.

For the POJOSession aspect, we extend the abstract aspect EJBResolver. This aspect is not used in the EntityBean interface implementation and will be described later in the "Resolving Object References" section.

Modularization of the Business Persistence

One important advantage of using aspects with entity EJBs is that persistence management can be inserted in a more generic manner by the aspects. Here, we insert a persistence protocol by using intertype declarations.

Since the POJOEntity aspect is abstract, these intertype declarations can be specialized depending on the targeted EJB, as shown in Listing 11-4, which illustrates the account example.

Listing 11-4. *An Aspect to Transparently Introduce Persistence into the Account POJO*

```
package aop.j2ee.business.aspect.sql;

import java.sql.*;
import java.util.*;
import java.math.*;
import javax.ejb.*;
import aop.j2ee.commons.exception.*;
import aop.j2ee.commons.util.Debug;
import aop.j2ee.business.entity.account.AccountPOJO;
import aop.j2ee.business.aspect.POJOEntity;

public privileged aspect SQLAccount extends POJOEntity {

// EJB- or EJBHome-specific methods

public String AccountPOJO.ejbCreate(String accountId,String type,
```

```
  String description,BigDecimal balance,BigDecimal creditLine,
  BigDecimal beginBalance,java.util.Date beginBalanceTimeStamp,
  ArrayList customerIds)
  throws CreateException, MissingPrimaryKeyException {
  if ((accountId == null) || (accountId.trim().length() == 0)) {
    throw new MissingPrimaryKeyException(
      "ejbCreate: accountId arg is null or empty");
  }
  this.accountId = accountId;
  this.type = type;
  this.description = description;
  this.balance = balance;
  this.creditLine = creditLine;
  this.beginBalance = beginBalance;
  this.beginBalanceTimeStamp = beginBalanceTimeStamp;
  this.customerIds = customerIds;
  try {
    insertRow();
  } catch (Exception ex) {
    throw new EJBException("ejbCreate: " + ex.getMessage());
  }
  return accountId;
}

public void AccountPOJO.ejbPostCreate(String accountId,String type,
  String description,BigDecimal balance,BigDecimal creditLine,
  BigDecimal beginBalance,java.util.Date beginBalanceTimeStamp,
  ArrayList customerIds) {}

public Collection AccountPOJO.ejbFindByCustomerId(
  String customerId) throws FinderException {
  Collection result;
  try {
    result = selectByCustomerId(customerId);
  } catch (Exception ex) {
    throw new EJBException("ejbFindByCustomerId " +
      ex.getMessage());
  }
  return result;
}

private void AccountPOJO.setExtraContext() {
  customerIds = new ArrayList();
}

private void AccountPOJO.setEntityId(String id) {
  this.accountId = id;
```

```
  }

  private String AccountPOJO.getEntityId(String id) {
    return this.accountId;
  }

  // SQL persistence methods (implementation)

  private Connection AccountPOJO.con;

  // see AccountBean for implementations
  private void AccountPOJO.makeConnection() { [...] }
  private void AccountPOJO.releaseConnection() { [...] }
  private void AccountPOJO.insertRow() throws SQLException { [...] }
  private void AccountPOJO.deleteRow(String id)
  throws SQLException { [...] }
  private boolean AccountPOJO.selectByPrimaryKey(String primaryKey)
  { [...] }
  private Collection AccountPOJO
    .selectByCustomerId(String customerId) throws SQLException { [...] }
  private void AccountPOJO.loadEntity() throws SQLException { [...] }
  private void AccountPOJO.storeEntity() throws SQLException { [...] }

  // SQL implementation for methods accessing collections
  void around(AccountPOJO account) throws Exception :
    execution(private void AccountPOJO.loadCustomerIds())
    && this(account) {
      account.makeConnection();
      String selectStatement = "select customer_id "
        + "from customer_account_xref where account_id = ? ";
      PreparedStatement prepStmt =
      account.con.prepareStatement(selectStatement);
      prepStmt.setString(1, account.accountId);
      ResultSet rs = prepStmt.executeQuery();
      account.customerIds.clear();
      while (rs.next()) {
        account.customerIds.add(rs.getString(1));
      }
      prepStmt.close();
      account.releaseConnection();
    }
}
```

The implementation of the SQL requests does not differ from the regular implementation. The development work is therefore similar in both versions. However, since the implementation is well modularized, it is easy to completely change the persistence mechanism by removing the SQLAccount aspect.

With these two aspects, the business object is now implemented as shown in Listing 11-5.

Listing 11-5. *The Account POJO Implementation*

```
package aop.j2ee.business.entity.account;

import java.util.*;
import java.math.*;
import aop.j2ee.commons.to.AccountDetails;
import aop.j2ee.business.aspect.marker.EntityBeanProtocol;

public class AccountPOJO implements EntityBeanProtocol {

  private String accountId;
  private String type;
  private String description;
  private BigDecimal balance;
  private BigDecimal creditLine;
  private BigDecimal beginBalance;
  private java.util.Date beginBalanceTimeStamp;
  private ArrayList customerIds;

  // business methods
  public AccountDetails getDetails() {
    try {
      loadCustomerIds();
    } catch (Exception ex) {
      throw new EJBException("loadCustomerIds: "
                            + ex.getMessage());
    }
    return new AccountDetails(accountId, type,description,balance,
      creditLine, beginBalance, beginBalanceTimeStamp,customerIds);
  }

  public BigDecimal getBalance() { return balance; }
  public String getType() {return type; }
  [...] // other Account methods implementations

  // protocol to load related objects
  private void loadCustomerIds() throws Exception {}
}
```

This implementation is done as a regular POJO or JavaBean. It can be easily reused in its original form in the context of a framework or technology other than EJBs or JDBC. For instance, you can write an aspect that will make the object persistent through another framework such as Hibernate or Spring.

Careful readers would have noted the use of the empty method loadCustomerIds at the end of the AccountPOJO class, which is used by the method getDetails. As the name suggests, loadCustomerIds loads the customer IDs that are related to the current account. It is not implemented in the business object but in the SQLAccount aspect (see the "around" advice of Listing 11-4). This is a common technique used to delegate the implementation of a function within a dedicated aspect, performed in two phases as described here:

1. You define one or several empty methods within an object. These methods define a generic but inactive protocol.

2. You implement these methods within aspects, by using "around" advice codes that replace the empty implementation by not calling proceed.

This technique is more flexible and explicit than an object-oriented design based on inheritance, for instance. Within this book, we refer to this technique as the *implicit protocol* technique for three reasons:

- It defines a protocol as methods.

- This protocol is private to the object but can be made public, for example, within an interface that would be implemented by the object.

- Its implementation is implicitly handled by an external aspect.

The following section uses this technique for object references resolving with research protocols similar to the loadCustomerIds method.

AOP VS. DESIGN PATTERNS

As explained previously in Chapter 8, AOP offers alternate solutions to design patterns. Whether or not to use AOP depends on the needs of the programmer. The choice is guided mostly by implementation concerns such as code modularity, complexity, and evolution. However, these criteria are subjective and often difficult to evaluate up front. They become important during development, when the need for new functions makes the application's code more complex. Therefore, it is important to possess experience in developing real-world applications in order to accurately evaluate the advantages and disadvantages of a chosen solution, whether with AOP or otherwise.

AOP is a young field, and feedback from those using it is still needed. This feedback should go far beyond regular design patterns, since AOP opens new possibilities. In the long term, good AOP practice should be identified and stated in a guide similar to the GoF's book. In such a guide, aspect-oriented design patterns would most likely handle problems such as code reuse, complexity, modularity, and evolution. As of now, these problems are rarely ever handled by regular design patterns.

In this book, we provide a set of aspect-oriented techniques that allow programmers to deal with some of the aforementioned problems. These solutions include the implicit protocol, the anchoring protocol techniques, and the internationalization aspect, depicted later in Chapter 12 in the section "Using AOP for UI Concerns." However, even though these techniques are reusable and open the door to good AOP practice, they do not replace designer expertise. It is the designer who is the key for identifying the crosscutting concerns that may appear at any level of the application.

Business Tier Improvement: Beyond Design Patterns

Certain concerns can be crosscutting to the business tier and difficult to handle with J2EE design patterns. With these concerns, the GoF design patterns may be useful.

As stated in Chapter 8, concerns not compatible with design patterns can often be implemented by using AOP. Indeed, AOP often offers simpler solutions than those proposed by design patterns.

In this section, we study a solution for modularizing reference resolving and preconditions in the context of our case study, the banking application.

Resolving Object References

Resolving object references is usually implemented through a well-defined protocol that allows the search based on certain criterions. Within the EJB context, the Home interface defines this protocol, which is implemented by the EJB.

Listing 11-6 illustrates the protocol for the account business object.

Listing 11-6. *The Home Interface of Account*

```
package aop.j2ee.business.entity.account;

01    import java.util.*;
02    import java.math.*;
03    import javax.ejb.*;
04    import java.rmi.RemoteException;
05    import aop.j2ee.commons.exception.MissingPrimaryKeyException;
06
07    public interface AccountHome extends EJBHome {
08
09      public Account create (String accountId, String type, String description,
10         BigDecimal balance, BigDecimal creditLine, BigDecimal beginBalance,
11         Date beginBalanceTimeStamp, ArrayList customerIds)
12            throws RemoteException, CreateException, MissingPrimaryKeyException;
13
14      public Account findByPrimaryKey(String accountId)
15         throws FinderException, RemoteException;
16
17      public Collection findByCustomerId(String customerId)
18         throws FinderException, RemoteException;
19
20    } // AccountHome
```

The create method allows for the creation of a new account by a client object. For instance, the Bank session EJB uses this method in the implementation of createAccount. It is a typical method for a Home interface. The findByPrimaryKey(String) method is also a classical method. It allows the client objects to access a given account instance through its primary key. Finally, findByCustomerId(String customerId) reveals the relation between the customers

(Customer) and the accounts (Account). This method is used to access the customer's accounts. For each relation between the EJB, a similar method can be defined in the Home interface.

The use of the Home interface implies a dependency to the EJB model. Even though it is a light dependency, it has a crosscutting effect because each client object (typically a session EJB such as Bank and TxController) must implement the Home interface accessing code, which uses some EJB and JNDI primitives. The technological dependency can be reduced by using the locator pattern. However, then the use of the locator itself becomes a crosscutting concern and requires additional design efforts.

In order to illustrate the complications related to reference resolving, we use our original design of the Duke's Bank example, which does not use the service locator pattern.

Let us refer again to the TxController session EJB implementation. Remember that the account resolving is implemented in the checkAccountArgsAndResolve method, as shown in Listing 11-7.

Listing 11-7. *The checkAccountArgsAndResolve Method*

```
01   private Account checkAccountArgsAndResolve(
02     BigDecimal amount,String description,String accountId)
03   throws InvalidParameterException, AccountNotFoundException {
04
05   Account account = null;
06     if (description == null)
07       throw new InvalidParameterException("null description");
08     if (accountId == null)
09       throw new InvalidParameterException("null accountId");
10     if (amount.compareTo(bigZero) != 1)
11       throw new InvalidParameterException("amount <= 0");
12     try {
13       account = accountHome.findByPrimaryKey(accountId);
14     } catch (Exception ex) {
15       throw new AccountNotFoundException(accountId);
16     }
17     return account;
18   } // checkAccountArgsAndResolve
```

The accountHome field (line 13) has been initialized with other similar fields when the EJB was created, as shown at line 4 of Listing 11-8.

Listing 11-8. *The EJBCreate Method*

```
01   public void ejbCreate() {
02     try {
03       txHome = EJBGetter.getTxHome();
04       accountHome = EJBGetter.getAccountHome();
05     } catch (Exception ex) {
06       throw new EJBException("ejbCreate: " + ex.getMessage());
07     }
08   } // ejbCreate
```

The EJBGetter class factorizes the EJB Home resolving code, as shown in Listing 11-9.

Listing 11-9. *The EJBGetter Class*

```
package aop.j2ee.business.util;

import javax.rmi.PortableRemoteObject;
import javax.naming.InitialContext;
import javax.naming.NamingException;
import aop.j2ee.commons.util.CodedNames;
import aop.j2ee.business.entity.account.*;
[...] // other imports

public final class EJBGetter {
  public static AccountHome getAccountHome()
    throws NamingException {
    InitialContext initial = new InitialContext();
    Object objref = initial.lookup(CodedNames.ACCOUNT_EJBHOME);
    return (AccountHome)
      PortableRemoteObject.narrow(objref, AccountHome.class);
  }
  [...] // other resolving methods
}
```

In the original Duke's Bank design, the account resolving and the transaction parameters testing are factorized within a single method. These two independent concerns are mixed because of the need to hide the use of the Home interface. This choice makes the transactional method code less explicit.

Listing 11-10 is an example of a business service implementation that corresponds to an account withdrawal.

Listing 11-10. *A Withdrawal Business Service Implementation*

```
01  public void withdraw(BigDecimal amount,String description,
02    String accountId)
03  throws InvalidParameterException, AccountNotFoundException,
04        IllegalAccountTypeException, InsufficientFundsException {
05
06    Account account =
07    checkAccountArgsAndResolve(amount, description, accountId);
08    try {
09      String type = account.getType();
10      if (DomainUtil.isCreditAccount(type))
11        throw new IllegalAccountTypeException(type);
12      BigDecimal newBalance = account.getBalance().subtract(amount);
13      if (newBalance.compareTo(bigZero) == -1)
14        throw new InsufficientFundsException();
15      executeTx(
16        amount.negate(),
17        description,
```

```
18          accountId,
19          newBalance,
20          account);
21       } catch (RemoteException ex) {
22          throw new EJBException("withdraw: " + ex.getMessage());
23       }
24    } // withdraw
25
26    private void executeTx(BigDecimal amount, String description,
27       String accountId, BigDecimal newBalance, Account account) {
28
29       try {
30          makeConnection();
31          String txId = DBHelper.getNextTxId(con);
32          account.setBalance(newBalance);
33          Tx tx = txHome.create(txId,accountId,new java.util.Date(),
34                                 amount,newBalance,description);
35       } catch (Exception ex) {
36          throw new EJBException("executeTx: " + ex.getMessage());
37       } finally {
38          releaseConnection();
39       }
40    } // executeTx
```

The executedTx method of line 15 gathers two independent functions that would benefit from being explicitly coded within the functional implementation: the Tx EJB creation (line 33), and the invocation of setBalance (line 32) on an account.

As shown in the code, the Tx EJB creation uses a database-related method: DBHelper.getNextTxId (line 31), which returns the next available transaction identifier. This operation is a low-level operation that should probably not be used within a business method.

Conceptually speaking, we can classify all the presented operations—Home interface resolving, account lookup from a primary key, and instantiation of the Tx EJB—within a reference-managing concern. This concern depends highly on the J2EE infrastructure and on the EJB model. This is clearly a crosscutting concern for all EJB accessing or for the creation of EJBs, particularly the session EJBs.

The use of design patterns such as the locator can make the code less dependent on the infrastructure and minimize the design efforts through reuse. However, it is then the use of the pattern that becomes a crosscutting concern. Furthermore, the use of a locator pattern still requires an indirect use of the EJB model.

Using AOP

AOP, and more precisely the previously discussed implicit protocol technique, significantly simplifies the design and efficiently modularizes the reference-resolving crosscutting concern.

First, we defined the reference accessing protocol in the EJB itself, as shown in Listing 11-11. In our program, it is a POJO since it automatically implements the javax.ejb.SessionBean interface through the POJOSession aspect. This POJO, named TxControllerPOJO, will be detailed in the rest of the chapter, once all the applied aspects have been presented.

Listing 11-11. *The Implicit Protocol for EJB Resolving*

```
[...]
// excerpt of the TxControllerPOJO implicit resolving protocol implementation
private Collection findTxByAccountId(Date startDate,
  Date endDate,String accountId) throws Exception {return null;}
private Tx findTxByPrimaryKey(String txId)
  throws Exception {return null;}
private Account findAccountByPrimaryKey(String accountID)
  throws Exception {return null;}
private Tx createTx(String accountId, Date date,
  BigDecimal amount, BigDecimal newBalance, String description)
throws Exception {return null;}
```

We now define the aspect implementing this protocol. In our study, this aspect is called the EJBResolver aspect, which is an abstract aspect extended by the POJOSession and POJOEntity concrete aspects. The purpose of the EJBResolver aspect is to implement common behaviors for reference-resolving implementation, as shown in Listing 11-12.

Listing 11-12. *The Aspect Implementation of the EJB Resolving Implicit Protocol*

```
01  package aop.j2ee.business.aspect;
02
03  import java.util.Collection;
04  import java.util.Date;
05  import java.math.BigDecimal;
06  import aop.j2ee.business.entity.account.AccountHome;
07  import aop.j2ee.business.entity.account.Account;
08  import aop.j2ee.business.entity.tx.TxHome;
09  import aop.j2ee.business.entity.tx.Tx;
10  import aop.j2ee.business.aspect.sql.DBUtil;
11
12  public abstract aspect EJBResolver {
13
14    static protected TxHome txHome;
15    static protected AccountHome accountHome;
16    [...] // Other homes...
17
18    Account around(String accountID) throws Exception: execution(
19    private Account *.findAccountByPrimaryKey(String) && args(accountID) {
20      return accountHome.findByPrimaryKey(accountID);
21    }
22
23    Tx around(String txID) throws Exception:
24    execution(private Tx *.findTxByPrimaryKey(String)) && args(txID) {
25      return txHome.findByPrimaryKey(txID);
26    }
27
```

```
28    Collection around(Date start,Date end,String accountId) throws Exception:
29    execution(private Collection *.findTxByAccountId(Date,Date,String))
30    && args(start,end,accountId) {
31      return txHome.findByAccountId(start,end,accountId);
32    }
33
34    Tx around(String accountId, Date date, BigDecimal amount,
35                      BigDecimal newBalance, String description)
36    throws Exception:
37    execution(private Tx *.createTx(String, Date, BigDecimal, BigDecimal, String))
38    && args(accountId,date,amount,newBalance,description) {
39      return txHome.create(DBUtil.getNextTxId(),accountId,date,
40                                    amount,newBalance,description);
41    }
42
43    [...] // other resolving methods
44  }
```

With EJBs, the implementation of these methods is fairly simple since they only delegate to the Home interfaces.

Note the use of the DBUtil.getNextTxId method (line 39), which makes the database identifier creation transparent to the POJOs when creating a new transaction. The references on the required Home interfaces are stored in noninitialized private attributes. The attributes can be initialized by the concrete aspects that implement this abstract one.

Thus, the subaspects can implement session or entity EJB specificities, and must initialize the Homes. For instance, the POJOSession aspect performs this initialization in the ejbCreate method, as shown in Listing 11-13.

Listing 11-13. *EJB References Initialization in the POJOSession Aspect*

```
package aop.j2ee.business.aspect;

[...] // imports

public aspect POJOSession extends EJBResolver {

  declare parents: SessionBeanProtocol
    extends javax.ejb.SessionBean;

  [...] // see above for the other methods implementations

  public void SessionBeanProtocol.ejbCreate() {
    try {
      if(txHome==null)
        txHome = EJBGetter.getTxHome();
      if(accountHome==null)
        accountHome = EJBGetter.getAccountHome();
    } catch (Exception ex) {
```

```
        throw new EJBException("ejbCreate: " + ex.getMessage());
    }
  }
}
```

Once these aspects are applied, the withdrawal method of the TxControllerPOJO class is as shown in Listing 11-14.

Listing 11-14. *The Aspectized Withdrawal Method*

```
01  public void withdraw(BigDecimal amount,String description,
02                                  String accountId) throws
03      InvalidParameterException, AccountNotFoundException,
04      InsufficientFundsException, InsufficientCreditException {
05
06      checkAccountArgs(amount, description, accountId);
07      Account account;
08      try {
09        account = findAccountByPrimaryKey(accountId);
10      } catch (Exception ex) {
11        throw new AccountNotFoundException(accountId);
12      }
13      try {
14        String type = account.getType();
15        if (DomainUtil.isCreditAccount(type))
16            throw new IllegalAccountTypeException(type);
17        BigDecimal newBalance = account.getBalance().subtract(amount);
18        if (newBalance.compareTo(bigZero) == -1)
19            throw new InsufficientFundsException();
20        account.setBalance(newBalance);
21        createTx(amount.negate(),description,accountId,newBalance,account);
22      } catch (RemoteException ex) {
23        throw new EJBException("withdraw: " + ex.getMessage());
24      }
25  } // withdraw
```

Lines 9 and 21 show the use of the implicit protocol.

The withdrawal and other business method implementations have the following characteristics:

- They are clearer than the method that used the Home protocol. This protocol requires the resolving of the references through JNDI, the managing of these references, and the identification of the newly created EJBs. None of these are required with the implicit protocol technique, and the programmer simply uses the protocol methods without knowing their implementation.

- They are more modular. The implementation of the EJB-resolving logic is located within a unique aspect instead of being dispatched in all the EJBs. Then it becomes easier to factorize common reference-resolving mechanisms.

- They are less technologically dependent. If the defined implicit protocol is of the right detail level, it is then simple to change the actual implementation of the resolving.

Precondition Factorization

In Chapter 9, we presented the use of AOP for transparently adding constraints within a program, particularly for adding pre- and postconditions.

Here, we apply the same principles to the reference application.

Regular Implementation

The implementation of the TxController session facade shows that the arguments of an account operation must be checked by preconditions.

If we focus on the withdrawal operation discussed before in the context of TxControllerPOJO, the implementation shown in Listing 11-15 is obtained.

Listing 11-15. *The Withdraw Implementation, with Arguments Checks Included*

```
01  [...]
02  public void withdraw(BigDecimal amount,String description,
03                       String accountId)
04    throws
05      InvalidParameterException, AccountNotFoundException,
06      InsufficientFundsException, InsufficientCreditException {
07
08    checkAccountArgs(amount, description, accountId);
09    Account account;
10    try {
11      account = findAccountByPrimaryKey(accountId);
12    } catch (Exception ex) {
13      throw new AccountNotFoundException(accountId);
14    }
15    try {
16      String type = account.getType();
17      if (DomainUtil.isCreditAccount(type))
18        throw new IllegalAccountTypeException(type);
19      BigDecimal newBalance = account.getBalance().subtract(amount);
20      if (newBalance.compareTo(bigZero) == -1)
21        throw new InsufficientFundsException();
22      account.setBalance(newBalance);
23      createTx(amount.negate(),description,accountId, newBalance,account);
24    } catch (RemoteException ex) {
25      throw new EJBException("withdraw: " + ex.getMessage());
26    }
27
28  } // withdraw
29
30  [...]
```

```
31   private void checkAccountArgs(BigDecimal amount,String descr, String accountId)
32     throws InvalidParameterException, AccountNotFoundException {
33     if (descr == null)
34       throw new InvalidParameterException("null description");
35     if (accountId == null)
36       throw new InvalidParameterException("null accountId");
37     if (amount.compareTo(bigZero) != 1)
38       throw new InvalidParameterException("amount <= 0");
39   }
```

In the preceding code, we can see the different tests implementing the preconditions (lines 8, 17, and 20). In this case, the preconditions can be split into two parts:

- The part that checks the consistency of the parameters, implemented in checkAccountArgs (line 8). This is the *parameter precondition* part.

- The part that is more business-related and that checks that the type of account allows the current withdrawal operation (line 17) and that the balance is high enough to perform the withdrawal (line 20). This is the *business precondition* part.

AOP-based Implementation

The following sections describe the use of AOP to implement the two precondition types previously encountered.

Parameter Preconditions Aspect

It is obvious that the first precondition part benefits from an AOP implementation. It is a generic test, which is systematically executed before each account operation, for instance, before credit and withdrawal operations. It is therefore a crosscutting concern that can be implemented as a pre-/postcondition aspect. With an aspect, the implementation is modular (see Listing 11-16).

Listing 11-16. *An Aspect to Check the Arguments of a Transaction*

```
package aop.j2ee.business.aspects;

01   import java.math.BigDecimal;
02   import aop.j2ee.business.session.txcontroller.TxControllerBean;
03
04   import aop.j2ee.commons.exception.*;
05
06   public aspect TxCheckArgs {
07
08     private BigDecimal TxControllerBean.bigZero = new BigDecimal("0.00");
09
10     before(TxControllerBean controller,BigDecimal amount,
11           String description,String accountId)
12       throws InvalidParameterException:
13       execution(void aop.j2ee.business.session.txcontroller.
```

```
14                        TxControllerBean.*(BigDecimal,String,String))
15                        && args(amount,description,accountId) && this(controller) {
16          controller.checkAccountArgs(amount,description,accountId);
17       }
18
19       before(TxControllerBean controller,BigDecimal amount,
20             String description,String fromAccountId, String toAccountId)
21          throws InvalidParameterException:
22          execution(void aop.j2ee.business.session.txcontroller.
23          TxControllerBean.*(BigDecimal,String,String,String)) && this(controller)
24          && args(amount,description,fromAccountId,toAccountId) {
25          controller.checkAccountArgs(amount,description,fromAccountId);
26          controller.checkAccountArgs(amount,description,toAccountId);
27       }
28
29       private void TxControllerBean.checkAccountArgs(
30          BigDecimal amount,String description,String accountId)
31          throws InvalidParameterException {
32          if (description == null)
33             throw new InvalidParameterException("null description");
34          if (accountId == null)
35             throw new InvalidParameterException("null accountId");
36          if (amount.compareTo(bigZero) != 1)
37             throw new InvalidParameterException("amount <= 0");
38       }
39    }
```

The TxCheckArgs parameter precondition aspect introduces the checkAccountArgs method in TxControllerBean through an intertype declaration (line 29). It also defines two advice codes applied on the prototypes that correspond to an account operation (line 10), and that correspond to an account transfer (line 19).

Business Preconditions Aspect

As stated previously, the second set of preconditions correspond to the business concerns and are part of the business rules set. We call them business preconditions. Note that, in general, preconditions can also be completed with postconditions in order to implement, for instance, potential invariants. For more details on this generic issue, you can refer to Chapter 9.

In our current case study, externalizing the preconditions within an aspect is useful for three principal reasons:

- These preconditions may evolve with time. We can imagine, for instance, that the precondition changes and ensures that a minimum amount is necessary for a withdrawal in order for it to accept a negative balance.

- These preconditions can be applied depending on the context. We can imagine that we do not want to apply the preconditions if the withdrawal operation is executed within another service that would already have applied its own preconditions. In this case, the use of aspects, particularly the AspectJ cflows, is well suited to easily implement contextual tests.

- The use of an aspect simplifies the code, which reflects the main behavior of the service. Analogously to use cases, the service's implementation only contains the main scenario, with no errors. This allows the programmer to better understand the service and to more easily identify the strategic joinpoints where other concerns can be inserted. For instance, if preconditions are code within aspects, it becomes easier to add a transaction management concern, as you will see later on.

In general, postconditions are defined within the same aspect. However, that is not the case here.

The implementation of the business preconditions is slightly different from the parameter preconditions (see Listing 11-17).

Listing 11-17. *An Aspect to Check the Business Preconditions of the Accounts*

```
01  package aop.j2ee.business.aspect;
02
03  import java.math.BigDecimal;
04  import java.rmi.RemoteException;
05  import javax.ejb.EJBException;
06  import aop.j2ee.business.entity.account.Account;
07  import aop.j2ee.business.session.txcontroller.TxControllerPOJO;
08  import aop.j2ee.commons.exception.*;
09  import aop.j2ee.commons.util.DomainUtil;
10
11  public aspect CheckBusinessConditions {
12
13    pointcut setBalance(Account account, BigDecimal amount):
14      call(void Account.setBalance(BigDecimal))
15      && args(amount) && target(account) && within(TxControllerPOJO);
16
17    before(Account account, BigDecimal amount) throws
18      InsufficientFundsException, InsufficientCreditException :
19        setBalance(account,amount) {
20
21      try {
22        String type = account.getType();
23        if (DomainUtil.isCreditAccount(type)) {
24          if (amount.compareTo(account.getCreditLine()) == 1)
25            throw new InsufficientCreditException();
26        } else {
27          if (amount.compareTo(DomainUtil.bigZero) == -1)
28          throw new InsufficientFundsException();
29        }
30      } catch (RemoteException ex) {
31        throw new EJBException("transferFunds: " + ex.getMessage());
32      }
33    }
34  }
```

We chose to implement the precondition in a generic manner by applying the test to the account setBalance function (see pointcut line 13).

The application of the two precondition aspects finally simplifies the business code, as shown in Listing 11-18 in the new implementation of the withdraw method extracted from the TxControllerBean class.

Listing 11-18. *The Final WithdrawIimplementation, with All Concerns Aspectized*

```
public void withdraw(BigDecimal amount,String description,
                              String accountId)
  throws AccountNotFoundException, EJBException {

  Account account;
  try {
    account = accountHome.findByPrimaryKey(accountId);
  } catch (Exception ex) {
    throw new AccountNotFoundException(accountId);
  }
  try {
    BigDecimal newBalance = account.getBalance().subtract(amount);
    account.setBalance(newBalance);
    createTx(amount.negate(),description,ccountId,
             newBalance,account);
  } catch (RemoteException ex) {
    throw new EJBException("withdraw: " + ex.getMessage());
  }
}
```

Business Tier Aspects Synthesis

The aspect-oriented version of the business tier contains three generic aspects:

- aop.ejb.business.aspect.EJBResolver (abstract), for reference resolving and EJB creation

- aop.ejb.business.aspect.POJOSession (extends EJBResolver), for transforming the POJOs that implement the aop.ejb.business.aspect.maker.SessionBeanProtocol into session EJBs

- aop.ejb.business.aspect.POJOEntity (abstract and extending EJBResolver), for transforming the POJOs that implement the aop.ejb.business.aspect.maker.EntityBeanProtocol into entity EJBs

Through the application of these aspects, the session and entity objects of the application can be implemented as POJOs, independently from the J2EE/EJB technology. The global design of the application is more modular, and certain concerns such as pre-/postcondition checking and reference resolving are made simpler and localized.

As an example, the TxController session facade can be implemented (see Listing 11-19).

Listing 11-19. *The Final Aspectized TxControllerPOJO*

```
package aop.j2ee.business.session.txcontroller;

import java.util.*;
import java.math.*;
import javax.ejb.*;
import java.util.Date;
import java.rmi.RemoteException;
import aop.j2ee.business.entity.tx.Tx;
import aop.j2ee.business.entity.account.Account;
import aop.j2ee.commons.exception.*;
import aop.j2ee.commons.util.*;
import aop.j2ee.commons.to.*;
import aop.j2ee.business.aspect.marker.SessionBeanProtocol;

public class TxControllerPOJO implements SessionBeanProtocol {

  public void withdraw(BigDecimal amount,String description,
                       String accountId)
  throws
    InvalidParameterException,AccountNotFoundException,
    InsufficientFundsException, InsufficientCreditException {

    Account account;
    try {
      account = findAccountByPrimaryKey(accountId);
    } catch (Exception ex) {
      throw new AccountNotFoundException(accountId);
    }
    try {
      BigDecimal newBalance = account.getBalance().subtract(amount);
      account.setBalance(newBalance);
      createTx(amount.negate(),description,accountId,newBalance,account);
    } catch (RemoteException ex) {
      throw new EJBException("withdraw: " + ex.getMessage());
    }
  } // withdraw

  public void transferFunds(BigDecimal amount,String description,
                       String fromAccountId, String toAccountId)
  throws
    InvalidParameterException,AccountNotFoundException,
    InsufficientFundsException,InsufficientCreditException {

    Account fromAccount;
    Account toAccount;
```

```
    try {
      fromAccount = findAccountByPrimaryKey(fromAccountId);
    } catch (Exception ex) {
      throw new AccountNotFoundException(fromAccountId);
    }
    try {
      toAccount = findAccountByPrimaryKey(toAccountId);
    } catch (Exception ex) {
      throw new AccountNotFoundException(toAccountId);
    }

    try {
      String fromType = fromAccount.getType();
      BigDecimal fromBalance = fromAccount.getBalance();
      BigDecimal fromAmount=
        DomainUtil.isCreditAccount(fromType)?amount.negate():amount;
      BigDecimal fromNewBalance = fromBalance.subtract(fromAmount);
      fromAccount.setBalance(fromNewBalance);
      createTx(fromAmount,description,fromAccountId,fromNewBalance,fromAccount);

      String toType = toAccount.getType();
      BigDecimal toBalance = toAccount.getBalance();
      BigDecimal toAmount=
        DomainUtil.isCreditAccount(fromType)?amount.negate():amount;
      BigDecimal toNewBalance = toBalance.subtract(toAmount);
      toAccount.setBalance(toNewBalance);
      createTx(toAmount,description,toAccountId,toNewBalance,toAccount);
    } catch (RemoteException ex) {
      throw new EJBException("transferFunds: " + ex.getMessage());
    }

  } // transferFunds

  [...] // other business methods

  // implicit resolving protocol
  private Collection findTxByAccountId(Date startDate, Date endDate,
    String accountId) throws Exception {return null;}
  private Tx findTxByPrimaryKey(String txId) throws Exception {return null;}
  private Account findAccountByPrimaryKey(String accountID) throws Exception
    {return null;}
  private Tx createTx(String accountId, Date date, BigDecimal amount,
    BigDecimal newBalance, String description) throws Exception {return null;}
}
```

As stated before, we can note the independence of the code from the EJB and the simplicity of the business code. For a persistent entity POJO, we can refer to the `AccountPOJO` implementation, previously given in the section "The Business Object."

Figure 11-1 shows an overview of the piece of code added by the aspects in `AccountPOJO` (left bar) and `TxControllerPOJO` (right bar). Each bar corresponds to a file, and the size of the bar depends on the number of lines in the represented file. Each line where an aspect adds code is shown with a color that corresponds to the particular aspect.

Note that the graphics produced by the Aspect Visualizer of the AJDT Eclipse plug-in does not show the intertype declarations. This explains why `AccountPOJO` does not seem to be modified a great deal by the aspects. Note the line at bottom of the left bar, which corresponds to the protocol implicit implementation, and more precisely to the implementation of the `getCustomerIds` method within `AccountPOJO`.

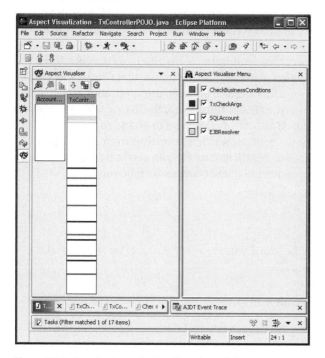

Figure 11-1. *Synthesis and visualization of the aspects*

AOP As an Integration Technique

Application servers rely on component containers. Their ultimate goal is to integrate all the concerns that are linked to distributed enterprise application development into the middleware layer as transparently as possible. The best integration support is provided when a concern can be integrated in a declarative manner. The programmer then needs to consider container-oriented management systems such as container-managed persistence (CMP) and container-managed transaction (CMT), also called declarative transaction management (DTM). In J2EE, the integration is parameterized within an XML deployment descriptor.

In this section, we study the container-oriented management of transactions. After describing the underlying mechanisms and limitations, we show how AOP offers an alternative solution for flexible and transparent transaction management in J2EE.

Managing Distributed Transactions with JTA

Java Transaction API (JTA) defines a set of interfaces and mechanisms for using distributed transactions. A transaction is distributed when several data sources are involved. In general, data sources are located on different servers, but this is not mandatory. JTA can also be used for only one data source. Within J2EE, JTA is typically used to make a session EJB facade service transactional.

The reference banking application only has one data source: a PointBase database. It is interesting to evaluate possible data distributions. For example, accounts and transactions could be stored in two distinct databases in order to balance the load and the data volume. In addition, it is useful for the system administration since transactions can call for a different maintenance process than the accounts. In this case, the use of JTA and an architecture that supports distribution is important.

In short, JTA relies on the definition of three communication interfaces between three main entities: the application, the transaction manager, and the transactional resources. In the context of an application server, JTA defines an interface between the application server and the transaction manager. This interface permits the notification of the manager for operations occurring on EJBs within the transactions. It also allows the client to access an automatically and transparently transmitted transactional context, which is accessible from any EJB participating in a transaction. Within a transaction, a participating EJB can access through the transactional context an object that represents the transaction: an instance of `javax.transaction.UserTransaction`.

A JTA Solution

The code in Listing 11-20 is a rewrite of the transfer function of `TxControllerBean` so that it ensures transactional properties by using JTA.

Listing 11-20. *Manual Control of Transactions with JTA*

```
01  // a modified version of aop.j2ee.business.session.TxControllerBean to use JTA
02  [...]
03  javax.transaction.UserTransaction ut;
04
05  public void transferFunds(BigDecimal amount,String descr,
06                      String fromAccountId,String toAccountId)
07  throws
08    InvalidParameterException,AccountNotFoundException,
09    InsufficientFundsException,InsufficientCreditException {
10
11    Account fromAccount;
12    Account toAccount;
13
14    fromAccount= checkAccountArgsAndResolve(amount, descr, fromAccountId);
15    toAccount= checkAccountArgsAndResolve(amount, descr, toAccountId);
16
17    ut= context.getUserTransaction();
18
```

```
19    try {
20      ut.begin();
21    } catch (Exception e) {
22      throw new EJBException("transferFunds: " + e.getMessage());
23    }
24
25    try {
26
27      String fromType= fromAccount.getType();
28      BigDecimal fromBalance= fromAccount.getBalance();
29
30      if (DomainUtil.isCreditAccount(fromType)) {
31        BigDecimal fromNewBalance= fromBalance.add(amount);
32        if (fromNewBalance.compareTo(fromAccount.getCreditLine()) == 1)
33          throw new InsufficientCreditException();
34        executeTx(amount,descr,fromAccountId,fromNewBalance,fromAccount);
35      } else {
36        BigDecimal fromNewBalance= fromBalance.subtract(amount);
37        if (fromNewBalance.compareTo(bigZero) == -1)
38          throw new InsufficientFundsException();
39       executeTx(amount.negate(),descr,fromAccountId,fromNewBalance,fromAccount);
40      }
41
42      String toType= toAccount.getType();
43      BigDecimal toBalance= toAccount.getBalance();
44
45      if (DomainUtil.isCreditAccount(toType)) {
46        BigDecimal toNewBalance= toBalance.subtract(amount);
47        executeTx(amount.negate(),descr,toAccountId,toNewBalance,toAccount);
48      } else {
49        BigDecimal toNewBalance= toBalance.add(amount);
50        executeTx(amount, descr, toAccountId, toNewBalance, toAccount);
51      }
52
53      ut.commit();
54
55    } catch (Exception ex) {
56      try {
57        ut.rollback();
58      } catch (Exception e) {
59        throw new EJBException("transferFunds: " + e.getMessage());
60      }
61      throw new EJBException("transferFunds: " + ex.getMessage());
62    }
63  } // transferFunds
```

As shown, managing transactions with JTA complicates the application code. Furthermore, it is a crosscutting concern since it must be handled with each participating EJB.

This concern adds the following elements:

- A field that stores the `UserTransaction` object and allows it to be quickly accessed (line 3)

- The initialization of this field at the beginning of the transactional method (line 17)

- A call to `begin`, which indicates a transaction start (line 20)

- A call to `commit` to ask for the realization of the transaction (line 53)

- A `rollback` invocation to ask for the cancellation of the transaction in case of an error (line 57)

In addition, we need to manage the exceptions that can be thrown by the transaction itself. Here, we handle them in a generic way.

EJBs As an Infrastructure for the Automatic Integration of Transactions

The J2EE specification given by Sun Microsystems allows the transactions to be declaratively defined through dedicated attributes, which are defined in deployment descriptors. These attributes are applied to EJB methods and parameterize the behavior of the container regarding the transaction manager when these methods are invoked.

These attributes are the following:

- `TX_NOT_SUPPORTED`: Indicates that the method is not transactional. If this method is invoked within a transaction, this transaction is suspended during the method execution.

- `TX_SUPPORTS`: Indicates that the bean that supports the method will be included in the transaction as a participant. If the client does not define any transaction, the container can create a new transaction depending on the implementation.

- `TX_REQUIRED`: Indicates that the method must be executed within the context of a transaction. If not, the container automatically creates a new one.

- `TX_REQUIRES_NEW`: Indicates that the method triggers the creation of a new transaction, even if the client has already defined one. In this later case, the transaction of the client is replaced by the newly created transaction.

- `TX_BEAN_MANAGED`: Indicates that the EJB method manually implements the transaction management by using JTA, for instance.

- `TX_MANDATORY`: Indicates that the method has to be executed within a transaction. If not, the container throws a `TransactionRequired` exception.

Figure 11-2 shows the messages that are sent from the application to the transaction manager, and to the transactional resources when the `transferFunds` method is set to `TX_REQUIRES_NEW`—which means that a transaction will automatically be created by the container, even if a transaction has already been defined by the client—and that the methods `Account.setBalance` and `AccountHome.create` are set to `TX_REQUIRED`.

The call to the transferFunds method triggers the begin message to the manager, which in turn creates a new transaction. This transaction is added to the current thread's context and is automatically transmitted to the participating EJBs. When the Account EJBs are used and the Tx bank-level transactions are created, they are added to the current transaction as participants. The successful end of the transferFund method triggers the commit, while an EJBException catch implies a rollback.

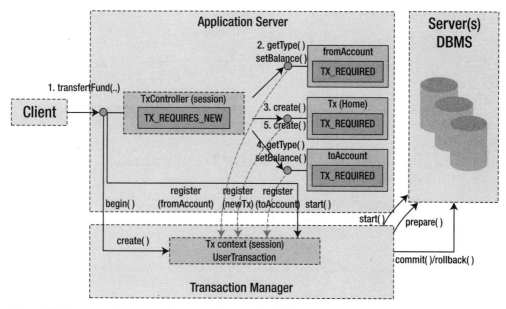

Figure 11-2. *Declarative transactions mechanism in J2EE*

The existence of container-managed transactions allows the program's code to remain free from the transaction concern. However, this technique has its limitations.

The attributes defined by the EJB standard are too simple to cover all the possible cases that can arise when developing complex applications. For instance, the programmer may need to retry a transaction if it did not complete successfully in the first place. It is also common to optimize the application by not applying a transaction within some contexts, which depends on the application or environment state. Nevertheless, when it comes to optimization, it is sometimes useful to limit the transaction application scope to an instruction group rather than to the whole method code. In this case, the only way is to use the TX_BEAN_MANAGED attribute and to manually code the transactional logic.

Even in the cases when the provided attributes allow the description of the transactional logic, this technique still requires some code to be written in order to handle the client-side exceptions and some rollback management cases.

In particular, the programmer may need to force the rollback of a transaction within a participant. In this case, the setRollbackOnly method shall be used (see line 7 of Listing 11-21) in order to cancel the transaction, even if higher-level participants try to commit the transaction.

As an example, the code in Listing 11-21 prevents a negative setBalance from occurring in any transactional context:

Listing 11-21. *An Example of Use for the setRollbackOnly Method*

```
01   [...]
02   public void setBalance(double amount)
03     throw InsufficientFundsException {
04     if( balance >= 0 ) {
05       balance = amount;
06     } else {
07       context.setRollbackOnly();
08       throw new InsufficientFundsException(balance);
09     }
10   }
11   [...]
```

As you can see, the declarative transaction management is not an ideal solution. The following sections show how AOP can be used in its place.

AOP and the Modular Integration of Transactions

Because of its flexibility, AOP is helpful for integrating transactions in a modular way, and by avoiding the limitations previously encountered.

Indeed, to make a method transactional (here transferFunds), the transaction aspect shown in Listing 11-22 can be used.

Listing 11-22. *An Aspect for Modularizing Transaction Management Code*

```
01   package aop.j2ee.business.aspect;
02
03   import javax.ejb.EJBException;
04   import aop.j2ee.business.session.txcontroller.TxControllerPOJO;
05
06   public privileged aspect Transaction {
07     Object around(TxControllerPOJO controller) :
08       execution(* TxControllerPOJO.transferFunds(..)) && this(controller) {
09
10       Object result;
11       try {
12         controller.context.getUserTransaction().begin();
13       } catch (Exception e) {
14         throw new EJBException("transferFunds: " + e.getMessage());
15       }
16       try {
17         result=proceed(controller);
18         controller.context.getUserTransaction().commit();
19       } catch (Exception ex) {
20         try {
21           controller.context.getUserTransaction().rollback();
22         } catch (Exception e) {
```

```
23            throw new EJBException("transferFunds: " + e.getMessage());
24        }
25        throw new EJBException("transferFunds: " + ex.getMessage());
26      }
27      return result;
28    }
29  }
```

Contrary to the container-managed transactions, the code that implements the start of a transaction (line 12) is fully open and accessible to the programmer, who can then implement all the variants required for the application.

To limit the transaction's scope to a group of instructions within a given method, you use the *anchoring protocol* technique.

This technique is similar to the implicit protocol technique, which has already been used several times in this book. The main difference is that the aspect does not implement the protocol methods but uses them as anchor points to add code within the target method.

For instance, we define two methods, beginTx (lines 4 and 19) and endTx (lines 5 and 28), as the anchoring protocol in Listing 11-23.

Listing 11-23. *Using an Anchoring Protocol in the transferFunds Method*

```
01  // modification of TxControllerBean by using a anchoring protocol
02  [...]
03  // protocol definition
04  private void beginTx() {};
05  private void endTx() {};
06
07  public void transferFunds(BigDecimal amount,String description,
08    String fromAccountId,String toAccountId)
09  throws
10    InvalidParameterException,AccountNotFoundException,
11    InsufficientFundsException,InsufficientCreditException {
12
13    Account fromAccount;
14    Account toAccount;
15
16    fromAccount= checkAccountArgsAndResolve(amount, description, fromAccountId);
17    toAccount= checkAccountArgsAndResolve(amount, description, toAccountId);
18
19    beginTx();
20
21    try {
22      String fromType= fromAccount.getType();
23      BigDecimal fromBalance= fromAccount.getBalance();
24
25      if (DomainUtil.isCreditAccount(fromType)) {
26      [...] // transfer implementation (see before)
27
```

```
28      endTx();
29
30   } catch (RemoteException ex) {
31      throw new EJBException("makePayment: " + ex.getMessage());
32   }
33
34 } // transferFunds
```

Then, the aspect shown in Listing 11-24 introduces the transaction management logic for the code placed between the beginTx and endTx anchors.

Listing 11-24. *Using an Aspect to Inject the Transaction Management Code with the Anchoring Protocol*

```
package aop.j2ee.business.aspect;

import javax.ejb.EJBException;
import aop.j2ee.business.session.txcontroller.TxControllerPOJO;
import aop.j2ee.business.entity.account.Account;

public privileged aspect Transaction {

  javax.transaction.UserTransaction ut;

  after(TxControllerPOJO controller) : execution(
    void TxControllerPOJO.beginTx())
    && withincode(* TxControllerPOJO.transferFunds(..))
    && this(controller) {
    ut= controller.context.getUserTransaction();
    try {
      ut.begin();
    } catch (Exception e) {
      throw new EJBException("transferFunds: " + e.getMessage());
    }
  }

  after() : call(void TxControllerPOJO.endTx())
    && withincode(* TxControllerPOJO.transferFunds(..)) {

      ut.commit();    try {
      ut= null;
    } catch (Exception ex) {
      try {
        ut.rollback();
      } catch (Exception e) {
        throw new EJBException("transferFunds: " + e.getMessage());
      }
```

```
        throw new EJBException("transferFunds: " + ex.getMessage());
    }
}

after()throwing(Exception ex)
  throws
    EJBException : call(* Account +.* (..))
    && withincode(* TxControllerPOJO.transferFunds(..)) {
  try {
    if (ut != null)
      ut.rollback();
  } catch (Exception e) {
    throw new EJBException("transferFunds: " + e.getMessage());
  }
  throw new EJBException("transferFunds: " + ex.getMessage());
}
```

The anchoring protocol technique, however, does not allow a precise management of exceptions. This can be solved by testing the variable that indicates we are within the delimited zone (here ut).

When the environment allows, it is also important to take multithreading into account (it is not used in our example). The use of the threadlocals for the variables that have to be shared by advice codes is then necessary. The aspect instantiation directive per thread can also be an elegant solution.

Summary

In this chapter, we have presented the use of AOP to improve the design of the business tier.

From a separation of concerns perspective, we can conclude that the AOP is successfully applied to our case study since many crosscutting concerns have been more clearly separated, including the following:

- Dependencies towards the EJB/J2EE technology

- Management and resolving of business object references

- Persistence

- Preconditions (including technical and business preconditions)

- Transactions

It is still possible to modularize other concerns, such as logging, that we have not shown here.

Figure 11-3 shows the components that form the business tier when all the aspects are applied. Each gray bar corresponds to a regular EJB. Indeed, the gray color indicates that no aspects have been applied. The first bar corresponds to the Entity EJB AccountBean, the second corresponds to the AccountPOJO, and so on for each component.

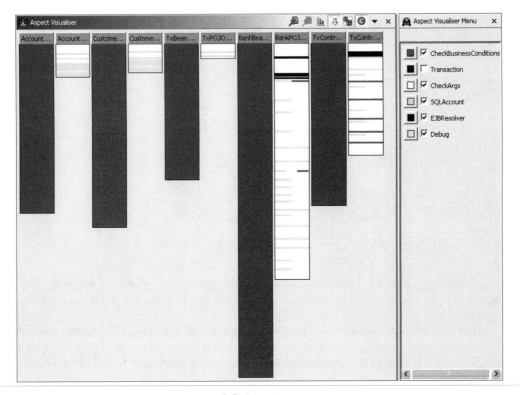

Figure 11-3. *Business tier components and their aspects*

We can note that the sizes of the business components implementations are clearly smaller for the POJO versions. This comes from the persistence externalization.

Advice codes are used more in facade components (like the last two) than in the business components. This comes from an implementation choice, which makes a great use of inter-type declarations on business components.

CHAPTER 12

■■■

Using AOP in the Sample Application's Presentation and Client Tiers

In Chapter 11, we used AOP to improve the business tier design of the Duke's Bank case study application presented in Chapter 10. In this chapter, we'll investigate the use of AOP in other tiers—in particular, the Java (Swing) client tier and the presentation tier. We will not use the data tier since it cannot benefit from Java-based AOP techniques (as we explained previously in Chapter 11).

The original design of the case study does not adapt completely to AOP because it uses ad hoc design solutions. The web presentation tier, for example, uses the Struts framework, which encapsulates some difficult design issues. This does not mean that AOP cannot be useful, especially for improving Struts implementation or integration. However, because of the inherent complexity, in this chapter we introduce simplified pieces of design to more clearly illustrate the advantages of AOP.

We first show the use of AOP in the Java Swing client, and then we elaborate on its impacts for the web (Servlets/JSP) presentation tier.

Using AOP for Distributed Communications

Communication issues can arise when clients access the business servers in a three-tier J2EE environment. The client tier contains several design patterns that are designed to deal with the concerns that come with distributed communications.

The J2EE design patterns for communication and data transfer most often impact the client side and occasionally impact the server side. Thus, these patterns represent an important source of crosscutting, especially when building multiclient applications.

As previously explained, the use of J2EE design patterns is not mandatory. However, by using them, we can contrast aspect-oriented implementations with well-documented, well-known, and proven reference designs.

Design Patterns for Business Layer Access

The three main J2EE design patterns for client/server communication are the business delegate, the service locator, and the data transfer object. In this chapter, we illustrate these patterns used with and without the help of AOP.

For simplicity, we use a basic Java client that accesses the sample application presented in Chapter 11 as well as this one. We discuss its limitations and show how aspects improve the client implementation independence with regard to the technology and the design choices.

Business Delegate

The goal of the *business delegate* is to hide the implementation details of the server remote access protocol, such as the lookup of the EJB container, through a JNDI repository or the processing of remote invocations. As a consequence, this design pattern reduces the coupling between the presentation tier clients and the business tier.

However, this design pattern does not completely eliminate the dependence, because its interface is subject to change if the business services are modified. Moreover, the systematic reference to the business delegate layer within each client implementation constitutes by itself a crosscutting concern.

Even though the location and the transparency of the distribution layers are benefits of this pattern, the business delegate can induce some subtle utilization problems. Indeed, the client cannot use a business delegate as if it was a local object, since doing so may generate serious performance issues, such as network overloads. Therefore, client-side programmers must be aware that the manipulated objects are proxies for remote objects.

Listing 12-1 defines a simple Java client, which we have developed to illustrate the issues discussed in this section. These issues can be transposed into real bank clients: the Java Swing administration client and the servlet-based presentation layer.

Listing 12-1. *A Simple Client for the Bank Application*

```
01  package aop.j2ee.client.java.regular;
02
03  import java.math.BigDecimal;
04  import java.util.Date;
05  import aop.j2ee.client.delegate.BankDelegate;
06  import aop.j2ee.commons.to.AccountDetails;
07
08  public class Simple {
09
10    public static void main(String[] args) {
11      try {
12        BankDelegate deleguate = new BankDelegate();
13        String customerId = deleguate.createCustomer("Pawlak","Renaud","P",
14                "Frederick St","Hartford","CT","06105","NA",
15                "renaud@aopsys.com");
16        System.out.println("Created new customer " + customerId);
17        String accountId = deleguate.createAccount(customerId,"Debit",
18                "This is a test.",new BigDecimal(100),new BigDecimal(0),
19                new BigDecimal(100),new Date());
```

```
20          System.out.println("Created new customer " + accountId);
21          deleguate.setAccountBalance(new BigDecimal(200), accountId);
22          System.out.println("Changed balance");
23          AccountDetails details = deleguate.getAccountDetails(accountId);
24          System.out.println("Account details:");
25          System.out.println(details);
26        } catch (Exception e) {
27          System.err.println(e.getMessage());
28          e.printStackTrace();
29        }
30      }
31    }
```

Here, the client uses only the business delegate created in line 12. All the code related to remote communication is modularized in this object.

As shown in the code in Listing 12-2, the business delegate is quite complex, as it integrates the calls to the getServiceFacade method, which implements the EJB lookup in the JNDI repository of the application server (line 34). This code uses a locator object, which we present later (see line 26 for its initialization).

Listing 12-2. *A Business Delegate Implementation for the Bank Application*

```
001  package aop.j2ee.client.delegate;
002
003  import java.math.BigDecimal;
004  import java.rmi.RemoteException;
005  import java.util.ArrayList;
006  import java.util.Date;
007  import java.util.ResourceBundle;
008
009  import javax.ejb.CreateException;
010  import javax.naming.NamingException;
011
012  import aop.j2ee.commons.exception.*;
013  import aop.j2ee.commons.to.AccountDetails;
014  import aop.j2ee.commons.to.CustomerDetails;
015  import aop.j2ee.commons.util.locator.ServiceLocator;
016
017  import aop.j2ee.business.session.bank.BankHome;
018  import aop.j2ee.business.session.bank.Bank;
019
020  public class BankDelegate {
021
022    private ResourceBundle messages;
023    private static ServiceLocator locator;
024    Bank bank = null;
025
026    private void init() throws SystemException {
027      try {
```

```
028        locator = ServiceLocator.getInstance();
029      } catch (NamingException ne) {
030        throw new SystemException(ne.getMessage());
031      }
032    }
033
034    private Bank getServiceFacade() throws SystemException {
035      if(bank!=null) return bank;
036      try {
037        BankHome home = (BankHome) locator.lookupHome(Bank.class);
038        bank = home.create();
039      } catch (ClassNotFoundException cne) {
040        throw new SystemException(cne.getMessage());
041      } catch (NamingException ne) {
042        throw new SystemException(ne.getMessage());
043      } catch (CreateException ce) {
044        throw new SystemException(ce.getMessage());
045      } catch (RemoteException re) {
046        throw new SystemException(re.getMessage());
047      }
048      return bank;
049    }
050
051    public BankDelegate() throws SystemException {
052      if (locator == null)
053        init();
054    }
055
056    public void addCustomerToAccount(String customerId,
057                                     String accountId)
058    throws RemoteException, AccountNotFoundException,
059         CustomerNotFoundException, CustomerInAccountException,
060         InvalidParameterException {
061      Bank bank;
062      try {
063        bank = getServiceFacade();
064      } catch (SystemException ex) {
065        ex.printStackTrace();
066        return;
067      }
068      bank.addCustomerToAccount(customerId, accountId);
069    }
070
071    public String createAccount(String customerId,String type,
072      String description,BigDecimal balance,BigDecimal creditLine,
073      BigDecimal beginBalance, Date beginBalanceTimeStamp)
074    throws
```

```
075    RemoteException, IllegalAccountTypeException,
076    CustomerNotFoundException,InvalidParameterException {
077
078    Bank bank;
079    try {
080      bank = getServiceFacade();
081    } catch (SystemException ex) {
082      ex.printStackTrace();
083      return null;
084    }
085    return bank.createAccount(
086      customerId,type,description,balance,creditLine,beginBalance,
087      beginBalanceTimeStamp);
088    }
089
090  public String createCustomer(String lastName,String firstName,
091    String middleInitial,String street,String city,String state,
092    String zip,String phone,String email)
093  throws InvalidParameterException, RemoteException {
094    Bank bank;
095    try {
096      bank = getServiceFacade();
097    } catch (SystemException ex) {
098      ex.printStackTrace();
099      return null;
100    }
101    return bank.createCustomer(lastName,firstName,middleInitial,
102      street,city,state,zip,phone,email);
103  }
104
105  public AccountDetails getAccountDetails(String accountId)
106  throws RemoteException, AccountNotFoundException,
107        InvalidParameterException {
108
109    Bank bank;
110    try {
111      bank = getServiceFacade();
112    } catch (SystemException ex) {
113      ex.printStackTrace();
114      return null;
115    }
116    return bank.getAccountDetails(accountId);
117  }
118
119  [...] // same delegation pattern
120        // to the bank for the other services
121 }
```

With each business delegate method, we retrieve the instance of the session facade introduced in Chapter 11 (line 63) and we call the corresponding service of this facade with the needed arguments (line 68).

Another advantage of the business delegate is that it encapsulates the remote communication strategies. For instance, timeout, retry, and caching policies can be implemented within the delegate so that the client code becomes more independent from these nonfunctional concerns.

Next, the code in Listing 12-3 shows the implementation of a simple retry policy within a delegate. This policy makes the application more stable if the network or server is temporarily unavailable. In this case, if the service resolving fails, we stop the current thread during one second (line 17) before retrying (line 18). Similarly, if we encounter an error during the invocation, we wait one second (line 33) and recursively retry (line 35). Note that we force the resolution of the facade in line 34.

Listing 12-3. *Adding a Retry Policy to the Bank Delegate*

```
01  public class BankDelegate {
02
03    [...]
04
05    public String createAccount(String customerId, String type, String descr,
06         BigDecimal balance, BigDecimal creditLine, BigDecimal beginBalance,
07         Date beginBalanceTimeStamp)
08      throws
09         RemoteException, IllegalAccountTypeException, CustomerNotFoundException,
10         InvalidParameterException {
11
12      Bank bank;
13      try {
14        bank= getServiceFacade();
15      } catch (SystemException ex) {
16        try {
17          Thread.sleep(1000);
18          bank= getServiceFacade();
19        } catch (SystemException ex2) {
20          ex2.printStackTrace();
21          return null;
22        } catch (InterruptedException ex2) {
23          ex2.printStackTrace();
24          return null;
25        }
26      }
27      String result=null;
28      try {
29        result = bank.createAccount(customerId, type, descr, balance, creditLine,
```

```
30                         beginBalance, beginBalanceTimeStamp);
31      } catch (RemoteException ex) {
32        try {
33          Thread.sleep(1000);
34          bank= null;
35          createAccount(customerId, type, description, balance, creditLine,
36                          beginBalance, beginBalanceTimeStamp);
37        } catch (InterruptedException ex2) {
38          ex2.printStackTrace();
39        }
40      }
41      return result;
42    }
43    [...]
```

The implementation in Listing 12-3 is clearly better than a simple implementation that would resolve and invoke the facade directly from the client code. However, this improvement is not entirely satisfactory for several reasons. First, to keep a clean business-level API, it is preferable to implement one business delegate for each business object. Even though this work is done only once in theory, coding the delegates is an error-prone and tedious task. Second, the accesses to the business delegate API constitute a crosscutting concern. Finally, delegates are not easy to reuse since they depend on the communication layer of the underlying J2EE infrastructure.

Notice that the business delegate implementation uses a class called ServiceLocator, which implements another client-side design pattern explained in the next section.

Service Locator

The *service locator* design pattern reduces the complexity resulting from the client's need to locate and create remote services access stubs. This concern is typical of J2EE environments. The modularization of this concern within a service locator does not remove all the technological dependencies.

First, a service locator user, such as a business delegate, must reference the javax.ejb. EJBHome and javax.ejb.EJBLocalHome interfaces. In addition, the exceptions of the javax.ejb, java.rmi, and javax.naming packages must be handled by the utilizing codes. These dependencies are shown in the BankDelegate code, which uses the service locator.

Some crosscutting concerns will remain when using the service locator within distinct client codes—for example, within a servlet-based presentation tier client and a business delegate of a Swing client. These crosscutting concerns implement the references to the EJB interfaces, the handling of the aforementioned exceptions, and the service locator reference, which we find within each client.

Recall that the service locator is also an implementation of the GoF singleton design pattern. Chapter 8 shows how a regular class can be automatically transformed into a singleton with a dedicated aspect (see the section "The Singleton Design Pattern" in Chapter 8 for more details).

Data Transfer Object

Within the client code given at the beginning of this chapter, we see the use of a service called getAccountDetails, which returns an object instance of the AccountDetails type. This object aggregates the attributes' values of an account and presents an interface close to Account. This object is one instantiation of a participant of a J2EE design pattern: the *data transfer object*.

A data transfer object can be used in two main cases:

- When a client computation unit needs to access more than one piece of data returned by the business layer (multiple downloads)

- When a client computation unit needs to send more than one piece of data to be completed (multiple uploads)

It is possible to reduce the number of remote calls by using the data transfer object design pattern, as shown in Listing 12-4. This pattern then proposes the use of a transfer object, which is designed to transfer a set of data from the client to the server, or vice versa. In this case, we use an AccountDetails transfer object. Since the transfer objects must be accessed from the client as well as from the server, all the transfer objects of the application are placed in the aop.j2ee.commons.to package (to means transfer object).

Listing 12-4. *A Transfer Object for the Bank Application*

```
01  package aop.j2ee.commons.to;
02
03  import java.math.BigDecimal;
04  import java.util.Date;
05  import java.util.ArrayList;
06
07  public class AccountDetails implements java.io.Serializable {
08
09      private String accountId;
10      private String type;
11      private String description;
12      private BigDecimal balance;
13      private BigDecimal creditLine;
14      private BigDecimal beginBalance;
15      private Date beginBalanceTimeStamp;
16      private ArrayList customerIds;
17
18      public AccountDetails(String accountId, String type, String descr,
19              BigDecimal balance, BigDecimal creditLine, BigDecimal beginBalance,
20              Date beginBalanceTimeStamp, ArrayList customerIds) {
21
22          this.accountId = accountId;
23          this.type = type;
24          this.description = descr;
25          this.balance = balance;
26          this.creditLine = creditLine;
```

```
27      this.beginBalance = beginBalance;
28      this.beginBalanceTimeStamp = beginBalanceTimeStamp;
29      this.customerIds = customerIds;
30   }
31
32   public String getAccountId() {return accountId;}
33   public String getDescription() {return description;}
34   public String getType() {return type;}
35   public BigDecimal getBalance() {return balance;}
36   public BigDecimal getCreditLine() {return creditLine;}
37   public BigDecimal getBeginBalance() {return beginBalance;}
38   public Date getBeginBalanceTimeStamp() {return beginBalanceTimeStamp;}
39   public ArrayList getCustomerIds() {return customerIds;}
40   public void setAccountId(String accountId) {this.accountId = accountId;}
41   public void setType(String type) {this.type = type;}
42   public void setDescription(String descr) {this.description = descr;}
43   public void setBalance(BigDecimal balance) {this.balance = balance;}
44   public void setCreditLine(BigDecimal n) {this.creditLine = n;}
45   public void setBeginBalance(BigDecimal n) {this.beginBalance = n;}
46   public void setBeginBalanceTimeStamp(Date beginBalanceTimeStamp){
47     this.beginBalanceTimeStamp = beginBalanceTimeStamp;
48   }
49   public void setCustomerIds(ArrayList ids) {this.customerIds= ids;}
50   public String toString() {
51      return "account "+accountId+" ("+type+")\n"+
52      "description: "+description+"\n"+
53      "balance: "+balance+"\n"+
54      "creditLine: "+creditLine+"\n"+
55      "beginBalance: "+beginBalance+"\n"+
56      "beginBalanceTimeStamp: "+beginBalanceTimeStamp+"\n"+
57      "customerIds: "+customerIds+"\n";
58   }
59
60 }
```

To be remotely transferable trough Remote Method Invocation (RMI), the transfer object must implement the java.io.Serializable interface. If the client is located on the same virtual machine as the server object (for instance, a local EJB), the client does not use RMI and the Serializable interface is then just redundant information.

For our case, with the Simple client, it is possible to optimize the client/server transfer of the data (upload). To do so, the client can use a CustomerAndAccountInfos transfer object, which aggregates the set of data for a given account and customer couple. The calls will then be reduced to one unique invocation to Bank.createAccountWithCustomer(CustomerAndAccountInfos), which is a new service to be added to the server for this specific optimization.

The main problem of the data transfer object pattern comes from the introduction of new server-side services. These services target the remote data exchange's optimization and depend greatly on how the clients use the servers. They pollute the business interfaces and make the global application less maintainable. For instance, when the business's needs evolve, important changes may have to be made to these patterns.

In conclusion, even though transfer objects can be employed in some cases (for instance, to aggregate the state of a given object), they are more difficult (and dangerous) to use in general (for example, when trying to optimize communication costs like CustomerAndAccountInfos). These objects are difficult to anticipate and can change depending on the application's architecture. Thus, a better modularization of this concern's implementation would be a great help for maintainability reasons. In the following section, we explain how AOP implements this separation.

Aspect-oriented Implementation of the Access Design Patterns

In the previous sections, we presented the three main design patterns for the business layer access: the business delegate, the service locator, and the data transfer object. These patterns work together to manage the business layer access within a distributed J2EE environment. We have discussed their limits and defects.

In this section, we propose an aspect-oriented implementation of these design patterns, which can be used as an alternative, elegant solution.

Eliminating Business Delegates

With an aspect-oriented design, the business delegate design pattern is not frequently needed. Indeed, the purpose of this pattern is to encapsulate the communication with the business facade (resolution, error handling, retry, and timeout). However, all this can be easily encapsulated within an "around" advice code.

This advice is to be applied to the direct invocations of a facade, which is called by a remote client through its Remote interface. The resolution of this interface can be done similarly to the business tier, by using the implicit protocol technique.

A first aspect of J2EE service locator can be implemented as shown in Listing 12-5.

Listing 12-5. *The Locator Aspect*

```
01  package aop.j2ee.client.java.aspect;
02
03  import java.rmi.RemoteException;
04  import javax.ejb.CreateException;
05  import javax.naming.NamingException;
06
07  import aop.j2ee.business.session.bank.BankHome;
08  import aop.j2ee.commons.exception.SystemException;
09
10  import aop.j2ee.commons.util.locator.*;
11
12  public aspect Locator {
13    public static final String BANK_SERVICE = "aop.j2ee.business.session.Bank";
14
15    public pointcut ejbservice(Class aClass) : call(
16    * aop.j2ee.client.java.aspectized..*.getServiceFacade(Class))&&args(aClass);
```

```
17
18    protected pointcut connectionservice(String aDataSource) :
19    call(* aop.j2ee.client.java.aspectized..*.getDatabaseConnection(String))
20    && args(aDataSource);
21
22    protected pointcut jmsservice(String aJMSObject) : call(
23    * aop.j2ee.client.java.aspectized..*.getJMSObject(String))&&args(aJMSObject);
24
25    protected Object createService(Class aClass, Object home)
26      throws Exception {
27      if (aClass.getName().equals(BANK_SERVICE)) {
28        BankHome bankhome = (BankHome) home;
29        return bankhome.create();
30      }
31      throw new Exception("Cannot create service for " + aClass);
32    }
33
34    public pointcut exception() :
35      call(* aop.j2ee..*+.*(..) throws *Exception)
36      && within(aop.j2ee.client.java.aspectized.* +);
37
38    private EJBServiceLocator ejbLocator;
39    private JDBCServiceLocator jdbcConnectionLocator;
40    private JMSServiceLocator jmsObjectLocator;
41
42    Object around(Class aClass)
43      throws SystemException : ejbservice(aClass) {
44        Object service = null;
45      try {
46        if (ejbLocator == null)
47          ejbLocator = new EJBServiceLocator();
48        Object home = ejbLocator.lookup(aClass);
49        service = createService(aClass,home);
50      } catch (NamingException ne) {
51        throw new SystemException(ne.getMessage());
52      } catch (ClassNotFoundException cne) {
53        throw new SystemException(cne.getMessage());
54      } catch (CreateException ce) {
55        throw new SystemException(ce.getMessage());
56      } catch (RemoteException re) {
57        throw new SystemException(re.getMessage());
58      } catch (Exception e) {
59        throw new SystemException(e.getMessage());
60      }
61      return service;
62    }
63
```

```
64   Object around(String aDataSource)
65     throws SystemException : connectionservice(aDataSource) {
66     Object connection = null;
67     try {
68       if (jdbcConnectionLocator == null)
69         jdbcConnectionLocator = new JDBCServiceLocator();
70       connection = jdbcConnectionLocator.lookup(aDataSource);
71     } catch (Exception ne) {
72       throw new SystemException(ne.getMessage());
73     }
74     return connection;
75   }
76
77   Object around(String aName)
78     throws SystemException : jmsservice(aName) {
79     Object jmsObject = null;
80     try {
81       if (jmsObjectLocator == null)
82         jmsObjectLocator = new JMSServiceLocator();
83       jmsObject = jmsObjectLocator.lookup(aName);
84     } catch (Exception ne) {
85       throw new SystemException(ne.getMessage());
86     }
87     return jmsObject;
88   }
89 }
```

This aspect goes beyond EJB service resolution because it also allows for the resolution of JMS services and data sources. It relies on a simple implicit protocol that hides the implementations of the actual resolution, which is transparently inserted by the aspects.

Hence, for each resolving type, the client can define one of these empty methods:

- aclass.getServiceFacade(Class) (pointcut line 15)

- aclass.getDatabaseConnection(Class) (pointcut line 18)

- aclass.getJMSObject(Class) (pointcut line 22)

The actual implementations are then provided by the corresponding "around" advice codes (lines 42, 64, and 77).

Thanks to this aspect, the Simple client defined previously can be modified as shown in Listing 12-6.

Listing 12-6. *The Simple Client Aspectized*

```
package aop.j2ee.client.java.aspectized;

import java.math.BigDecimal;
import java.util.Date;
```

```
import aop.j2ee.business.session.bank.Bank;
import aop.j2ee.commons.to.AccountDetails;
import aop.j2ee.commons.exception.SystemException;


public class Simple {

  public static void main(String[] args) {

    try {
      BankDelegate deleguate = new BankDelegate();
      String customerId =
        deleguate.createCustomer("Pawlak","Renaud","P",
        "Frederick St","Hartford","CT","06105","NA",
        "renaud@aopsys.com");
      System.out.println("Created new customer " + customerId);
      String accountId =
        deleguate.createAccount(customerId,"Debit",
        "This is a test.",new BigDecimal(100),new BigDecimal(0),
        new BigDecimal(100),new Date());
      System.out.println("Created new customer " + accountId);
      deleguate.setAccountBalance(new BigDecimal(200), accountId);
      System.out.println("Changed balance");
      AccountDetails details =
        deleguate.getAccountDetails(accountId);
      System.out.println("Account details:");
      System.out.println(details);
    } catch (Exception e) {
      System.err.println(e.getMessage());
      e.printStackTrace();
    }
  }

  // implicit protocol for service resolving/locating
  static Object getServiceFacade(Class cl) throws SystemException {
    return null;
  }
}
```

This technique is particularly well suited for clients accessing the service through a business interface, which is most often the case. In the rare case in which the client needs to access the business layer through a dedicated interface (which should be avoided for maintainability reasons), it is still possible to use a classic business delegate pattern.

Like a regular client, the business delegate can use an implicit resolving protocol. It then relies on the aspects in case a communication layer–related problem occurs. We explain this in further detail next.

Managing Communication Layer–Related Problems

As stated previously in this chapter, to improve the reliability of the application in a distributed environment, which is by nature subject to service interruptions, it is important to implement policies such as retry or cache. Since we have eliminated the business delegate pattern, these policies cannot be implemented in the delegate any longer; they must be implemented in aspects.

AOP offers a natural framework to separate some subconcerns within the main remote communication concern. For instance, it is possible to separate retry and cache within two independent aspects. This design choice depends on the designers and their needs. It must be done after a careful analysis of the maintainability and evolution needs.

The aspect shown in Listing 12-7 implements a retry policy for account creation in the case of a physical communication error between the client and the server. This aspect can be considered as a simple fault tolerance aspect.

Listing 12-7. *The Retry Aspect*

```
01  package aop.j2ee.client.java.aspect;
02
03  import java.math.BigDecimal;
04  import java.rmi.RemoteException;
05  import java.util.Date;
06  import aop.j2ee.business.session.bank.Bank;
07  import aop.j2ee.commons.exception.*;
08  import aop.j2ee.client.java.aspectized.Simple;
09
10  public aspect Retry {
11
12     pointcut retry(String customerId,String type,String description,
13                    BigDecimal balance,BigDecimal creditLine,
14                    BigDecimal beginBalance,
15                    Date beginBalanceTimeStamp):
16     call(public String Bank+.createAccount(..))
17     && within(Simple) && args(customerId,type,description,
18     balance,creditLine,beginBalance,beginBalanceTimeStamp);
19
20     String around(String customerId,String type,String description,
21                    BigDecimal balance,BigDecimal creditLine,
22                    BigDecimal beginBalance,Date beginBalanceTimeStamp)
23     throws RemoteException,IllegalAccountTypeException,
24            CustomerNotFoundException,InvalidParameterException:
25     retry(customerId, type, description, balance, creditLine,
26           beginBalance, beginBalanceTimeStamp) {
27       String result=null;
28       try {
29         result = proceed(customerId,type,description,
30            balance,creditLine,beginBalance,beginBalanceTimeStamp);
31       } catch (RemoteException ex) {
```

```
32       try {
33         Thread.sleep(1000);
34         result = proceed (
35           customerId,type,description,
36           balance,creditLine,beginBalance,beginBalanceTimeStamp);
37       } catch (InterruptedException ex2) {
38         ex2.printStackTrace();
39       }
40     }
41     return result;
42   }
43 }
```

The advice code of the aspect in Listing 12-7 is linked to the retry pointcut, which denotes the calls to the implementations of the remote Bank interface (line 16). The initial call of the service is done through the first call to proceed (line 29). If an error occurs, the retried call is done through a second call to proceed (line 34) after having waited one second (line 33). This aspect code can fall into an infinite loop when the communication layer systematically throws a RemoteException. This problem must be handled by modifying the implementation or by defining a new advice code to detect and break the infinite loops in a generic way.

To apply this aspect to a set of methods, instead of one particular method, we can use the nontyped generic AOP, which uses wildcards and the joinpoint API to access the base level information reflectively. Thus, the solution presented in Listing 12-8 is applied to all the facade's methods.

Listing 12-8. *Applying the Retry Aspect to All Bank Methods*

```
Object around():
call(public * Bank+.*(..))
&& within(Simple) {
  Object result=null;
  try {
    result = proceed();
  } catch (RemoteException ex) {
    try {
      Thread.sleep(1000);
      result = proceed();
    } catch (InterruptedException ex2) {
      ex2.printStackTrace();
    }
  }
  return result;
}
```

TYPED VS. GENERIC AOP

Some AOP technologies allow advice codes and pointcuts to be statically typed; this is called *typed AOP*. The Prose project, for example, allows for the typing of certain advice parameters, which results in optimization possibilities. Rickard Oberg proposes an implementation technique, based on abstract schemas, that provides static typing. AspectJ is certainly the most advanced language for this issue. In particular, it permits the binding of the different elements composing a joinpoint to some pointcut variables that can be used within the advice implementations.

When AOP is nontyped, or generic, and when joinpoint information needs to be accessed, the best alternative is to use reflection. Advice codes can introspect a joinpoint and access the current object (`this` or `target`), the currently invoked or executed method, and its parameters. All this information is available through untyped objects (`java.lang.Object` or `java.lang.reflect.Method`). Programmers then manually cast and unbox the objects as needed. In typed AOP, the program can pass an `int` parameter to an advice code, whereas in the generic case, the same parameter will be an `Object` to be cast into an `Integer` instance.

Both techniques have their advantages and drawbacks. Typed AOP permits a certain degree of program validation during the compilation and weaving phases. As a consequence, the IDE can potentially offer better support in terms of code completion, contextual help, and browsing. On the other hand, typed AOP is less flexible and makes it more difficult to write reusable advice code, as previously shown in the retry aspect. Typed AOP implies a strong dependency between the base program and the aspects. If the base program interface changes, it is likely to have an impact on the aspect's implementation, including the advice code, which can prevent reusability and evolution. This is the separation of concerns paradox: the better the concerns are separated, the less likely they are to evolve separately. Conversely, generic AOP allows the creation of generic and reusable aspects. However, it almost completely disables the compile- and weaving-time tests. Consequently, programmers should be more careful when programming with generic AOP.

With regard to performance, typed AOP has a great advantage over generic AOP, especially when advice code uses the advised method parameters. Indeed, the reflexive access to the arguments implies the creation of an array of objects, which is the primary reason for performance loss in generic AOP and, more generally, in reflective programming (see the `java.lang.reflect` API). We should note that this performance issue is completely insignificant for most real-world applications, where the complexity of the aspects and the business layer make the overhead insignificant in comparison. For instance, the generic retry aspect presented earlier creates an insignificant overhead in comparison to the remote call, which is done to invoke the facade's service.

For an optimal aspect-oriented design, both typed and generic AOP techniques should be used in a judicious way, so that the advantages of each can be realized when possible.

THE SEPARATION OF CONCERNS PARADOX

The ultimate goal of AOP is to provide better separation of concerns. This goal is reached with aspects since they allow the modularization of concerns that are not clearly modularized using regular programming techniques. However, with the separation of concerns into different modules, another kind of dependency appears when different modules are integrated. This dependency, which we can refer to as *association coupling*, is particularly important when using statically typed AOP.

For instance, with the statically typed retry aspect, a change in the method signature captured by the pointcut invalidates this pointcut definition, as well as the associated advice codes. Any evolution of the application can then become tedious in the long run. It is a paradox in the sense that separation of concerns makes the application more understandable and, at the same time, more difficult to maintain. This is the *separation of concerns paradox*.

The use of generic AOP minimizes this problem, but a coupling still remains within pointcuts or aspect configurations when supported (within the configuration interfaces of JAC, the XML configuration files of JBoss AOP or AspectWerkz, or even the annotations when using the upcoming Java 5–based technologies).

Even though we cannot deny the separation of concern paradox, aspect-oriented design is still a better alternative. With this design, the coupling of aspects is more localized than the coupling of the same implementation without any aspects. Additionally, it allows for faster refactoring in the case that the application changes. In other words, AOP does not remove the dependencies, but it allows for better control over them. Tool support can also help to control these dependencies. In JAC, for instance, the configuration level reduces the dependencies to a minimum. In AspectJ, we can improve the decoupling with the systematic use of abstract aspects (see Chapter 3) and the actual definitions of the pointcuts within concrete aspects extending the abstract aspects. The *pointcut library* technique can also be useful. For more details about these techniques, please refer to AspectJ's specific guides.

Introducing the Data Transfer Objects Transparently

As previously explained, the data transfer object pattern allows for the optimization of client/ server communications. It gathers a set of elementary requests into higher-level requests, which use transfer objects to aggregate the parameters of the elementary requests.

In specific cases, this design pattern greatly benefits from AOP; however, it is not recommended for modifying the business API for the purpose of optimizing the communications. Also, complicating the clients' implementation for the same reasons would be an anti-pattern.

With the help of AOP, we can define two aspects, one for the client and one for the server, so we can entirely free the application code from this optimization concern. First, we need to find the server utilization schemas (use cases) within the clients code that could benefit from a data transfer object optimization. If we take the code of the Simple client, we will see that the account creation is done in two consecutive remote invocations: a call to Bank.createCustomer and a call to Bank.createAccount, which take as a parameter the current created customer. This use case occurs, for instance, when registering a new customer and assigning that user a default account. This is a frequent operation that we would like to implement with only one remote call, to reduce network traffic. It can also be interesting to deal with one unique call/ transaction so that the rollback can be implemented in a more efficient way (only a local client-side cancellation is needed until we actually perform the call).

Once the use case code has been identified, we will define the transfer object that aggregates the needed data. Since this object will be used by the aspects, it can be useful to define it in a different package than the transfer objects that are explicitly used by the business layer (located in aop.j2ee.commons.to).

In Listing 12-9, the CustomerAndAccountInfos class defines a transfer object that gathers all the needed data.

Listing 12-9. *The CustomerAndAccountInfos Transfer Object*

```
package aop.j2ee.commons.aspect.to;

import java.math.BigDecimal;
import java.util.Date;
import java.io.Serializable;

public class CustomerAndAccountInfos implements Serializable {

    private String type;
    private String description;
    private BigDecimal balance;
    private BigDecimal creditLine;
    private BigDecimal beginBalance;
    private Date beginBalanceTimeStamp;
    private String lastName;
    private String firstName;
    private String middleInitial;
    private String street;
    private String city;
    private String state;
    private String zip;
    private String phone;
    private String email;

    public CustomerAndAccountInfos() {}

    public String getDescription() {return description;}
    public String getType() {return type;}
    [...]

    public void setType(String type) {this.type = type;}
    public void setDescription(String description) {
        this.description = description;
    }
    [...]
}
```

We now define a service (see Listing 12-10) that creates a new customer with a default account, using this data transfer object. As expected, this new service is defined by an aspect using intertype declarations. Two declarations are needed: one for adding the service prototype in the Remote interface of the bank facade (line 10) and another to add its implementation within BankBean or its POJO version, depending on whether we have used the business tier aspects presented in the previous chapter (line 16).

Listing 12-10. *A Transfer Object Aspect (Server Side)*

```
01  package aop.j2ee.business.aspect;
02
03  import java.rmi.RemoteException;
04  import aop.j2ee.commons.aspect.to.*;
05  import aop.j2ee.business.session.bank.*;
06  import aop.j2ee.commons.exception.*;
07
08  public aspect ServerSideTO {
09
10    public abstract String Bank
11      .createAccountWithCustomer(CustomerAndAccountInfos infos)
12    throws
13     RemoteException,IllegalAccountTypeException,
14     CustomerNotFoundException,InvalidParameterException;
15
16    public String BankBean
17      .createAccountWithCustomer(CustomerAndAccountInfos infos)
18    throws
19     RemoteException,IllegalAccountTypeException,
20     CustomerNotFoundException,InvalidParameterException {
21
22      String customerId = createCustomer(infos.getLastName(),
23        infos.getFirstName(),infos.getMiddleInitial(),
24        infos.getStreet(),infos.getCity(),infos.getState(),
25        infos.getZip(),infos.getPhone(),infos.getEmail());
26
27      String accountId = createAccount(customerId,infos.getType(),
28        infos.getDescription(),infos.getBalance(),
29        infos.getCreditLine(),infos.getBeginBalance(),
30        infos.getBeginBalanceTimeStamp());
31
32      return accountId;
33    }
34  }
```

For the client side, we define an aspect that allows the transparent use of this service when the aggregated invocation sequence is used, as shown in Listing 12-11.

Listing 12-11. *A Transfer Object Aspect (Client Side)*

```
01  package aop.j2ee.client.java.aspect;
02
03  import java.math.BigDecimal;
04  import java.util.Date;
05  import aop.j2ee.commons.aspect.to.*;
06  import aop.j2ee.business.session.bank.Bank;
07  import aop.j2ee.client.java.aspectized.Simple;
08
09  public aspect TransferOptimizer {
10
11    ThreadLocal to = new ThreadLocal();
12
13    Object around(String lastName,String firstName,
14      String middleInitial,String street,String city,
15      String state,String zip,String phone,String email) :
16    call(String aop.j2ee.business.session.bank.Bank+
17        .createCustomer(..))
18    && args(lastName,firstName,middleInitial,street,city,
19          state,zip,phone,email)
20    && withincode(void Simple.main(String[])) {
21      CustomerAndAccountInfos infos=new CustomerAndAccountInfos();
22      infos.setLastName(lastName);
23      infos.setFirstName(firstName);
24      infos.setMiddleInitial(middleInitial);
25      infos.setStreet(street);
26      infos.setCity(city);
27      infos.setState(state);
28      infos.setZip(zip);
29      infos.setPhone(phone);
30      to.set(infos);
31      return null;
32    }
33
34    Object around(Bank bank,String customerId,String type,
35      String description,BigDecimal balance,BigDecimal creditLine,
36      BigDecimal beginBalance,Date beginBalanceTimeStamp) :
37    call(String aop.j2ee.business.session.bank.Bank+
38        .createAccount(..))
39    && args(customerId,type,description,balance,creditLine,
40          beginBalance,beginBalanceTimeStamp)
41    && withincode(void Simple.main(String[]))
42    && target(bank) {
```

```
43    CustomerAndAccountInfos infos =
44      (CustomerAndAccountInfos)to.get();
45    if (infos == null) {
46      return proceed(bank,customerId,type,description,balance,
47        creditLine,beginBalance,beginBalanceTimeStamp);
48    } else {
49      infos.setType(type);
50      infos.setDescription(description);
51      infos.setBalance(balance);
52      infos.setCreditLine(creditLine);
53      infos.setBeginBalance(beginBalance);
54      infos.setBeginBalanceTimeStamp(beginBalanceTimeStamp);
55      String id = bank.createAccountWithCustomer(infos);
56      // reset the transfer object
57      to.set(null);
58      return id;
59    }
60  }
```

The implementation of the communication optimization aspect `TransferOptimizer` relies on a simple idea. When the first method of the sequence is called (the first advice code), we replace the call by the creation of the transfer object and its partial initialization (line 21). This transfer object is then locally saved in a threadlocal variable (lines 11 and 30). The threadlocal makes the aspect thread safe. Hence, the `TransferOptimizer` aspect behaves like an upload cache.

When the second method of the sequence is called, we complete the transfer object initialization with the parameters and invoke the `createAccountWithCustomer` remote service (line 55). This service is transparently added by the server-side aspect. If the thread local returns `null` (line 44), we assume that we are not within a sequence to optimize and we directly invoke the service (line 46). This technique can be generalized to any sequence.

Optimization aspects depend on the application code. If the program changes, the aspect is likely to be invalidated. For instance, if the program were using the `createCustomer` method's result, the optimization would not be valid any longer, since the program would have to return a `null` value for `createCustomer`. This coupling is stronger than the separation of concern paradox coupling. In this case, the aspect can be invalidated even if the object interfaces are stable, since the aspect heavily relies on their internal implementation.

Client Tier Communication Aspects Synthesis

So far, we have presented three aspects to manage typical concerns found in a distributed context, and we have applied them to a simple Java client (`aop.j2ee.client.java.aspectized.Simple`). These aspects are illustrated Figure 12-1.

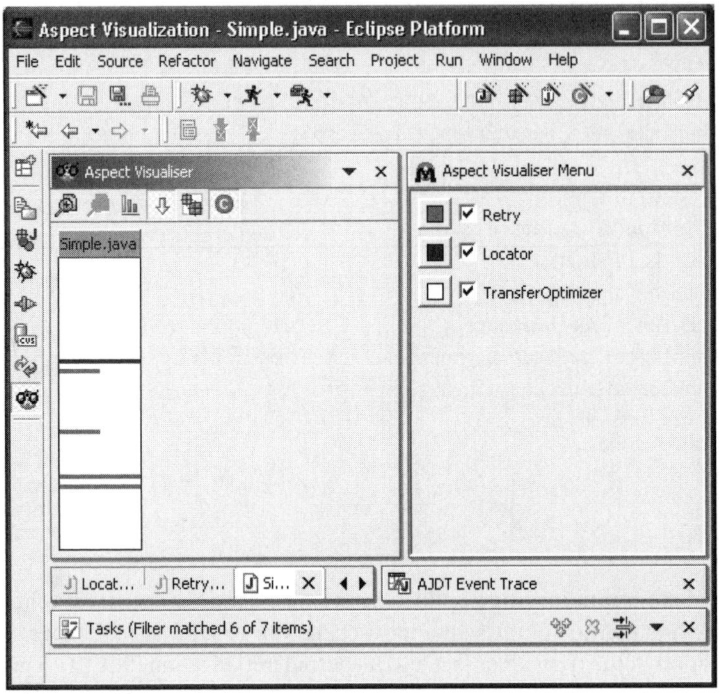

Figure 12-1. *Three aspects for client/server communication*

The three aspects have the following roles:

- `aop.j2ee.client.java.aspect.Locator` uses an implicit protocol to resolve the business facades. The darkest line of the `Simple.java` bar corresponds to the implementation of the `getServiceFacade` method, which is defined but not implemented by the client.

- `aop.j2ee.client.java.aspect.Retry` implements a retry policy to minimize the impacts of potential communication errors. We use the generic aspect, which applies to all the methods (three lines).

- `aop.j2ee.client.java.aspect.TransferOptimizer` enhances the client's performance by seamlessly introducing a transfer object. The two lines related to this aspect correspond to the `createCustomer` and `createAccount` calling sequence, which we optimize with the transfer object.

This is not a complete design of a distributed concern. Coverage of all the possible subconcerns of this complicated concern is beyond the scope of this book, but this design gives you some indication of how to build well-designed distributed applications by using AOP. Note that the same design has also been successfully applied to the administration client of the bank.

Using AOP for the Presentation of the Client Tier

Once the communication concerns are managed, the client handles the presentation, which is usually a complicated task. In the case of Swing-based clients, the techniques do not differ from non-J2EE applications. For a thin web client, the implementation differs, since the presentation is located on the server side within a web container over JSP/Servlets.

This section presents use cases for AOP in the presentation tier. First, we show examples of the UI in general. Next, we study the web presentation tier by enhancing the design patterns commonly used for this tier.

Using AOP for UI Concerns

Because of its complexity, the UI often represents an important part of an application's development. Although these concerns are not J2EE specific, aspects can help in their development.

In the sections that follow, we illustrate the use of AOP for two generic UI concerns: internationalization and condition verification on input data. To do so, we rely on the Java Swing administration client of the banking application.

Application Internationalization

An ongoing concern during development of J2EE applications is application internationalization. *Internationalization* consists of supporting several languages within the same application. Property files are frequently used to support this concern. In Java, however, numerous operations need to be performed in order to implement internationalization.

For instance, a common solution for handling error messages is to define the error message set within a property file, which can be translated into different languages. The client-side configuration indicates which file to use in the program. For the banking administration client, this configuration is done by a launching parameter:

```
%JAVA_HOME%\bin\java -Daop.j2ee.config.applicationname=BankAdmin
  -Daop.j2ee.config.applicationconfigdir=c:/aop/config
  -Daop.j2ee.config.applicationpropertyfile=bankadmin.properties
  aop.j2ee.client.java.BankAdmin
```

When necessary, the client program manages the access mechanism to the messages defined in the file. Generally, these accesses are scattered all over the code, particularly in the exception handling code, as illustrated in Listing 12-12.

Listing 12-12. *Sample Application Excerpt That Illustrates Exception Handling*

```
01  // excerpt of aop.j2ee.client.java.regular.DataModel
02  [...]
03  protected void createActInf(int currentFunction, String returned) {
04      AccountDetails details = null;
05      //View Account Information
06      if ((currentFunction == 4) && (returned.length() > 0)) {
```

```
07        try {
08            details = bank.getAccountDetails(returned);
09            boolean readonly = true;
10            frame.setDescription(details.getDescription());
11            ArrayList alist = new ArrayList();
12            alist = details.getCustomerIds();
13            frame.createActFields(
14                readonly,
15                details.getType(),
16                details.getBalance(),
17                details.getCreditLine(),
18                details.getBeginBalance(),
19                alist,
20                details.getBeginBalanceTimeStamp());
21        } catch (AccountNotFoundException ex) {
22            frame.resetPanelTwo();
23            frame.messlab3.setText(
24                messages.getString("AccountException")
25                + " " + returned + " "
26                + messages.getString("NotFoundException"));
27        } catch (RemoteException ex) {
28            frame.messlab.setText(
29                messages.getString("Remote Exception"));
30        } catch (InvalidParameterException ex) {
31            frame.messlab.setText(
32                messages.getString("InvalidParameterException"));
33        }
34    } [...]
```

Lines 24, 26, 29, and 32 show where the application accesses the international messages, which are indexed by string keys. As demonstrated, internationalization is a crosscutting concern, which can be difficult to handle. In addition, maintenance is more difficult since the accesses are scattered in the client code and closely tangled with exception handling.

The externalization of the error handling concern in the internationalization context is performed in the i18n aspect. However, the internationalization concern must also deal with issues such as measurement units, currencies, and labels in graphical components.

The i18n aspect shown in Listing 12-13 is the first step toward a modular internationalization.

Listing 12-13. *A Simple Internationalization Aspect*

```
01  package aop.j2ee.client.java.aspect;
02
03  import java.rmi.RemoteException;
04  import aop.j2ee.commons.exception.*;
05  import aop.j2ee.client.java.aspectized.BankAdmin;
```

```
06
07  public privileged aspect I18n {
08
09      // translation of common exception messages
10      Object around() throws RemoteException, InvalidParameterException:
11          call(* aop.j2ee.business.session.bank.Bank+.*(..) throws *Exception)
12          && within(aop.j2ee.client.java.aspectized.*+) {
13
14      Object value = null;
15      try {
16        value = proceed();
17      } catch (RemoteException ex) {
18        throw new RemoteException(BankAdmin.messages.getString(
19            "Remote Exception"),ex);
20      } catch (InvalidParameterException ex) {
21        throw new InvalidParameterException(BankAdmin.messages.getString(
22            "InvalidParameterException"),ex);
23      }
24      return value;
25    }
26
27    // handling of joinpoint-specific exceptions
28    Object around(String accountId) throws AccountNotFoundException:
29    call(* aop.[...].Bank+.getAccountDetails(String) throws *Exception)
30    && args(accountId) && within(aop.j2ee.client.java.aspectized.*+) {
31
32      Object value = null;
33      try {
34        value = proceed(accountId);
35      } catch (AccountNotFoundException ex) {
36          throw new AccountNotFoundException(
37          BankAdmin.messages.getString("AccountException")
38            + " " + accountId + " "
39            + BankAdmin.messages.getString("NotFoundException"),ex);
40      }
41      return value;
42    }
43
44    [...] // other specific exceptions
45  }
```

For each exception thrown, the aspect builds a new exception that contains an internationalized message (lines 18, 21, and 36) in order to modularize the management of error message internationalization.

Figure 12-2 gives an overview of where the aspect is applied by showing the advised calls within the bank administration client (see aop.j2ee.client.java.aspectized.DataModel).

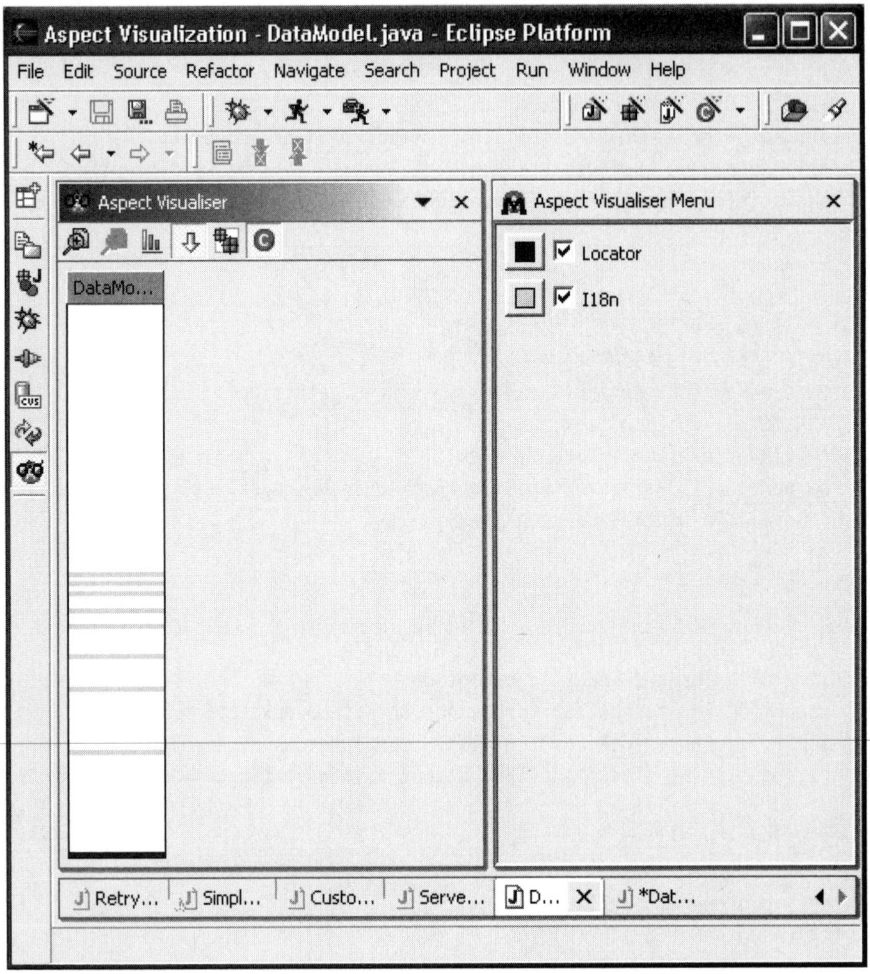

Figure 12-2. *Application of the i18n aspect to the Swing Java client of Duke's Bank*

With the previous aspect, the internationalized exceptions are sent to the client. The client does not have to handle this concern itself. For instance, the createActInf method of the administration client can be simplified as shown in Listing 12-14.

Listing 12-14. *Aspectizing the Administration Client with the i18n Aspect*

```
// excerpt of aop.j2ee.client.java.aspectized.DataModel
[...]
protected void createActInf(int currentFunction, String returned) {
  AccountDetails details= null;

  if ((currentFunction == 4) && (returned.length() > 0)) {
    try {
      details= bank.getAccountDetails(returned);
```

```
      boolean readonly= true;
      frame.setDescription(details.getDescription());
      ArrayList alist= new ArrayList();
      alist= details.getCustomerIds();
      frame.createActFields(
        readonly,
        details.getType(),
        details.getBalance(),
        details.getCreditLine(),
        details.getBeginBalance(),
        alist,
        details.getBeginBalanceTimeStamp());

    // exception messages are already internationalized by the i18n aspect
    } catch (AccountNotFoundException ex) {
      frame.resetPanelTwo();
      frame.messlab3.setText(ex.getMessage());
    } catch (RemoteException ex) {
      frame.messlab.setText(ex.getMessage());
    } catch (InvalidParameterException ex) {
      frame.messlab.setText(ex.getMessage());
    }
  }
}
```

The client can access the original exception by using the ex.getCause method. After Java 1.4, the cause of the exception is also included in the stack trace and is shown by the ex.printStackTrace method below the "caused by" line. This works only if the aspect passes the original exception as a parameter while constructing the internationalized exception (see lines 18, 21, and 36 of the i18n aspect).

Input Constraints Verification

When developing UIs, verifying constraints on the data entered by the users is a recurring issue. For example, all data entered to create a new client should be verified and checked for accuracy. The program should test that the e-mail, ZIP code, and so forth are correctly formatted. The program can also force the user to enter additional information.

It is important to clearly modularize this concern for three main reasons:

- First, it is a concern that crosscuts all the functions related to data input and validation.

- Second, in general, it is a concern that evolves and is refined over time, sometimes independent of other concerns.

- Third, for the security of the application, the entered data should be controlled on the server side. For client latency reasons, it is also preferable to implement some control on the client. Aspect-oriented modularization makes it easier to maintain consistency between the client and server sides.

To clarify the second point, we can compare the aspect-oriented development of the constraint verification to a use case–based development methodology. In a use case–based methodology, we find primary use cases, which correspond to the normal behavior of the application (here, the entering of the data by the user), and secondary use cases, which correspond to the abnormal behavior of the application (here, errors and input error handling). Among secondary cases, a use case–guided analysis generally assigns priorities to the use cases. Some of them are not critical and do not need to be implemented during the first iterations (for instance, checking that the entered name starts with an uppercase letter).

Similarly, when developing UI and data verification, we start with primary cases (verifications) and critical secondary cases. Only after the development of these cases is completed can we implement the noncritical cases (verifications). If the verification concern is not correctly modularized, testing a new case will be difficult because its code will be tangled up with the code of the preexisting cases.

Thus, the use of AOP helps to handle the growing complexity of the verification concern. In particular, the use of well-chosen pre-/postcondition aspects (such as the ones explained in Chapters 9 and 11) allow the modularized implementation of the verification concern.

Using AOP in the Design Patterns of the Web Presentation Tier

In a J2EE context, the web presentation logic relies on Servlets technology. Servlets are Java components that reply to HTTP requests coming from the web server and are transmitted to the J2EE web container. Some well-known containers are Apache Tomcat (reference implementation) and Caucho Resin (http://www.caucho.com/resin-2.1/index.xtp). To help with the programming of GUI dedicated servlets, Sun Microsystems defined the JavaServer Pages (JSP) standard.

Since servlets are low-level components, certain J2EE design patterns have been defined to manage the presentation efficiently. Here we will evaluate how aspects enhance the design of the presentation tier when compared to J2EE design pattern–based solutions.

In this section, we introduce the presentation tier design patterns and discuss how they can be improved with AOP. We do not rely directly on the sample application since the presentation would be too complicated to discuss here. Furthermore, the sample application uses the Struts framework, which provides a packaged and ready-to-use implementation of a set of J2EE design patterns.

To fully understand this section, knowledge of Servlets/JSP technologies (http://java.sun.com/products/jsp/docs.html) and of presentation tier J2EE design patterns (http://java.sun.com/blueprints/corej2eepatterns/Patterns/index.html) is necessary.

Front Controller

The role of a *front controller* design pattern is to centralize the base management logic of the requests and to forward them to the appropriate managers. Thus, the client's requests go through the front controller, which contains a command dictionary.

Command objects are usually instances of the application controller design pattern, even though it is still possible to choose alternate designs. More precisely, the controller's behavior handles the requests by looking up the appropriate command for the given request's URL and delegating this request to the command. In addition, the controller can encapsulate server-specific data in a context object. *Context objects* are regular Java objects used to make the GUI logic as independent as possible from the HTTP protocol.

Listing 12-15 presents the important parts of a simple front controller.

Listing 12-15. *A Simple Front Controller*

```
package aop.j2ee.client.web.controller;

01  import java.io.IOException;
02  import java.util.Hashtable;
03  import javax.servlet.RequestDispatcher;
04  import javax.servlet.http.HttpServlet;
05  import javax.servlet.http.HttpServletRequest;
06  import javax.servlet.http.HttpServletResponse;
07  import aop.j2ee.client.web.protocol.RequestContextFactory;
08  import aop.j2ee. client.web.protocol.RequestContext;
09
10  public class FrontController extends HttpServlet {
11    static final String ERROR_VIEW = "/error.jsp";
12    [...] // other URLs
13    static Hashtable pathInfoCommandMap = new Hashtable();
14
15    public void init(javax.servlet.ServletConfig config) throws ServletException {
16      super.init(config);
17      pathInfoCommandMap.put("/logon","aop.j2ee.[...].LoginController");
18      pathInfoCommandMap.put("/subscribe","aop.j2ee. [...].SubscribeController");
19      [...] // other paths of application controllers
20    }
21
22    public void doGet [...] // process method invocation
23    public void doPost[...] // process method invocation
24
25    protected void process(HttpServletRequest request, HttpServletResponse resp)
26          throws ServletException, IOException {
27      String pathInfo = request.getPathInfo();
28
29      try {
30        // lookup the real path by delegating to the application controller
31        pathInfo=invokeApplicationController(pathInfo,request,resp );
32      } catch(Exception e) {
33        pathInfo = ERROR_VIEW;
34      }
35      // forward the control to the view / command
36      RequestDispatcher dispatcher = request.getRequestDispatcher(pathInfo);
37      dispatcher.forward(request,resp );
38    }
```

```
39
40    private String invokeApplicationController(
41                String aRequestPathInfo,
42                HttpServletRequest aRequest,
43                HttpServletResponse aResponse) throws Exception {
44      ApplicationController controller = null;
45      String className = (String)pathInfoCommandMap.get(aRequestPathInfo);
46      if(className != null) {
47        Class controllerClass = Class.forName(className);
48        controller = (ApplicationController)
49        controllerClass.newInstance();
50        if(controller != null)
51        aRequestPathInfo = (String)controller.process(aRequest,aResponse);
52      }
53      return aRequestPathInfo;
54    }
55  }
```

The process method of line 25 is a common method for handling requests. It checks if the user is logged. If so, it forwards the request to the requested URL; otherwise, it forwards the request to the login page.

When the application evolves, the front controller code becomes more complicated and handles more specific cases. A strategy to avoid this problem is to create an inheritance hierarchy to replace excessive conditional logic. For instance, for an application containing three distinct functional zones, we can factorize the commonalities within a superclass. Even though this design seems simple, it is complicated and tedious to program since the presentation layer and its associated needs are complex and often permanently redefined.

The use of an aspect improves the application's modularity by separating the base logic of a front controller from a given piece of application logic. For instance, in Listing 12-16, the FrontController aspect handles the delegation and encapsulation of the requests toward the application controllers.

Listing 12-16. *A Simple Front Controller Aspect*

```
01  package aop.j2ee.client.web.aspect;
02
03  import java.util.Hashtable;
04  import javax.servlet.http.HttpServlet;
05  import javax.servlet.http.HttpServletRequest;
06  import javax.servlet.http.HttpServletResponse;
07  import aop.j2ee.client.web.protocol.RequestContextFactory;
08  import aop.j2ee.client.web.protocol.RequestContext;
09  import aop.j2ee.client.web.controlleur.*;
10
11  public aspect FrontController {
12    static Hashtable pathInfoCommandMap = new Hashtable();
13
14    static {
```

```
15    pathInfoCommandMap.put("/logon","aop.j2ee.[...].LoginController");
16    pathInfoCommandMap.put("/subscribe","aop.j2ee.[...].SubscribeController");
17  }
18
19  pointcut trapApplicationController(String aRequestPathInfo,
20    HttpServletRequest aRequest, HttpServletResponse aResponse):
21    call(private String FrontController.invokeApplicationController(
22         String,HttpServletRequest,HttpServletResponse) throws Exception)
23    && args(aRequestPathInfo,aRequest,aResponse);
24
25  String around(String aRequestPathInfo,
26                HttpServletRequest aRequest,
27                HttpServletResponse aResponse)
28    throws Exception: trapApplicationController(aRequestPathInfo,
29                                          aRequest,aResponse) {
30    ApplicationController controller = null;
31    String className =
32      (String)pathInfoCommandMap.get(aRequestPathInfo);
33    if(className != null) {
34      Class controllerClass = Class.forName(className);
35      controller = (ApplicationController)controllerClass.newInstance();
36      if(controller != null) {
37        RequestContextFactory factory = RequestContextFactory.getInstance();
38        RequestContext context = factory.getRequestContext(aRequest);
39        aRequestPathInfo = (String)controller.process(context);
40      }
41    }
42    return aRequestPathInfo;
43  }
44 }
```

Note that here we use the implicit protocol technique, through the invokeApplicationController protocol method captured by the pointcut of line 11.

With this aspect, the front controller code implements the implicit protocol (line 23), as shown in Listing 12-17.

Listing 12-17. *The Aspectized Implementation of the Front Controller*

```
01  package aop.j2ee.client.web.controller;
02
03  import java.io.IOException;
04  import javax.servlet.RequestDispatcher;
05  import javax.servlet.ServletException;
06  import javax.servlet.http.HttpServlet;
07  import javax.servlet.http.HttpServletRequest;
08  import javax.servlet.http.HttpServletResponse;
09
10  public class FrontController extends HttpServlet {
```

```
11    static final String ERROR_VIEW = "/error.jsp";
12
13    public void doGet [...] // process invocation
14    public void doPost [...] // process invocation
15
16    protected void process(HttpServletRequest request,
17                                        HttpServletResponse response)
18    throws ServletException, IOException {
19      [...] // no changes
20    }
21
22    // implemented by the aspect
23    private String invokeApplicationController(
24          String aRequestPathInfo,
25          HttpServletRequest aRequest,
26          HttpServletResponse aResponse)
27    throws Exception { return aRequestPathInfo; } // default
28  }
```

Thus, the front controller code is independent from the application. The application's specific paths are defined within the aspect. HTTP requests are encapsulated in the application-level requests (RequestContextFactory and RequestContext) of the aop.j2ee.client.web. protocol package.

Application Controller

The *application controller* design pattern centralizes the control and the invocation of the application-specific views and commands. Similar to the front controller, a typical design implies that a base class implements the commonalities of the controllers. Also, the use of an aspect can be more efficient than inheritance for factorization.

Listing 12-18 shows that AOP simplifies the design of the application's presentation for the factorization of common functions. In any case, it allows the centralization of object initializations (see advice code lines 15 and 23).

Listing 12-18. *An Application Controller Aspect*

```
01  package aop.j2ee.client.web.aspect;
02
03  import aop.j2ee.client.web.bean.*;
04  import aop.j2ee.client.web.controller.*;
05  import aop.j2ee.client.web.protocol.RequestContext;
06  import aop.j2ee.client.web.protocol.LoginRequestContext;
07  import aop.j2ee.client.web.protocol.SubscriptionContext;
08
09  public aspect ApplicationController {
10
11    // initialization, through getRequestData, of the application controllers
12
```

```
13    void around(Object aBean,RequestContext aContext):
14         call(* LoginController.getRequestData(..)) && args(aBean,aContext) {
15      LoginRequestContext context=(LoginRequestContext)aContext;
16      UserBean bean = (UserBean)aBean;
17      bean.setUser(context.getUserName());
18      bean.setPassword(context.getUserPassword());
19    }
20
21    void around(Object aBean,RequestContext aContext):
22         call(* SubscribeController.getRequestData(..)) && args(aBean,aContext) {
23      SubscriberBean bean = (SubscriberBean)aBean;
24      SubscriptionContext context = (SubscriptionContext)aContext;
25      bean.setFirst(context.getFirstName());
26      bean.setLast(context.getLastName());
27      bean.setEmail(context.getEmail());
28    }
29    [...] // other controllers
30  }
```

With this aspect, the implementation of an authentication controller, for instance, focuses only on the request treatment implementation, as shown in Listing 12-19, still by using an implicit protocol (line 18).

Listing 12-19. *An Aspectized Login Controller*

```
01  package aop.j2ee.client.web.controller;
02
03  import aop.j2ee.client.web.controller.ApplicationController;
04  import aop.j2ee.client.web.command.Command;
05  import aop.j2ee.client.web.command.LoginCommand;
06  import aop.j2ee.client.web.protocol.RequestContext;
07  import aop.j2ee.client.web.protocol.LoginRequestContext;
08
09  // ApplicationController is an interface which defines process()
10  public class LoginController implements ApplicationController {
11    static final String USERBEAN_ATTR = "userbean";
12    static final String SUCCESS_VIEW = "/subscribe.html";
13    static final String FAILURE_VIEW = "/login.jsp";
14
15    public LoginController() {}
16
17    // implemented by the aspect (implicit protocol)
18    public void getRequestData(Object aBean,
19                               RequestContext aRequestContext) {}
20
21    public Object process(RequestContext aRequestContext)
22      throws Exception {
23      Command logon = new LoginCommand();
```

```
24      LoginRequestContext context = (LoginRequestContext)aRequestContext;
25      // initialize the bean which receives the request's data
26      getRequestData(logon.getReceiver(),context);
27      // execute the login command
28      String logicalRequest = ((Boolean)logon.executeCommand()).booleanValue()?
29          SUCCESS_VIEW:FAILURE_VIEW;
30      // put the bean in the context
31      context.setSessionAttribute(USERBEAN_ATTR,logon.getReceiver());
32      return logicalRequest;
33    }
34  }
```

Context Object

The *context object* design pattern encapsulates a contextual state linked to a request but independent of the HTTP protocol. The context object can then be used in the different roles of the presentation tiers.

The use of context objects makes the treatments simpler, more generic, and less dependent on a particular web container. The context object classes are generally part of an inheritance hierarchy, where the parent classes deal with the specificities of the HTTP protocol; they contain references to the javax.servlet.http package.

With AOP, the whole context object design pattern can be made independent from the HTTP protocol. The code of HttpRequestContext shows how to introduce the specificities of the HTTP protocol (see Listing 12-20).

Listing 12-20. *A Context Object Aspect*

```
package aop.j2ee.client.web.aspect;

import javax.servlet.http.HttpServletRequest;
import aop.j2ee.client.web.protocol.*;

public aspect HttpRequestContext {
  public static final String USER_PARAM = "subscriber";
  public static final String PASSWORD_PARAM = "password";

  // implementation of the tag interface
  declare parents: LoginRequestContext implements HttpRequestContext;
  declare parents: SubscriptionContext implements HttpRequestContext;
  [...] // other contexts types...

  public HttpServletRequest HttpRequestContext.request;
  public HttpServletRequest LoginRequestContext.loginRequest;
  public HttpServletRequest SubscriptionContext.subscriptionRequest;

  // implementation of the common behaviors

  public void HttpRequestContext.initialize(HttpServletRequest aRequest) {
```

```
      request = aRequest;
   }

   public void HttpRequestContext.setHttpRequest(HttpServletRequest aRequest) {
      request = aRequest;
   }

   public HttpServletRequest HttpRequestContext.getHttpRequest() {
     return request;
   }

   public String HttpRequestContext.getAuthType() {
     return getHttpRequest().getAuthType();
   }

   // same principle...
   public String HttpRequestContext.getCharacterEncoding() {...}
   public int HttpRequestContext.getContentLength() {...}
   public String HttpRequestContext.getContentType() {...}
   public String HttpRequestContext.getContextPath() {...}
   public String HttpRequestContext.getPathInfo() {...}
   public String HttpRequestContext.getPathTranslated() {...}
   public String HttpRequestContext.getProtocol(){...}
   public String HttpRequestContext.getQueryString(){...}
   public String HttpRequestContext.getRemoteAddress(){...}
   public String HttpRequestContext.getRemoteHost(){...}
   public String HttpRequestContext.getRemoteUser(){...}
   public String HttpRequestContext.getRequestedSessionID(){...}
   public String HttpRequestContext.getRequestURI(){...}
   public String HttpRequestContext.getScheme(){...}
   public String HttpRequestContext.getServerName(){...}
   public String HttpRequestContext.getServletPath(){...}
   public Object HttpRequestContext
   .getSessionAttribute(String aAttribute) {...}
   public void HttpRequestContext.setSessionAttribute(String attr,Object val) {...}
   public Object HttpRequestContext.getRequestAttribute(String aAttribute){...}
   public void HttpRequestContext.setRequestAttribute(String attr,Object val) {...}

   // login

   public void LoginRequestContext.setHttpRequest(HttpServletRequest aRequest) {
      loginRequest = aRequest;
   }

   public HttpServletRequest LoginRequestContext.getHttpRequest() {
     return loginRequest;
   }
```

```
public void LoginRequestContext
  .initialize(HttpServletRequest aRequest) {
  loginRequest = aRequest;
  setUserName(aRequest.getParameter(USER_PARAM));
  setUserPassword(aRequest.getParameter(PASSWORD_PARAM));
}

// subscription

public void SubscriptionContext.setHttpRequest(
  HttpServletRequest aRequest) {
  subscriptionRequest = aRequest;
}

public HttpServletRequest SubscriptionContext.getHttpRequest() {
  return subscriptionRequest;
}

public void SubscriptionContext
  .initialize(HttpServletRequest aRequest) {
  subscriptionRequest = aRequest;
  setFirstName(aRequest.getParameter(FIRST_PARAM));
  setLastName(aRequest.getParameter(LAST_PARAM));
  setEmail(aRequest.getParameter(EMAIL_PARAM));
}

// other requests
[...]
}
```

Interception Filter

The role of the *interception filter* is to intercept the incoming requests and outgoing responses so that extra functions can be applied. The web container is responsible for calling the filters, which can be declaratively added and removed in the web.xml file, as shown in Listing 12-21.

Listing 12-21. *Declarative Configuration of the Filters*

```
<filter>
<filter-name>silverMembership</filter-name>
<filter-class>
aop.j2ee.presentation.controller.MembershipFilter
</filter-class>
<init-param>
<param-name>subscriptionType</param-name>
<param-value>silver</param-value>
```

```
</init-param>
<init-param>
<param-name>denyPage</param-name>
<param-value>/secure/denied.jsp</param-value>
</init-param>
</filter>
```

The filters encapsulate recurring logic within reusable objects and thus enhance the code modularity. For instance, they can add/remove or activate/deactivate presentation elements depending on the user's profile.

Listing 12-22 shows part of a filter that changes the response to deny a page if the user is not authorized to access the current application space.

Listing 12-22. *An Authorization Filter Example*

```
01   package aop.j2ee.client.web.controller;
02
03   import java.io.IOException;
04   import javax.servlet.*;
05   import javax.servlet.http.*;
06   import aop.j2ee.presentation.bean.SubscriberBean;
07
08   public class MembershipFilter implements Filter {
09     [...]
10     private String subscriptionType;
11     private String denyPage;
12
13     public MembershipFilter() {}
14
15     public void init(FilterConfig config) throws ServletException {
16       subscriptionType = config.getInitParameter("subscriptionType");
17       denyPage = config.getInitParameter("denyPage");
18     }
19
20     public void doFilter(ServletRequest request,
21                            ServletResponse response,
22                            FilterChain chain)
23     throws IOException, ServletException {
24       [...] // applies a treatment on the request
25       // go on with the application of the filters
26       chain.doFilter(request,response);
27       [...]/ / applies a treatment on the response
28     }
29
30     public void destroy() {}
31   }
```

In the *filter object* design pattern, we can identify a typical structure of AOP: the "around" advice code. To get the same effect, we could replace the MembershipFilter class with an aspect, and the filter method doFilter (line 20) with "around" advice code. Indeed, the invocation of the doFilter method on the chain (line 26) has a similar effect as proceed within "around" advice code.

The use of AOP does not greatly improve the code modularity, because the resulting implementation is very similar to that of the filter object pattern. However, it can improve performance in an outstanding way since the web container handles the interception chain in a transparent and noncontrollable manner. The mechanism is dynamic and may induce overhead. Due to compile-time weaving such as in AspectJ, the interception code can be inserted directly within the target class code, thus removing the implementation of the chain initialization and iteration mechanism.

Listing 12-23 shows an aspect-oriented implementation of a filter.

Listing 12-23. *An Implementation of the Authorization Filter Using AOP*

```
01  package aop.j2ee.client.web.aspect;
02
03  import java.io.IOException;
04  import javax.servlet.*;
05  import javax.servlet.http.*;
06  import aop.j2ee.presentation.bean.SubscriberBean;
07
08  public class SilverMembershipFilterAspect {
09      declare precedence: GoldMembershipFilterAspect,
10                                       SilverMembershipFilterAspect, *;
11
12      private String FrontController.subscriptionType="silver";
13      private String FrontController.denyPage="/secure/denied.jsp";
14
15      pointcut filter(ServletRequest request,ServletResponse response):
16        execution(protected void process(HttpServletRequest, HttpServletResponse))
17                      && args(request,response);
18
19      around(ServletRequest request,
20              ServletResponse response): filter(request,response) {
21
22      throws IOException, ServletException {
23        [...] // applies a treatment to the request
24        // continues the filters application
25        proceed(request,response);
26        [...] // applies a treatment to the response
27      }
28  }
```

In the aspect-oriented solution, proceed implements the call to the next filter (line 25). The order in which the filters are applied is defined by the precedence declaration (line 9). Here, we apply the filter with the pointcut that corresponds to the execution of the request processing of the front controller (line 15). This ensures that all the incoming requests and outgoing responses are filtered out. The pointcut could have been factorized in a superclass, since it is the same for all the filters.

Note that this technique is more flexible than the original. By modifying the pointcut we can, for instance, install the filters on the application controllers rather than only the front ones. The only disadvantage of this technique is that the filters are not defined in a declarative way (in the web.xml file). When a change is made, the application then needs to be recompiled.

View Helper

The *view helper* is a Java object that implements subparts of a JSP page's logic. This design pattern externalizes Java code out of the JSP for maintenance and performance reasons. Indeed, when the Java logic of a JSP is implemented in a view helper, the code is compiled and loaded only once, thus avoiding the handling of too much Java code by the web servlet container.

In specific cases, the implementation of the view helper is improved by using AOP. For instance, we can add filters to modify the behavior of the helper regarding some session-based criteria such as user preferences. This use of AOP can be considered as a generalization of the interception filters previously described. Note that the systematic use of AOP for filtering can lead to better separation of concerns. Filtering, for example, can be used to implement some internationalization features in a modular way.

Web Presentation Tier Summary

AOP improvements are less systematic in the presentation tier than in the business and client tiers. This is due to two main reasons:

- The web tier uses Java and the Servlet model to handle the requests, as well as screen linking. It is a low-level, interaction-based implementation, and there is no explicit or stable business model where the aspects can be applied in a systematic way. It is also interesting to note that, for the controller design pattern aspect-oriented implementation, business specificities are implemented within the aspects.

- The presentation tier already uses non-Java technologies for separating concerns. For instance, the layout is defined in HTML within JSP pages. Except for the view helpers, presentation cannot be improved by Java-based AOP technologies. Other technologies, such as eXtensible Stylesheet Language Transformations (XSLT), should be preferred or combined for maximum efficiency.

Summary

In this chapter, we studied the use of AOP in the client and presentation tiers. When possible, we used the sample application in our examples. We showed that AOP offers many improvements for modularizing remote communication–related issues. The three main J2EE design patterns for distribution present many drawbacks that can be avoided through the use of AOP.

For the presentation tier, AOP is useful for modularizing typical concerns, such as internationalization and pre- and postcondition checks. Existing presentation frameworks such as Struts and Swing already provide abstraction for and deal with presentation-related concerns. In these contexts, AOP is less efficient; however, the study of the J2EE design patterns for the presentation tier shows that AOP can be used efficiently to build or enhance such frameworks.

INDEX